T0385697

DAYS OF TWILIGHT
NIGHTS OF FRENZY

DAYS OF TWILIGHT

NIGHTS OF FRENZY

WERNER SCHROETER

with Claudia Lenssen

Translated from the German by Anthea Bell

A MEMOIR

The University of Chicago Press
Chicago and London

The University of Chicago Press, Chicago 60637
The University of Chicago Press, Ltd., London
© 2017 by The University of Chicago
Published 2017
Printed in the Unites States of America

Originally published as *Tage im Dämmer, Nächte im Rausch: Autobiographie.*
© Aufbau Verlag GmbH & Co. KG, Berlin 2011

26 25 24 23 22 21 20 19 18 17   1 2 3 4 5

ISBN-13: 978-0-226-01911-6 (cloth)
ISBN-13: 978-0-226-01925-3 (e-book)
DOI: 10.7208/chicago/9780226019253.001.0001

 GOETHE
INSTITUT

The translation of this work was supported by a grant from the Goethe-
Institut, which is funded by the German Ministry of Foreign Affairs.

Library of Congress Cataloging in Publication Data

Names: Schroeter, Werner, 1945–2010, author. | Lenssen, Claudia, 1950– |
    Bell, Anthea, translator.
Title: Days of twilight, nights of frenzy : a memoir / Werner Schroeter, with
    Claudia Lenssen ; translated from the German by Anthea Bell.
Other titles: Tage im Dämmer, Nächte im Rausch. English
Description: Chicago : The University of Chicago Press, 2017. | Includes
    index.
Identifiers: LCCN 2017010067 | ISBN 9780226019116 (cloth : alk. paper) |
    ISBN 9780226019253 (e-book)
Subjects: LCSH: Schroeter, Werner, 1945–2010. | Motion picture producers
    and directors—Germany—Biography.
Classification: LCC PN1998.3.S359 A313 2017 | DDC 791.4302/33092 [B]—dc23
LC record available at https://lccn.loc.gov/2017010067

♾ This paper meets the requirements of ANSI/NISO Z39.48-1992
(Permanence of Paper).

CONTENTS

PREFACE

CLAUDIA LENSSEN

In 2012 the Museum of Modern Art in New York City presented the first North American retrospective of Werner's Schroeter's films, drawing comprehensively on a career that had spanned four decades. Ranging from experimental shorts to dramatic releases to documentaries, more than forty works were shown. As film aficionados know, in the States, MoMA's recognition—one might say, stamp of approval—is essential for any filmmaker who wishes to be considered an auteur in the modern sense of the term. Certainly this had been true for German directors Wim Wenders and Rainer Werner Fassbinder, both of whom had benefited from the museum's attentions. Now it was Schroeter's turn, though the recognition came late—two years after his death. While revered in Germany, indeed throughout Europe, as a founder of the New German Cinema and for his dazzling and affective productions, Schroeter was barely known in America, apart from a small sphere of film historians and festivalgoers. If his name was recognized at all, it was as a director for the opera and theater and for his close collaborations with the great soprano and diva Maria Callas.

The idea of this memoir first came up in spring 2009, when I had caught up with Werner Schroeter at a café to interview him about the impending German première of his film *Diese Nacht* [This night] in Berlin. He had emerged briefly from the studio where he was working on the German version of the script, and with typical compulsiveness and vigor, he told me all about his situation at the moment, his history, his universe. *This Night*, which had been originally produced in French as *Nuit de chien*, was Schroeter's newest film for the German market, the first in a long time, and that made it worth his while to oversee the dubbing himself. I discovered that he liked best to work at night and, if possible, with the actors in his "theatrical family," whom he knew so well. He mentioned Markus Boysen, Almut Zilcher, and Martin Wuttke, as well as other leading specialists in the art of dubbed dialog, with brief assessments of their qualities.

Schroeter was proud of the increasing attention he was attracting. Ever since the international première of *This Night* at the 2008 Venice International Film Festival, when the director was awarded a Golden Lion for his life's work, receiving the award from his friend Wim Wenders, the media had been full of pictures of the extravagant figure he cut. He was being rediscovered as the great outsider of the modern German cinema. Soon after our conversation, the German première of the film was celebrated at the Berlin Volksbühne [People's Theater], and a tour was being planned. At the same time he was preparing to direct a play on the live stage. Our interview also covered several film projects in Hamburg, Amsterdam, and Lisbon.

Schroeter talked about his collaboration with Elfi Mikesch, the filmmaker and camerawoman who was preparing to make a documentary about him. This portrait, *Mondo Lux*, would eventually record, among other things, rehearsals for *Alles ist tot—Formen der Einsamkeit* [All is dead—forms of loneliness], a production staged in June 2009 in a temporary wooden amphitheater in front of the Berlin Volksbühne. With his dramaturge and friend Monika Keppler, Werner had devised a collage of fragments from tragedies about Antigone and Electra by Sophocles, Friedrich Hölderlin, and Hugo von Hofmannsthal. The result was a new play intensifying the tragic stories of Antigone, Electra, Clytemnestra, and Ismene/Chrysothemis, the relentless struggle between daughters, sisters, and their mother in situations involving guilt, revenge, and sacrifice, and making that struggle a parable of Werner Schroeter's lifelong theme of Eros and Thanatos. With the actresses Almut Zilcher, Dörte Lyssewski, Pascale Schiller, and Anne Ratte-Polle, the director and his dramaturge translated the complex linguistic structure step-by-step into a theatrical event. He was pleased that Elfi Mikesch was recording this intense process in images: the magical transformation of poetic literature into gesture, voice, sound, image space, and choreography was Werner Schroeter's calling, the essence of his art, his way of communicating. He did not like to explain it analytically.

In his last year of life, Werner Schroeter was busy with many projects that allowed him to look back upon his achievements, and this memoir was one of them. As we worked on it, he seemed secure in the idea that everything in his life would fit together organically. Although very sick, he wanted to link every new venture to what he had done before.

Early in 2009, Schroeter had directed Mozart's *Don Giovanni* in Leipzig, and he also exhibited his photographic oeuvre for the first time, at the Galerie Jörg Heitsch in Munich. He was, as I said, also working on the launch of *This Night* in German, rehearsing at the Volksbühne, and introducing a retrospective of his work at the Arsenal Cinema in Berlin. He took part in the Festival des deutschen Films in Ludwigshafen am Rhein, met Isabelle Huppert for a mini-retrospective of their films together, *Malina* and *Two*, and photographed her in a whirlwind of down feathers. In September he went to a symposium devoted to his work in Lugano and opened an exhibition in Munich on the actress Marianne Hoppe. All that was followed, in December, by the great exhibition of his photographic portraits of his friends, colleagues, and companions at the Berliner Galerie at Lützowplatz, in collaboration with the gallerist Christian Holzfuss. In the context of this exhibition, he staged a scene from the *Songs of Maldoror*, in parallel to the next play he was to direct at the Volksbühne, *Quai West*, which had its première in January 2010. He was anxious to use every minute to the full, to go on working tirelessly as long as he could.

Even with all these projects, the story of his own life was prominent in his mind. At our first meeting, he regaled me with wonderful anecdotes, speaking enthusiastically of his grandmother, of Maria Callas, and of Magdalena Montezuma. He talked about his childhood. He was born on 7 April 1945, four weeks before the end of World War II in Europe. He spent his early childhood in East Germany until his family fled to the West, where they lived in refugee barracks near Bielefeld until his father found employment in Heidelberg. Schroeter talked about his coming-out as gay, his wholehearted love of opera, and his dazzling self-invention in 1968, the year of revolution. He talked about visiting Italy, France, and Latin America, and about his life on the road over four decades as a director and adventurer. He set out the experiences and encounters that had molded his life in countless sketches. Some of them, which he told in different variants over several interviews, eventually seemed to merge into a kind of private mythology. But there was more: there were events that he had never put down on paper and organized consecutively. Schroeter laughed at his "elephantine" memory, saying that anyone listening to him for four weeks on end would have his complete memoir. His life story was on the tip of his tongue; he just didn't have time to write it. Eventually, after some serious reflection on both sides, we agreed to write the book together.

Schroeter would always try to find out in advance as much as he could about anyone who wanted to interview him. He read the newspapers every day, knew exactly who had written about him and where, and was inclined to think poorly of German reviewers. He loved his German mother tongue and, in particular, the literature and music of our culture, but not the German mentality. He was less than enthusiastic about living in Berlin and felt that his real self was always somewhere else. Yet the public recognition he was now receiving in Germany gave him satisfaction. It seemed time for him to complete his oeuvre by adding his memoirs.

Vous êtes pardonné, Werner

I first met the wonderful Maria Callas in Paris. It must have been in 1974, or just a bit later. I had been invited to a banquet at the Greek Embassy, and the ambassador's wife said, "I know you'd like to sit next to Maria." With my ripped jeans and boots, I must have looked very much a punk among the elegant Louis XIV and Louis XV furnishings. Then I was seated on one of those exquisite chairs beside Maria Callas. She was enthroned on several silk cushions and wore a beautiful emerald-green Balenciaga dress with magnificent jewelry, not an excessive amount of it but well chosen, and her hair was exquisitely arranged. She looked really beautiful at such close quarters. Then I thought: I'll stake everything on a single throw. If I lose, I lose. I'll act the way I am. Luckily my knowledge of music and of her life and work saved me.

But in the course of our serious conversation about the recording of the 1955 guest performance in Berlin of the La Scala, Milan, production of *Lucia di Lammermoor*, conducted by Herbert von Karajan, I suddenly succumbed to an impulse to take Signora Callas by the ear, turn her head, and look at her very closely. A moment's silence, a look, some ooh-ing and ah-ing. As we talked, we kept switching between English, French, and Italian, and I said, "You're so beautiful, I can't believe you haven't had a facelift. How can anyone be as beautiful as that?" She merely replied, "*Vous êtes pardonné, Werner!*" (You're forgiven, Werner). And so our conversation went on and was very amusing. At one point I didn't want to go on sitting with my nose in my cup; I wanted to be a towering figure myself, so I climbed up on the sofa and sat on the back, and she looked up and said,

"Well, does that really make any difference to you?" I slipped down again. She was a woman with a wonderful sense of humor. It was melancholy humor and expressed her vulnerability. I once heard her say, "I've lost everything. My voice is done, it seems. I don't have a man, I don't have a child, isn't it funny?"

But I had gained something. When the evening came to an end, and her chauffeur signaled that it was time to leave, she let me know that I could go to drink tea with her in the next few days. And so we developed a tentative friendship that I felt was wonderful—or no, a rapprochement. We'd have had to know each other longer to call it friendship. I was overjoyed.

In fact, the day I visited the Greek Embassy had begun with me crouching in the shower, puking. By the evening I had thrown up as much as Callas herself before a performance, which she did every time, purging herself both above and below so as to appear onstage as a figure of purity. I, on the other hand, was puking out of excitement. So that evening I felt light, almost airborne, when I arrived for the banquet—not that that prevented me from getting fresh with her, in my usual way.

She once told me that she knew only people who were afraid of her. That struck me as impossible, because I couldn't feel afraid of her myself. She was so friendly and warmhearted, still like a little girl at the age of fifty. I asked her what she'd think if I wrote a newspaper column saying that Maria Callas was looking for a man, because I was sure any number would reply. She thought that very amusing.

And here is an even better story: a few weeks before her death in September 1977, we were talking about music that can be sung even when the upper register of the voice is not what it used to be, a subject that I had to approach delicately. She told me that she wanted to go on trying to sing. By chance, I found a cassette on her piano, and when she briefly left the room, I switched on the recorder and listened to what she had been recording with her singing coach. It was Leonora's "Pace, pace," from the final act of *The Force of Destiny*, superbly sung. When she was alone, then, she could obviously still sing. There was a score open on the piano, from Rossini's *Barber of Seville*, that had been written out in the nineteenth century by the singer Maria Malibran.

Learning that Maria Malibran had also been a composer, I researched the songs that she had written. Like her sister, Pauline Viardot (later the muse of Hector Berlioz and later still Turgenev's lover in Baden-Baden), Maria Malibran was artistically extremely creative, but she died at the early age of twenty-eight after a concert in Manchester.

In the Bibliothèque nationale in Paris, Antoine, a friend of mine, finally found something that I was keen to track down: Malibran's song "Tac, tac, qui battera sera la mort" [Tap, tap, that will be Death knocking]. I had no new envelope, so I sent a copy of the score to Maria Callas in a used one, crossing out the names to which it had been sent before and writing her address over them. That was the behavior of a punk, careless and unforgivable, but the contents of the old envelope could have interested her. It must have been one of the last letters she ever received.

One day in September 1977 when I was sitting in the canteen of the Bochum theater where I was directing *Miss Julie*, Tamara Kafka came in and said, "Oh, there you are, Werner. Maria Callas died today." It shook me badly. What a terrible mistake on the part of the deity to take back that messenger of the gods! It seemed to me an inconceivable phenomenon.

My friend Maria Schell was rehearsing in Bochum at the same time for Fernando Arrabal's play *The Tower of Babel*, directed by Arrabal himself. After hearing Tamara's news, I instinctively changed into black leather. I was very thin at the time and looked funny. Back in the canteen, Maria Schell, who was still there, or maybe back there again, looked at me. I had an aura of mourning around me, radiating a broken heart, as I put it in my requiem on the death of Maria Callas, a piece that appeared in *Der Spiegel* [and is republished in this book as an appendix]. Maria Schell was to give a live radio interview in Cologne that evening and had a Mercedes available—at no expense to her, of course. And as she really was a dear friend to me, she said, "You come too, Werner. We'll stick together today." Maria drove us to Cologne herself. I was in a strange state of mind, there and not there at the same time. Maria took me with her into the studio, where the editor asked, "Who's that, Frau Schell? Some kind of weirdo?" To which she inquired, "Are you a racist? This is an extremely talented young artist, and I mean that seriously, my dear fellow." So although he gritted his teeth, he had to put up with my presence and my occasional contributions to the program.

Then it was late. We had something to eat in Cologne and drove back to Bochum at about midnight. I was all churned up with grief, a *pater dolorosa* and an orphaned child. The woman who was like the Mother of God to me, that messenger who determined my fate, was dead. Just as my real mother determined my corporeal life, Maria Callas inspired my artistic life. It was a dreadful loss. Somewhere between Cologne and Bochum, Maria felt exhausted, and I was at the end of my tether. We pulled into a parking bay just off the autobahn, she pushed the seats back, and we fell asleep. When the sun awoke us, we yawned and slowly moved off again. It was nine in the morning when we reached Bochum. We drank the contents of a huge pot of coffee, and then Maria went off to her rehearsal with Arrabal, and I to my own rehearsal of *Miss Julie* with Ingrid Caven, Wolfgang Schumacher, and Tamara Kafka. So that had been the day of the death of Maria Callas.

A day later *Der Spiegel* called to ask if I would write her obituary. I didn't have the patience to sit down and write, so I dictated the text between rehearsals to a charming secretary from the theater manager's office, ad hoc, without recording it or reading a proof. It took a little while, and the magazine even postponed printing the edition by a day so that the article could be included.

I think what I wrote was good. It contains the essentials about the damage that Maria Callas attracted to herself, the damage done to her. She wasn't able to cope with it because she came from another sphere, and her criteria of life and art had little to do with banality, so it brought her down. Her death was a strange one: she got up in the morning, went to eat breakfast, and died—maybe of heart failure. It was never fully explained. A few years ago I read that she suffered from a skin disease of unknown origin on her back and her throat, which were not on public view. Her death came when she was suffering from deep depression, involving all kinds of men. To me, it meant the loss of a great love, a divine gift taken from me too soon, for I would so much have wished for more meetings with her.

Spiritual mother, natural mother

A year before the death of Maria Callas, my mother died. A few hours earlier, I had had to go to Munich for the première of a show with Ingrid Caven, the first chanson recital that Ingrid ever gave. When she was still with Rainer Werner Fassbinder, Daniel Schmid and I had discovered her as a singer, before Yves Saint Laurent later arranged for her to appear at the Théâtre Pigalle in Paris.

After the show the phone rang. My brother was on the line, to tell me that our mother was dead. He and I had been caring for her together until the morning of that very day. I remember how we sat in our little house in Heidelberg-Dossenheim, talking, while our mother lay in her bed upstairs, knocked out with morphine. She was the first of many close to me to suffer from cancer. My whole family has died of that disease.

Her death was traumatic for me, as a mother's death is, I think, for anyone who is sensitive. Earlier, before anyone (including she) knew she was sick, I woke up suddenly in the night and fell out of bed, crying out that she was going to die. The mystic link between mother and child is extremely strong. That link, that mutual relationship, remains alive, transcending all boundaries. It was like that with my natural mother and also with my spiritual mother, Maria Callas.

I remember that, when my mother died, I retreated into myself. The year 1976 was a sad one. Her death marked the end of a kind of dream life in which everything seemed to happen at one remove, including my work. That's because her existence constituted home for me. I could be in Los Angeles, Mexico City, or somewhere at the back of beyond, and yet a moment would always come when I fell into a nest representing her. Lying in bed, with the windows darkened, dreaming and recuperating, was perhaps a case of leaving the nest in reverse. You can recover your strength in the place where you feel at home. When there was no such place for me anymore, I experienced self-alienation on a large scale. Yet I made the best of it, for I worked more after my mother's death than in the seven years before it.

But eventually things looked up again; I was asked to direct a play at the theater in Bochum. It was *Miss Julie*, with Ingrid Caven as Julie, Wolfgang Schumacher as the servant Jean, and Tamara Kafka as his fiancée, Christin. This Strindberg play, in a translation by Peter Weiss, was a great favorite of mine, and it was a fine production. Ingrid was excellent, prissy and at the same time erotic. My friend Alberte Barsacq created wild costumes; my companion Magdalena Montezuma worked with me and Jan Moewes to design a beautiful set. The struggle for power and love in the play turned into a curious hybrid between Strindberg's own period and an elegant Folies Bergère show. The life of Miss Julie celebrated life itself, even when trodden underfoot.

Looking back, I came to realize that things are always interconnected. Grief has always been a part of my life, as have loving relationships, friendship, and my artistic work, whether in movies, stage plays, or opera. I felt that, like Diderot's Jacques le fataliste, I had become a stoic: I understood that every aspect of life rises organically from another.

My model family

I was born in 1945, in Georgenthal in Thuringia, a resort near Gotha to which visitors came for its healthy air. When I was six, my father, Hans, said that after the Nazi period he didn't want to live under another repressive regime, so he emigrated from the German Democratic Republic with my mother, Lena, my Polish grandmother, Elsa, my elder brother, Hans-Jürgen, and me and started again from scratch.

At first we lived in a hastily constructed working-class housing development outside the city of Bielefeld. I still remember the gloomy ruins in the city. Everything I saw outside me was so alien to my feelings that my grandmother and her dreams became the world I lived in. Incidentally, the building of the Berlin Wall left me cold and had no effect on the rest of our family either. We had said goodbye to Georgenthal, and a great deal of time had passed since we left it and before the Wall was built in 1961.

My parents may have met in Berlin, where my mother, the daughter of a baroness, studied medicine. She originally wanted to be a medical doctor, but she became a housewife and mother instead. In those days, women hardly ever thought of pursuing a profession after marriage, and she probably did not want one by then. My father came from a farming family that ran a dairy in Thuringia. He himself was an engineer and inventor, and he developed special hand-brake power intensifiers for use in agricultural machinery, among other things. He had built up his factory in Georgenthal by his own efforts, and later he began again in Geretsried, near Munich, where the firm he founded still exists today.

I don't know how my father managed to avoid being conscripted into the army during the war. He never talked about it, but he was a clever man, and maybe his factory was needed at the time. We had a beautiful family villa in Georgenthal, and after the reunification of Germany I inherited it. I went to see the house that my father had left for the sake of freedom. By now it was a home for senior citizens, and it would have been so terrible to turn the old people out that I decided it could stay as it was. Furthermore, the dilapidated building on an unattractive plot of land was not worth much. Today it stands empty.

My father was a very liberal man who never complained of losing all he owned when we came to the West, and I think highly of him for that. As a child I thought that his tolerance was almost like indifference, and only years later did I realize that it was his way of accepting the nature of society. For instance, homosexuality was never an issue in my family, and there was a time when I alternated between boyfriends and girlfriends, although my erotic links to the men were always stronger than those I felt for the girls with whom I also slept.

It was the human qualities and not the sexual orientation of my partners of both sexes that my father appreciated, and he usually liked them. He took it all as perfectly normal. If I came home with a male partner, that was that. I couldn't be forbidden anything on that level; I might be quiet, calm, and gentle, but I had a certain forcefulness in which there was a kind of nonviolent authority.

My brother and I grew up with a good deal of freedom, if not to say actually running wild. My mother was a lovable and indeed a loving woman, although she had her flaws, like every other human being. She clung to the love of her sons, which was sometimes difficult for me and was even more difficult for my brother, who never entirely managed to break away from our parents.

I learned a great deal from my parents, my brother, and our relatives on my mother's side of the family, none of whom were materialists. But I had no real relationship with my paternal grandparents, and didn't like them. The way my father and mother lived showed us that life itself is what counts, and you have to grasp the present. I'm not interested in material things either. I see the ideal way of life as two or three suitcases, a good hotel, maybe a crate full of books and music as well. Although I'll admit that life is inconvenient if you don't have any money.

My beloved Polish grandmother Elsa Buchmann, born Baroness von Rodjow, would have loved to be an actress; it was her great dream. She had a real talent for the art of drama, but as a baroness and married off to a stout, choleric attorney at the age of seventeen, she could never live that dream. Our parents, too, took an interest in the arts, but the main influence on us came from our grandmother. She could neither stand repression nor exert it; instead, she turned everything into fantasy. When we went for walks with her, she told us crazy stories, until we came to the cemetery, where we would have a picnic on the grave of our great-grandparents. She read us fairy tales that I have never forgotten, and I keep rediscovering them in my work to this day.

I have much to thank my grandmother for; she awakened my imagination. I remember just how she could say that a chair was a palace, a flowerpot was the jungle. I was fascinated by such freedom in her way of treating inanimate objects; we had plenty of scope to move in her strange, daydream reality. She could transform everything: for instance, as if we were in a boat on the Nile, and there was a problem—then along came the Snow Queen, who found the weather too warm, and we had to find ice to keep her from melting. Or my grandmother would say that my brother and I—he was about ten and I was seven—should put our ears to the streetcar rails and hear the Indians come riding up. Or following her instructions we must piss everywhere to mark out our own part of Indian territory, something that really shocked the good bourgeois folk of the time. She designed a magical world that was very tolerant and incredibly creative. I owe such a great deal of my imagination to her.

The next anecdote shows that her sense of reality was also vitally ironic. After two world wars, my grandmother had lost all she had except for a few suitcases containing her beautiful silk dresses from the twenties and thirties. She wore them in our working-class housing estate in Bielefeld, where we lived in a kind of prefabricated apartment block. So my grandmother would walk along the street, elegantly and with a spring in her step, carrying her shopping bag, and she tinted her hair blonde. In her late sixties she was still a slender and remarkably beautiful woman. The boys whistled after her as I walked with her holding her hand. She smiled at me once, turned around, and told them, "There you are, then—a schoolgirl from behind, a museum piece from in front."

My grandmother still yearned for her lifelong dream of the theater, and it was up to my brother and me to make it come true for her by playing parts that she made up for us, thus revealing a dark and poetic parallel world. I recollect one crazy scene in which I was a princess sitting on top of a glass mountain, and my brother, as the prince, had to rescue me. The mountain consisted of a wobbly pile of chairs one on top of another, with an ironing board acting as a ramp. I went to school with my head full of such notions, which of course put a considerable distance between me and the normal school day, and provoked the other students, who were much more inhibited.

My grandmother lived close to us, in a one-room apartment. She came almost daily to do the housework, I think in return for something. She thought she owed her two daughters her love and attention, because she had not loved their father, the attorney. I inherited my love of cooking from her and my mother; I know a number of German and Polish dishes and love cooking in that style when it is well done. My grandmother owned a cookbook dating from 1896, in which there were many recipes calling for a pound of butter and thirty eggs. I particularly liked her shortcrust pastry with white peaches and whipped cream.

My grandmother led her own life and had friends of her own. In 1957 she converted to the Roman Catholic Church, and so did I—or at least I took a great interest in it, although I had been baptized as a Protestant. My mother, incidentally, knew nothing about this decision and was very much surprised at my grandmother's funeral when so many old people whom she didn't know turned up. I attended religious instruction lessons with great interest, as my teachers in Bielefeld always mentioned in my school reports. In connection with that, I remember the fact that long ago, after a very painful parting with someone I loved, I sought comfort from a young Catholic priest. While the pain of my loss grew worse and worse, I naturally spent time in bed with him. He didn't regret that; he enjoyed it.

My dear grandmother died the year after her conversion, either of suicide or a tramway accident, I don't know which. When I heard about it I went to my room and wrecked the furnishings in a fit of despair, rage, and grief. Then I felt better. It was clear to my parents and me that a violent temper lay concealed in the quiet, gentle child that their son Werner seemed to be. I never did anything like that again.

My school, the Max Planck High School in Bielefeld, was a disaster. The teachers, presumably former Nazis, didn't notice or didn't want to notice what was going on among their students. Without any idea why, or what was happening to me, I was beaten up by my classmates almost every day until my fourteenth year. I had a different concept of life from theirs, and didn't defend myself; it just made me sad. Things went so far that they emptied coffeepots full of urine over my head. I suffered several severe illnesses at this time, which surely arose from the fact that I felt entirely outside such forms of behavior, without holding anyone responsible or hating or even admiring them. I wasn't cultivating a stance of sadomasochism; I simply could not understand the constant insults and injuries. But afterward, I realized that those experiences made me what I am. Later, at the age of fifteen, I adopted an intellectual position, and everyone trembled before me. I was much respected and given cigarettes and beers. If that doesn't cast a spotlight on our society, I don't know what would . . .

All the same, I made friends—for instance, with an older boy called Siegfried, who talked to me and listened to me. I was allowed to ride on the handlebars of his bike when he cycled home with me after school. He was about fifteen, I was twelve, and he was my great love. I still remember how he described movies to me, and in that way I got to know about the big-bosomed film star Diana Dors. One day Siegfried was absent from the school yard, and I did not find out until much later that he had hanged himself in the attic of his parental home. He had been beaten by his stepfather, had gone through hell on earth, but never said a word about it to me or any of the others. Later, I set up a monument to him in my film *Deux*, in the scene where my alter ego, played by Isabelle Huppert, is given a ride like that on a bike.

At this time my family often went to the theater and the opera; that was simply a part of our life. So it was that I adored the actress Marianne Hoppe when I was twelve, and I saw her onstage in a touring production that came to Bielefeld. I was coerced into learning to play the piano in my childhood too, like every child at that time. I soon gave it up but later regretted it, if not often. I preferred listening to music on the radio or on records whenever I could, and the incomparable Caterina Valente was the star of my childhood. I also heard Hertha Töpper on the radio, as a confident Amneris in Verdi's *Aida*, and thought that her singing was like Valente's. And because I thought so highly of Caterina Valente, I also began to think highly of opera.

From time to time my father also took an interest in art, especially as he sometimes had a lover who was an opera singer. My mother did the same, by falling in love with a woman for once in her life, the Viennese actress Josefine Schult-Brasser, a wonderful woman, beautiful but austere, a first-rate tragic actor. My mother was certainly deeply in love with her, and my father, at almost the same time, with a blonde opera singer. Such were their connections with culture during our time in Bielefeld, although neither of them ever thought of separating or divorcing.

Josefine often came to our home. As a lover, she treated my mother badly; she was a real dominatrix. You have to imagine the way she went around—I had always imagined her type the way she was. She visited us in the early sixties, when we were living in Dossenheim, a suburb of Heidelberg. I collected her at the Upper Rhine railroad station. The villagers almost fainted in amazement at the sight of Josefine with her crazy hairstyle, her long, Medea-like locks, her leopard-skin coat, and her stiletto-heeled sandals. She had cherry-red lips and eyes outlined in black, and her finger- and toenails painted with blood-red nail polish. I was proud to have Josefine stalking through the village with me like that, while the locals froze in astonishment.

She visited us a couple of other times, and by then I had more to do with her than my mother did; for my mother, the story was over. So I adopted Josefine not as a lover but as a friend. I thought she was terrific, a beautiful woman. Josefine had had a career at the Burgtheater, Vienna; it came to an end because there is no doubt that she both insisted on quality and had a volcanic temper. She was very logical, and sometimes disagreeable, with the result that she lost her job in theater after theater. She landed in Flensburg, Heidelberg, and finally in Celle, where she played every kind of part from the witch in *Hansel and Gretel* to Medea. She always got what she wanted, but in tiny theaters. When she was nearly fifty, Hansgünther Heyme rediscovered her and engaged her for the theater in Cologne, where she had a great time, for she really was a fine actress.

Innocence has a friend in heaven

We moved to Dossenheim in 1959. First we had an apartment and then a small house with a garden. I traveled on the regional railroad to school in Heidelberg, where I spent a few months at Helmholtz High School, and after that I attended the private high school of the Anglo-American Institute. I was an adolescent by now and realized that, for me, learning French and English was no alternative to real life. My school report said that my behavior was good and I worked hard, but it was doubtful that I would move up to the next grade, just as it had been in Bielefeld. What can one say if education consists of copying out proverbial sayings from Schiller's *Wilhelm Tell* into an exercise book? "Innocence has a friend in heaven" and "A wise man takes precautions." Even switching to the Anglo-American school didn't help much.

After hearing Maria Callas sing in Italian in 1958, I just had to learn the language. It began when I switched on the radio, a Blaupunkt set. I was sitting in the kitchen one evening, I was thirteen, and at first there was nothing to hear but static. But then an orchestra began to play, and finally I heard a voice singing. It turned out to be the voice of Maria Callas, and I had no idea what to make of it. I remember that evening so clearly, because it was when I threw my math books into the garbage—I had always hated math—and that was more or less that. So I went ahead with learning Italian. My mother found a student, Luciano Rodolfo, to teach me. She cooked for him and paid for my lessons. He was strict with me, but as I loved Italian, I learned the language fast. I had the idea that I must get away from Dossenheim, get away from Germany itself. And so one thing led to another.

I devoted an album of memorabilia to Maria Callas and began collecting pictures and newspaper accounts of her appearances. For instance, I knew all about the opening of the 1960 season at La Scala, Milan: the newspapers said that Callas wanted to make her peace with Italy. I kept photos of menus from which you could deduce what she had eaten. I drew up a list of her appearances in 1962 when she went on tour to Munich, Hamburg, Essen, and Bonn; I collected reviews by Joachim Kaiser and Jürgen Serke. My "world of opera" was a great heap of material between the covers of a notebook, where I also found room for my discoveries about Joan Sutherland and Grace Bumbry at Bayreuth.

I would listen to music for hours on end. I had a tape recorder and began recording everything by and about Maria Callas that was transmitted over the radio. Later I seldom felt that constant need to hear her voice. She was still close to me after her death, she still represented something like my spiritual home, but I found it rather uncomfortable to call the sensuality of her voice into being again, as if she hadn't died. At heart, I didn't want that divine voice to be preserved on disks for infinite repetition, like a long-keeping sausage, as I once put it in conversation with my friend Daniel Schmid.

Once—it must have been in 1960 or 1961—I was at the amphitheater of Epidaurus in Greece with my parents. I had persuaded them to go there. To attend a performance you had to drive up into the mountains in a slow, nearly endless line of automobiles, as if in a convoy. The trip took four hours. Callas in *Medea* at Epidaurus would be a powerful performance, since the acoustics there are simply staggering. And the cicadas! Like a concert in the sky. When we went, Callas was to sing, but she had to cancel, so five thousand people got back into their cars and drove for four hours down the mountains again.

At sixteen I went to Naples, to study for a year at a school near the Stazione Garibaldi. Following the school subjects in Italian was no problem to me, none at all. The climate there was wonderful, marvelous. That was when my love of Naples began; it has lasted to this day. That also explains why, years later, my film *Regno di Napoli* [The Kingdom of Naples] was made in various different Neapolitan dialects.

Of course, I went to the opera house in Naples. There was a gay manager there, Commendatore Spizico. He used to assemble the city's faggots outside the opera house in the evening, climb onto a chair—because he was very short—and make inflammatory speeches: "Ragazzi di Napoli!" He was a genius, telling stories of who was fucking whom, stuff like that. I met him again years later when I was shooting parts of *Eika Katappa* in Naples and asked him to let me film a scene from *Aida* with Grace Bumbry in the opera house. He summoned his audience again, climbed onto his chair, and let fly. "Popolo de Napoli! Ascoltate tutti quanti! Questo signore avete visto, ragazzi! Impossibile questi ragazzi tedeschi, blah blah blah" [People of Naples, listen up! You've seen this gentleman, boys! These German lads are impossible]. But then, after all, he said, "Come along, then, we'll do it." So I went into the Opera San Carlo, but it didn't seem so interesting, and I didn't film the scene. However, Commendatore Spizico was a terrific Neapolitan character.

I was living in a boardinghouse kept by a real *mamma neapolitana*. She made a fuss over me, gave me *cornetti con prosciutto di Parma* and cappuccino for breakfast, and for lunch there was *spaghetti con vongole*, clams, still a favorite dish of mine. Then, in the evening, she would offer me *una bella cotoletta, caro*, and so forth. It was wonderful, and cost almost nothing.

By then I had fallen in love with the city—with all cities, in fact. At home, my mother and father had noticed that I was always disappearing into Heidelberg, but then I would come back. My parents were tolerant. They let me go, knowing that, even though I'm a gentle person, I have an iron will, so resisting me was useless. Of course, they questioned my wish to go to Italy, but they understood what kind of a son they had.

After Naples, I came back and went to the American school, but I was always roaming around. If I had been out all night and didn't come home until early morning, my mother would drive me to school in her VW Beetle. She would sometimes run me a bath and wash me in it; she liked to do that. My brother and I didn't help in the house, no cleaning or doing the dishes. No young man likes that sort of thing, nor did my father, another reason probably being that my mother hated to have men in her kitchen. She didn't approve of it. A young man in adolescence, with his way to make in the world, was out of place there, she thought. I took to cooking only later, because I really enjoyed it, and cooked very often.

Of course, there were conflicts with my mother. Once I was head over heels in love and wanted to bring my boyfriend home to meet my parents.

"Then we're having no more to do with you!" she told me on the telephone. We had a furious argument.

"This is my life, he's my friend. Welcome to the morgue!"

And even when I came to Dossenheim years later to visit my parents before making the film *Willow Springs*, I was overcome by depression. I was standing in the kitchen when my mother came in and said, "To think of all I've done for you! You're well off, after all."

I fell into a rage, reached for the kitchen drawer and took out a butcher's knife. I looked at the kitchen clock hanging over the sink, absorbed in my tragic concept of the world, and then I felt ridiculous and inadequate. I could have murdered my mother—she must never say such a thing to me again, I thought. The clock moved on and the impulse passed. I took her arm, escorted her out into our little garden, and explained what had come over me.

Much later, when I was staging a production that featured a tango with my sick partner Marcelo Uriona, I found myself in a similar situation. This time I was the one telling a depressive young man who was on edge and self-absorbed, "You're well off, after all." And he in his turn felt like killing me.

I took my graduation exam in 1966, both the German and the American versions of it, because you were recognized as passing the exam only if you took both together, which was ridiculous. I was good at German but didn't take much interest in the rest of it. "Works only at what he enjoys," said my school report.

After that I didn't know what to do. I wanted only to find out what love is like. I knew about passion but wanted to learn about love and experience it. "And so love seems to call a halt to lovers"—my school notes on a passage of dialog from Bert Brecht's *Rise and Fall of the City of Mahagonny* expressed my longing for a different life: See those cranes in a great curve flying high! / And the clouds that with them came / Moved on with them across the sky / From one life to another we cannot name.

During school I did have a wonderful relationship that at least resembled love, with a Sicilian waiter I met in a bar by Lake Garda. He came to see me in Germany in 1963, and I took him to the American school.

He sat beside me, and the other students said in English, "Look,

Miss Leube, who is that guy?" To which the teacher replied, "Please stand up."

I told him, "Stand up," and then said, "This is my friend."

"Ah," she said, "welcome, sit down. Now let's start the lesson." The tone was different from German schools: it partook of the American passion for freedom that was personified by Kennedy. His death was a huge shock to the German people; we had believed he could do anything. He had been a genuine *allianza per il futuro* for us. The Cold War, on the other hand, really did leave me cold. I was never afraid of a third world war, and I couldn't pretend to feel fear when I didn't. And no way could I influence a war. But I was sad about the loss of hope that came with Kennedy's death. At the time we were sure the United States was the land of liberty and would bring the world luck. But it just was not so.

By the time of my graduation exam I already had a certain amount of sexual experience, because I had started at fourteen, rather early for the time. Years later when I was invited to take my film *Nuit de chien* (*Diese Nacht*) to the Festival des deutschen Films in Ludwigshafen am Rhein, I remembered how I had walked the streets in that area, where there were extensive harbors. Along with a girl philosophy student from Karlsruhe, who also wanted to meet people, I hitchhiked from Heidelberg to Ludwigshafen to meet sailors in 1965 and 1966. How could it be anything but romantic to come close to others, and not only in one's thoughts and feelings? We wanted to experience real life.

Back then there were gas lamps everywhere, and the BASF chemical factories blinked like something in a science fiction movie— a wonderful image of the night. There was a friendly tart, getting on in years, who wanted to adopt me. But instead I hitchhiked home at four in the morning and was driven to school by my mother. Love was an unknown feeling that I still wanted to experience. To know love and then die—a death in love, a *Liebestod*—was an incredibly romantic notion.

The sun of the night

I met Pier Paolo Pasolini when I was very young. He was giving his film *Accatone* its première in Heidelberg at the Harmonie cinema, which may even still exist. This must have been in 1961 or 1962. Pasolini was introducing it, but his German interpreter translated phrases incorrectly. I was sitting up in the balcony, and after a while, when I'd heard enough of her inaccuracies, I said out loud, "Signore Pasolini, basta . . . ," and made her translate it properly, sometimes doing it myself. For instance, in his own language he said, "I know that I won't be understood here, in this commercial and uncultured German center, amid false student romanticism, in a capitalist city full of arrogant students. They will never understand *Accatone*, but I am showing the film here all the same, because I need money and because I believe that perhaps it may, in spite of everything, be understood." However, the interpreter's version ran, "Herr Pasolini is proud and glad to be in this wonderful city of students." And because I told them about this difference in both languages exactly as it was, Pasolini thanked me later. I was sixteen or seventeen years old, and his thanks really meant something to me.

Then I watched *Accatone*, my first Pasolini film. I thought it was magnificent; it really grabbed me. It's a film that does not date. I think Pasolini's *Salò* does date, but not *Accatone*. Its images are of sympathy in the midst of brutality, or rather while brutality and violence cannot be prevented, there is still sympathy in all the brutality, and that's what I call magnificent.

If I look at other models for my own work in the cinema and the theater, as well as *Accatone* I think of Carl Dreyer's *La Passion de Jeanne d'Arc*. It was also while I was in Heidelberg that I saw it in 1961, on German TV Channel One. There was only one TV channel, and it showed that silent film of Dreyer's in black and white from 8:30 in the evening. I thought it, too, was magnificent, and I consider it one of the greatest of all films to this day. There must have been an enormous number of phone calls to the TV station from viewers thinking there was something the matter with either their TV sets or the station itself. Just think of it: there were so many viewers then who took culture on television really seriously that Dreyer's masterpiece ran for two hours of normal evening viewing time, even though it is a silent film—that would be unthinkable today!

After passing my graduation exam, I did nothing at first. I had been through several serious illnesses—sepsis of the lungs, pulmonary tuberculosis—and I had often been beaten up at school. But things did improve at school when I returned from my time abroad in Italy. My health improved and I came to have a certain intellectual reputation and was not just a whipping boy. All the same, I had to take a lot of abuse. People shouted, "Julio Gréco" at me in the school yard, because I wore black and that somehow reminded them of Juliette Gréco. I was fluent in several languages and read a great deal, which made me seem even more eccentric to my classmates and helped me develop a certain tragic sensitivity to the world.

I was deep into the books of Cesare Pavese and translated them at night, because I was fascinated by his attitude to thoughts of suicide, and he did in fact kill himself. My "tragic sensitivity" became something like a code word for my longing for self-expression, but now that I look back I regard my feelings then more as comic melancholy. After all, I was living in a wonderful family, my mother was a great cook, and to this day I am a hedonist.

Reading, even to excess, was important to me, particularly in the silence of the night, when everything was asleep and I myself still awake. Night has enlightenment in store for the lonely, as we all know—or at least I do, for I have never slept much during the night, although I lie in late in the morning.

I have been an enthusiastic reader since my childhood, and at night I could always concentrate. "Watching lonely in the night," sings Brangäne in Wagner's *Tristan*, and in his *Hymns to Night* the poet Novalis writes: "What man alive, endowed with senses, loves not the wondrous vision of light above all else in the realm of space. . . . Away I turn to the sacred, inexpressible mystery of night." The riches of night have been my companion from an early age.

I read Cesare Pavese and Edgar Allan Poe particularly closely in my youth. Above all, however, I discovered the poet Lautréamont, whose works I found in a bookshop in original editions. Later, in France, I encountered him again. The people I met there, sensitive characters like the director Jean Eustache and many others, all knew Lautréamont and were sure I would like his writing. Lautréamont's main work, *Les chants de Maldoror* [The songs of Maldoror], is important to me, and Rainer Werner Fassbinder was perfectly right when, in an article, he associated my work with that of Novalis, Lautréamont, and Louis-Ferdinand Céline. In one of my very early films, *La morte d'Isotta*, shot in the spring of 1968, I was already quoting from *Les chants de Maldoror*. It has few equals for subtlety, depth, and a love-hate attitude to humanity; the images of "Diable et Dieu," come together in those poems. Lautréamont feels like my constant double.

Isidore Ducasse, who wrote under the pseudonym of the comte de Lautréamont, was the son of French parents who lived in Uruguay. He was born in Montevideo in 1846, lost his mother early, and at the age of five probably saw something of the fighting at the end of the war between Argentina and Uruguay, surely a terrible experience. His father sent him to school in France, where instead of aspiring to a bourgeois profession, he wrote *The Songs of Maldoror*, his one great work. Censorship prevented it from appearing complete in his lifetime. Very little is known about his life. He died almost alone in a hotel at the early age of twenty-four, and his work was nearly forgotten. Fortunately, there is a brilliant translation of *Songs* by Ré Soupault, who was born in Bublitz in Pomerania and was the wife of the famous surrealist Philippe Soupault. It was he who rediscovered Lautréamont and introduced his work to the surrealists, while his wife produced the German translation.

I was haunted by Lautréamont. He was the inspiration for my films *Neurasia*, *Argila*, and *The Death of Maria Malibran*, in which I quoted from the *Songs*. I returned to the subject in *Deux* and also referred to the *Songs* in my photography exhibition of 2009, *Autrefois et toujours* [In the past and always]. The title for the exhibition was inspired by the first song: "Do you not love the crystal-clear streams of water, in which thousands of little red, blue, and silver fishes play? You will catch them in a net so beautiful that they swim into it of their own accord until it is full." For the opening, I staged a relevant scene from the first song, in which Maldoror induces a boy to leave his family.

Of course, I did not really identify with the comte de Lautréamont, or with Maldoror, the ghost of the devil, the fallen angel, or Ahasuerus the Wandering Jew, all of whom are contained in that character. But Lautréamont's way of uniting irony and sensuality in his vision, *"malgré tout l'utopie"* [utopia in spite of everything], made him, along with Callas, a highly significant artist for me.

There was once an edition of the *Songs* published with beautiful illustrations. Antje Ellermann, of the publisher Rogner und Bernhard, helped me acquire a copy. Unfortunately, I have given it away, or perhaps lost it somewhere. Today, Lautréamont is disappearing again; in a bookshop recently, all I could find was a paperback edition of the *Songs* in which they are incorrectly described as a novel. The work is as much a poem as the *Odyssey* is, or the individual works of Virgil.

I often come upon rare and unusual works. For instance, take the song "Padre, padre" in the film *Palermo oder Wolfsburg*, which brings a note of kitsch to the effect of alienation in the courtroom scenes. It is a deliberate contrast with the harsh treatment of the characters in those scenes. I found this tearjerker of a song in Berlin while we were shooting that part of the film; there was a garbage bin in the street, with a 45 rpm record sticking out of it. I simply picked it up, washed it at home with distilled water and dishwashing detergent, put it on the record player—and there I had the song for my film.

My parents thought I wasn't doing enough. I was twenty-one years old; I had passed my graduation exam; I wanted to learn about love and then kill myself. Such was my long-term plan, in that order. As I saw it, suicide was not an expression of hostility to life; I could not imagine it as the outcome of depression. Instead, I wanted to kill myself in a state of grace and passion, a state of extreme lust. Admittedly, I see that wish as comically melancholy today, but it was how I felt at the time. And I looked the part: the photo taken for my draft card shows me in thick glasses with black frames and a rocker haircut. Fortunately, my earlier poor health and a bad back meant I didn't actually have to fear being called up for the draft.

I registered at the University of Mannheim to study psychology and medicine, but I dropped out after three weeks. I couldn't stand all the talk that went on in class, particularly as I could just as well read what the lecturers were saying in books. I had hoped the university would be something special, but it offered nothing I couldn't find in books anyway. So I said goodbye with a fine flourish, informing my professor that he could lick my ass. So much for my university studies.

My parents thought again. "He has to do something." They heard about the University of Television and Film in Munich, founded in 1967. I didn't want to study there, and did all I could not to be accepted, but the university took me all the same. In the entrance exam I was supposed to write a review of Luchino Visconti's *Rocco e i suoi fratelli* [Rocco and his brothers]. My essay ran to several pages and was solely about the fact that Visconti fancied Alain Delon—but that didn't help to get me turned down. I spent three months there, feeling very bored because I couldn't do anything practical. We weren't allowed to handle cameras or anything like that. Many students stayed on at the school, including my good friend Wim Wenders. Our friendship has lasted to this day. Wim took the whole course, but I was glad when, at the film festival of Knokke-le-Zoute, I met the first great love of my life. I never went back to the University of [Television and] Film in Munich until I began teaching there.

Muse, companion, friend—Magdalena Montezuma

I first met her in Heidelberg in the sixties, after a performance by the Living Theatre at the university there. The productions of *Mysteries* and *The Maids*, the exaggerated romanticism, had impressed us both very much. The woman I would later rename Magdalena Montezuma, in the sense of an imperious Mexican goddess, was really named Erika Kluge, and she had jumped off a wall intending to kill herself, but the wall was only two meters high, and she misjudged it. Her attempt to end her life was rather comic and seems to me today more of a suicidal urge in the pastoral tradition than anything.

I watched her that evening and thought she was wonderful. Her deep melancholy and those amazing eyes! We made friends, though only at a distance at first.

Erika was three years older than me, studying art history and Romance languages and literature. She was a deeply depressive woman, but with a strong temperament and a strong will to survive. She came from Dresden. As a child she had lived in Würzburg with her mother and sister and, unlike me, had been a model school student, with a brilliant mind.

When I met her I had been reading Patrick Dennis's *Little Me*, the imaginary biography of Maybelle Schlumpfert, who adopted the name of Belle Poitrine [Beautiful Breasts] and considered herself a film and TV star. Neil Simon turned this story into a successful Broadway musical. The book *Little Me* was not only a wonderful parody in fictional form of the cult of celebrity but also full of visual tricks with cleverly staged photos. Belle Poitrine's main opponent in the book was a star named Magdalena Montezuma, and the two clashed on the set of a film starring both rivals, *Viva tequila*. When I met my "Magdalena" I knew that was the only name for her. She simply was not an Erika Kluge. Someone had given her the wrong name. She had certainly been born under the aegis of the Aztec emperor Moctezuma.

In her youth Magdalena had a very bad time. As a child she had suffered from tuberculosis of the spinal marrow, and she was victimized by her frightful mother and sister. For years she was in a plaster cast and could view the street only in an outside mirror. When she was somewhat better, all she wanted was to get away from her family. But there was no compensation for a childhood like that. I once made her visit her mother against her will, because I always wanted harmony, but it was pointless. Her mother wrote, for instance, that she had seen Magdalena in my film *The Bomber Pilot*, was horrified to see her appear naked, and told her she was a disgrace to the family. That upset her. When she died, it was a while before I told her family; I wanted no more to do with them.

At first my mother had some difficulty with Magdalena, because she was so extreme. But then she took her to her heart, and so at least Magdalena had something like a family life. It was delightful to see her and my mother together, except that she sometimes walked in her sleep and mewed like a cat. My mother wasn't used to that kind of thing, but then she succeeded in domesticating Magdalena, who was a very expressive and exotic figure, as anyone can see from our films together. There was nothing artificial about her appearance; it was the real woman.

When I began making films in 1968, she was the first artist I wanted to work with. From the very first until her death in 1984 we worked together almost all the time. Magdalena was a great, gifted, ardent visual artist, but her drawings, pastels, and paintings were never good enough for her, so she tore up most of them and threw them away. I rescued a few, and with my friend Marcelo Uriona exhibited them in the Neue Räume of the Berlin Gallery after her death. You could see how talented she was at a glance.

But she also had a gift for performance art entirely removed from reality, and was unaware of it. I pointed it out to her, and we realized that we wanted to work together. She was my leading lady from my first venture into 8 mm film with the gay director Rosa von Praunheim, *Grotesque–Burlesque–Picturesque*, to *The Rose King* just before her death. In fact she was *the* leading lady, the expression of my soul and her talent, and her own soul and her ardor.

She moved to Munich with me at the end of the sixties. We had no money, but we went on filming all the same. Magdalena was splendid, and even took a job as a telephone operator at the BMW factory. I put a lot of work into styling her—work that was a pleasure, bringing out the best in her as an elegant, exotic beauty and an expressive woman. Later, she went to work in the delivery shop at the airport, where she was paid better. And then, at night, she and I worked together. At times Magdalena kept herself going on Captagon, a powerful stimulant. She would sleep for less than three hours; it was crazy, but that was how we made films like *Eika Katappa*.

She hardly ever went to the cinema or watched TV, certainly not to find inspiration for a film. We didn't think much of culture, and we couldn't afford to go to the opera. No one ever sent me invitations phrased along the lines of "It would be an honor, Herr Schroeter, if you would attend our première at the State Opera House." I was a drifter going around with Magdalena. Who was going to give us tickets to the opera? We thought up our imaginative ideas at home.

Back then, people were always pointing out that I cut an unusual figure, and they also made it clear that Montezuma didn't exactly resemble a dear old auntie working in a savings bank. But we hadn't yet moved far enough into the sphere that I wanted to inhabit with her. I had received my musical education at provincial opera houses when I was between thirteen and eighteen, and she had a wonderful visual sense, so by looking at images and listening to music, music, and more music, we created a kind of graphic environment for our visions.

We also liked going to cafés. Half my life with her consisted of hitchhiking and sitting in cafés. Even when I was making *Eika Katappa*, we were still hitching rides to Amsterdam and spending the night in youth hostels. Magdalena drew and painted, and we exhibited her pictures on the pavement. Now and then someone bought one, and we would treat ourselves to a gin in a café. We were free, except that when you were standing in the street with a suitcase, at night and in a snowstorm, that wasn't so much fun. But it was all part of our life, and we had the stamina to take it.

We succeeding in filming and traveling around in each other's company, although Magdalena was sometimes close to collapse. I think she was very much in love with me then. I valued her as a friend; to me, friendship was always more important than anything, and still is. But that wasn't enough for her, so there were conflicts.

At times we lived as a threesome in my thirty-five-square-meter apartment at 63 Kräpelinstrasse, Munich, opposite the Max Planck Institute of Psychiatry. Steven Adamczewski, known as Puttchen [Ducky], my great love, was living with us; he was a crazy and very young American. We had one bed, and when I was sleeping with him, I remember Magdalena coming along with a bucket and washing our socks beside the bed. It was wonderful, but sad for her too.

She managed all our correspondence with film labs, branches of the Goethe Institute, and distributors, and she did it all in perfect French and English. Well, someone had to do it. I couldn't, and anyway I was too lazy; I preferred fucking. Magdalena ran the business side of our filming from our apartment. We went away together as often as possible, when the films were being shown in Paris or Mexico City or other places. And sometimes she attended on her own, representing me and talking about the films to the audience, although it was a long time before that came easily to her.

When we were beginning to work in the theater together, Peter Zadek and Augusto Fernándes took an interest in her. It began in Hamburg in 1972, with Lessing's *Emilia Galotti*, in which I had also involved the actress Christine Kaufmann. The conventional, bourgeois audience thought the production was terrible, but Benjamin Henreich, writing in the *Süddeutsche Zeitung*, spoke of Montezuma's magnificent terraced dynamics—he used the musicological term indicating swift shifts of volume between crescendo and diminuendo. That was how we came to work in the theater at Bochum in 1973.

Our circle expanded, and Magdalena found she could fall in love with other people, though unfortunately, she made the wrong choices: for instance, a colleague who enjoyed her cooking but didn't want to be physically close. An unhappy love story yet again. And then there was an attorney who made advances to her. But when Magdalena's love for him was at its height, he sent her an invitation, addressed to the Frankfurt Theater, where we happened to be working, asking her to his wedding with another woman.

But as she got to know more people, Magdalena felt more independent. We were no longer living together. She had an apartment of her own, first in Bochum, then in Berlin. Working with her became freer, and I went on doing so as often as possible, with Magdalena as my companion, a part of my heart and my work. It made a great difference for us to be working together!

In our last film together, *The Rose King*, her magnificence and lucidity are clear to see. She was a wonderful woman, and I have never found one to succeed her fully. I did have women friends later: for instance, Bulle Ogier, Nathalie Delon, Ingrid Caven, and the photographer Roswitha Hecke, who was Peter Zadek's lover and with whom I had an affair, to his displeasure. But my first love, Magdalena, was unique. Everything fell into place, our work together, our life together. It was wonderful to find how two such strange people as the pair of us could stick together through thick and thin.

When we were shooting *The Rose King* in Portugal in 1984, I was already looking around for a grave for her. That sounds perverse, but it's the way it was. Magdalena was suffering from cancer, was very sick, and I didn't think she would want to travel back to Germany with us. She could have been buried in the cemetery at Sintra. But she did want to return to Berlin, where she lived and suffered, suffered and lived, for a few more weeks. At least she had a doctor and good girlfriends who were looking after her when she died in her apartment. I can count myself among the friends who stood by her in her sickness as well as we could. Magdalena had been dead for a few hours when I called my friend Antonio Orlando, who takes one of the three main parts in *The Rose King*, and told him, "Maddalena è morta." To which he replied with the fine remark, "Dunque è nata una stella" [Then a star has been born].

Magdalena was buried in Berlin's Südstern cemetery. I have never been back there. I like to visit cemeteries, but not to see the graves of particular people. For me a cemetery means all who have gone before us. I don't look for my dead friends there but carry them around with me. In my mother's case I did something special, marking her love of aquamarine gemstones by wearing jewelry made of them. That kind of thing is more important.

Rosa/Holger and Carla— the beginning of my artistic work

One Sunday morning
I come down the aisle
I'm very nervous
and he tries to smile

In 1967 I was bored to death studying film in Munich, so I traveled to Knokke-le-Zoute in Belgium for the excellent EXPRMNTL film festival. I was sick with anorexia, I felt unwell, and, though 1.81 meters tall, I weighed only sixty kilos. My mood resembled that of Jacques

Brel's "Knokke-le-Zoute Tango," which runs: "Il pleut sur Knokke-le-Zoute / Ce soir comme tous les soirs / Je me rentre chez moi / Le cœur en déroute / Et la bite sous l'bras" [It's raining on Knokke-le-Zoute / This evening like every evening / I'm going home / With my heart disturbed / And my prick under my arm].

This wonderful experimental film festival took place over Christmas and New Year's. It opened the door to another world, to American underground cinema, to Gregory Markopoulos, Andy Warhol, and Jackie Curtis. Great! It was a glimpse of something entirely strange, another kind of film, and the expression of my longings.

At that time everyone who had anything to do with films knew the Knokke festival and wanted to be there. I had brought along a ten-minute silent film in 8 mm that I had shot the previous year in beautiful squares in Verona, Venice, Milan, and elsewhere when I was traveling in Italy with my mother. I wanted to show it as a fringe event, but I was very shy. Today all I remember is that there were cats in it.

Anyway, what I wanted was to learn about love and then say goodbye to everything. I traveled to Knokke in a Volkswagen Beetle driven by a frustrated young dancer from the corps de ballet in Mannheim. She was probably hoping to find a lover there too—I don't know. Her name was Karin, Karin Müller. Anyway, I felt I was on my last journey. I was twenty-two years old and had no prospects.

That year was the last time, or the next-to-last time, the film festival was held, but that had nothing to do with me. Some of the audience protested during the screenings, insisting on discussions because they said the films, or some of them, were too apolitical. This was just before May 1968.

In Knokke I met a filmmaker from Berlin who took a great fancy to me. I fell in love with this Herr Holger Mischwitzky, alias Rosa von Praunheim—and guess what: all of a sudden I was cured of anorexia. I could drink a cognac again and eat something. Love conquered all.

So I discovered the true experience of love not in Naples but with Holger. He was the embodiment of love as passion. I had already made attempts at something like love, but I experienced the genuine thing with Holger. In January following the festival, I made the first 8 mm films that would start me on my real artistic path. Holger advised me to convert my energy into creativity, saying that he couldn't stand people who weren't active. "Why are you so lackadaisical?" he asked. I replied, as I always do, "It's my tragic perception of the world, that's all."

He inspired me in the true sense of the word, so that at last I was pointed toward my destiny. It was a revelation, and without it I probably would have hanged myself or drunk myself to death with friends. Holger started many people along the path of creativity, including Elfi Mikesch, the photographer and camerawoman, and her husband, the painter Fritz Mikesch. He impelled them in a direction that allowed them to give their talents full expression rather than just complaining passively. Holger could motivate you, give you strength, or, to put it more crudely, get you going by kicking your ass. That was his great quality.

This was also when Holger Mischwitzky adopted the name Rosa von Praunheim. He was three years older than me, was studying at the College of Art in West Berlin, and had just finished shooting his first film, *Von Rosa von Praunheim*. I called him Holger, because anything else would have been nonsense, but ultimately the name Rosa carried the day.

So in January and February 1968, I began shooting short films with my old 8 mm camera. For the time being I gave up my idea of pursuing love in death, a *Liebestod*, and went to Berlin to visit Holger. I found myself in a bizarre circle there, all of them superstars, outsiders, artists with crazy ideas. There is a fine photo from this period in which Holger is carrying me in his arms, like a Pietà. It is captioned "Our love was only brief, our friendship was eternal." And that was a fact.

I finally dropped out of my pseudotheoretical studies of film in Munich. I wanted to get at the camera and the cutting table; I wanted to work at my trade in practice and in my mind. Then I did apply to the College of Film in Berlin, and so did Rainer Werner Fassbinder and Holger, but all three of us were rejected. When we spoke at seminars later, the story of that rejection was always good for a laugh. The next year, in 1969, I was awarded the Josef von Sternberg Prize at the Mannheim Film Festival for my film *Eika Katappa*. So in a year and a half I had gone from zero to hero.

In fact, my path was one of organic, autodidactic development. Like my friends Rainer and Rosa, I was obliged to adopt an energetic approach and to overcome obstacles. I began as a dilettante, dealing with everything myself—the camera, the lighting, the cutting, and arranging the music too, because I enjoyed it. Then everything followed naturally, and I also came to direct in theater, from 1979 in opera, and later in ballet.

Of course, I was full of admiration for Maria Callas and the cinema as I knew it from Carl Dreyer's *La Passion de Jeanne d'Arc*. I loved the films of Alain Resnais—for instance, *L'année dernière à Marienbad* and *Muriel ou le temps d'un retour*. And the films of Michelangelo Antonioni, particularly *La notte*, were very much up my alley. I was in my early twenties, I had no experience, and making films is expensive. How could I dream of such a thing? But I always knew that I didn't want to direct the garbage of ordinary narrative cinema or the theatrical plays shown on television.

In the year 1968 alone, I shot about twenty short films with my old Austrian Normal-8 camera. They were little filmed collages and studies in black and white, featuring my actors and me, my stars Magdalena Montezuma, Carla Aulaulu, Steven Adamczewski, and other friends, both men and women. And there were films about my tormented love for Maria Callas, in which I used stage sets and portraits taken from magazines, record sleeves, and advertising. I had no idea that I would get to know her personally a few years later.

I experimented with assembling photos of Callas so that I could present her in movement, as if in an animated film, with her gestures and her tragic expression. I included texts about her appearance from opera critics, I tried out repetitions, double exposures, speech bubbles stuck to the film, and effects with a split screen. I included all kinds of diary-like shots, showing myself (it was from then on that I took to writing my name as Werner Schroeter, not Schröter) and the places and things surrounding my friends and me, the ambience in which we lived. My camera had no sound, so I took to compiling auditory collage tracks for my films, taken from my collection of records and transferred to tape—for instance, my favorite arias sung by Callas. I even had her singing duets with herself. I also used passages from hit songs performed by Caterina Valente, whom I revered, Christmas carols, and texts from Lautréamont's *Songs of Maldoror*, to contrast with the images on-screen. I can't offer any interpretation of exactly what was beginning then. I am an artist, I work intuitively.

Much later I gave my early works, as well as a carton of uncut material from that productive first year, to the Munich Museum of Film. They are mainly dramatic studies that we shot in Berlin with an 8 mm camera. I did not include them in my first retrospectives, which were as early as the year 1971, but I didn't destroy them either. A critic once said I made a poor decision giving them to the film archives, but never mind. I can be seen in one of those studies dancing in my room naked, except for socks on my feet. Another shows Carla Aulaulu miming the great Callas singing, holding up a microphone as if in playback or karaoke. There was no denying our sense of humor. Then I bought a 16 mm camera with money borrowed from my parents, who made me a present of half the price. My short films became more complex and comprehensive. The following year, *Neurasia* and *Argila* were shown in Hamburg, and so it went on. The effect of the events of 1968 is underestimated these days: there was a worldwide compulsion at the time among young people to communicate with others, with strangers.

But back to Knokke-le-Zoute. Holger was on the road then with his star "Carla Aulaulu," a petite blonde he had met in Berlin in the midsixties. Her stage name was wonderful; her actual name was Carla Egerer. Carla had a creative imagination far beyond what most people could grasp, and she had a gift for anarchic invention. I saw her in Rosa von Praunheim's first film, *Von Rosa von Praunheim*, a crazy parody, a travesty of melodrama, in which Carla played the oppressed maidservant of a middle-class family and sang such lines as "Ich leide bis zum Überdruss. Mein Besen in meinem Herzen ist vergoldet . . ." [I suffer to excess. The broom in my heart is gilded]. She had some great scenes in which, for instance, she collapses while serving tea but recovers, again and again.

There was something of Marilyn Monroe about Carla. This was the time of superstars as Andy Warhol portrayed them in films or as Jackie Davis, the housewives' diva, played them onstage in New York.

At Christmas and New Year in Knokke-le-Zoute, Carla was in top form. I was sharing a room in a boardinghouse with Karin, the dancer who drove the VW Beetle, but she disappeared, probably after finding a boyfriend. So I moved into the boardinghouse where Carla Aulaulu and Holger Mischwitzky were staying. There was a double bed, not a large one, but we all three slept in it. Now that I had recovered physically and was in love, I began to feel something again. My night of love with Holger was terrific, while Carla pretended to be asleep. After a short rest we were at it again. At that Carla went crazy, hit out with pillows and mattresses while we were fucking, and sang a parody of the folksong about a huntsman from the Palatinate, making it end, "He stumbles over chickenshit, he breaks his neck and then that's it."

So much for our night of love in Knokke. I came back to life; I became a film director, an author, all sorts of things. My health improved. I felt impelled to be active and creative. After the festival I didn't just visit Holger and his friends, I invited him to my mother's place in Dossenheim, shot *Grotesque–Burlesque–Picturesque* with him the same year, and assisted him with his own films. He financed one by marrying Carla, because a married couple could get a cheap loan then in West Berlin.

There was a major showdown in 1969. I was friendly with the artist Steven Adamczewski and loved him very much. Another friend was Ingo, who was mildly addicted to heroin and whom we all thought very attractive. Carla imagined he and I had something going—don't ask me why. I was lying on the bed at Rosa's place, where I stayed sometimes in Berlin. Ingo, Rosa, and I were feverishly talking about Ingo's withdrawal symptoms. Carla came into the room with a Bavarian tankard in her hand, bringing Ingo a beer. Or was it a large cup? "Have you guys been fucking?" she asked, to which Rosa replied, "Yes, it was great." That was just nonsense, but she threw the tankard right across the room to hit me on the forehead, so that a jet of blood shot out. I'd had a nasty blow, and shards of the tankard stuck to the wallpaper. Carla ran away, with Rosa in pursuit. Alix von Buchen was just coming in, and she almost fainted at the sight. I shouted, "Call a doctor!" Then I lost consciousness for a moment. Rosa had caught up with Carla and hit her—the sewerman's revenge. Alix von Buchen took me to the hospital.

It was horrible at hospitals at the beginning of 1969 because there were so many political confrontations in the street, and before treating me the medics wanted to know who had done it. I said it was a drunk in a bar, but no one believed me, because I looked suspiciously like a hippie anarchist. They left me sitting there with the blood flowing from that crazy wound. Finally, they said they were prepared to stitch it up. "Six stitches or twelve?"

"What's the difference?" I asked.

"With six you'll look like Nosferatu. With twelve you'll look all right."

Then they bungled the injection, which went in under my scalp and was uncomfortable. Finally, I was home, lying in bed with my head covered in Band-Aids. I don't have any doubts that it was really like that, but anyway it makes a good story. Carla came in. There was a photo of her on the nightstand close to me, and I threw it at her.

I still wanted to go on working with her on *Eika Katappa*, but there was something weird about her. Whenever I saw her, I felt I had to protect my head. I had wanted her to be in *Salome*, which we shot in Lebanon in 1971. But she had begun to change; she thought we were all bastards, exploiters, and assholes. I didn't see it that way. With her anarchical imagination, she had been a wonderful and amazingly expressive complement to Magdalena Montezuma: the actress with the philosophical profile against the philosopher Magdalena with her tragic face. But that was the end of our association.

Argila and *Neurasia*

I can't interpret my films, but I can say what led to them. As I see it, a description is profound if it clarifies the way themes from life lead to the cinema and the theater.

I experimented with 8 mm films for a good year, making more than ten of them in a short time. By now I had the 16 mm Beaulieu camera with which, in 1968, I shot *Neurasia* and *Argila*, two films of medium length this time, and they were very well received at the experimental Hamburg Film Show, the German equivalent of Knokke-le-Zoute.

I had made good friends during that year of working in 8 mm. I was thinking of those friends, Magdalena, Carla, and the others, and of a kaleidoscopic pattern, a selection from themes close to my heart that were developing in my mind like a wide horizon. The idea was to present our sense of life, the demands we made on ourselves, and achieve a change in our usual habits and the way we saw things. We involuntarily found ourselves expressing the spirit of the times. The group was an aesthetic movement, an aesthetic revolution, running parallel to the political events of 1968. I received compliments on that at the time, and I still do. My work was perceived as the breaking of windowpanes that had become dulled. The director Ulrike Ottinger, for instance, started a film club in Konstanz to which people traveled from Zurich to see my films. I didn't want anything to do with psychological cinema, preferring the free interplay of music and film. But of course I also encountered a great deal of hostility.

Someone from a Bavarian film club for young people called *Neurasia* a "Schroeter musical"; in Munich such films were shown in the Other Cinema. That was roughly the kind of reaction we wanted. The film critic Frieda Grafe called *Neurasia* a "stage for language." In the magazine *Filmkritik*, which was very important to me, she wrote: "*Neurasia* is a silent film with music. The tunes fit in with the images as they used to in the days when the pianist was still sitting in the auditorium. Sometimes you have the illusion of synchronicity,

time as space. Sound is of overriding importance only in one version; the sounds do not intersect. The acoustic plane is eternal, goes on forever, and so is present, past, and future; the pictorial plane is the present and memory. I was experimenting with aesthetically structural processes. The contents of the films, my reflections on relationships, on the archaic subjects of grief, love, and death, are themes that have always obsessed me. But I took great pleasure in *Argila* as an aesthetic experiment. It was my way of reacting counter to conventionally familiar narrative forms. I overshot the mark, going far into the sphere of the experimental. That gave me the confidence to find my own real work, merging the progressively aesthetic with eternal archaic problems.

Eika Katappa

In January 1969 I was in Mannheim, on my way to shoot some film with Magdalena Montezuma and Carla Aulaulu. Carla saw a poster that we couldn't read outside a cinema showing what were known as "films for guest workers." Carla didn't know any Turkish, nor of course did I. She deciphered it as best she could. "What does it mean, Werner? Look, it says *Eika Katappa*." I took that as the title of the film that we shot after *Neurasia* and *Argila*. Later, someone from the University of Bochum Film Club found out that, with some approximation to Greek, it can be translated as "scattered pictures." I thought that was amusing. There's no such thing as coincidence.

The titles of my films often came to me spontaneously as I went along, and that was what happened with *Eika Katappa*. Since I was carrying out experiments, the invented words seemed appropriate. If viewers associated *Neurasia* with neuroses, or *Argila* with the famous white clay used in sculptures, there's nothing I can add by way of explanation. I was interested only in what gave rise to such associations.

Carla, the actress with the Monroe hairstyle, and Magdalena the tragedian were both at the heart of *Eika Katappa*. It also drew on reminiscences of Carl Dreyer's silent film *La Passion de Jeanne d'Arc*, a work that had imprinted itself on my mind like a silhouette that would never fade. To be strictly honest, it was the only film that ever influenced me. It is extremely bold in its own way, with its close-ups, its concentrated framing, and its gestures of pain. At Knokke-le-Zoute I also fell in love with the films of Gregory Markopoulos, particularly *Twice a Man*, with those curiously slow, long-drawn-out sequences and frankly gay images of men. Although Holger thought them kitschy, they influenced me, but mainly it was the expression of the absolute in Dreyer's *Jeanne d'Arc* that left its mark on me, a mark comparable only to that also left by Maria Callas. With the strong intensity of Magdalena and Carla's crazy commedia dell'arte style, I found out what I could do in that line myself.

Like my other films, of course, *Eika Katappa* was made on a shoe-string. Well, not entirely, but it threw me into debt and so there wasn't much money for us to live on. Magdalena Montezuma con-tributed her own earnings, but when we were making *Eika Katappa*, we were on the scrounge anyway, living off other people. My parents were paying for my studies, although I'd dropped out, and financ-ing my Munich apartment. We were able to stay in the little house in Drossenheim when we were filming in the neighborhood, and my mother cooked for us. It was a way of life. In fact, we were to-gether the whole time, so the storyline developed in authentically close quarters.

As well as the 16 mm camera, I possessed a decent, professional Uher reel-to-reel tape recorder. I had a single piece of music on it, Leonora's cabaletta from act 3 of Giuseppe Verdi's opera *Il trovatore*: "Tu vedrai que l'amore in terra" [No love in the world is stronger than mine], she sings when she is in her lover's army camp in the middle of the war, thinking only of her wedding, which may at last be imminent. Three and a half minutes of singing by Maria Cal-las; I can still hear it in my mind. That music, plus us, the human beings involved—we and our equipment were in search of some-thing indefinable to do with life, joy, grief, and yearning. I had three handwritten pages of a draft script that I carried around with me, but I kept throwing them away and rewriting. That way, the film de-veloped like an organic life-form on our three-month journey. We weren't aiming for a conventional plot; it was all about gesture and movement, and emotional high points from the finest of operas, music that meant a great deal to me.

My mother drove us in her car to the places where we planned to shoot the film, to Heidelberg Castle and the abandoned amphitheater nearby that had been built by the Nazis as a *Thingplatz*, intending it to be a place of assembly in the style of the old Norse parliaments. The great, pseudoclassical flight of steps there was one of our locations for the slow sequences of walking, stopping, and sinking to the ground in *Eika Katappa*. Such flights of steps, which made the auditorium of the amphitheater into a stage, were also reminiscent of the tiers of steps in TV studios used for light entertainment, and I also employed them later in many productions for live theater.

Everything was improvised. I used my recording of the cabaletta from *Il trovatore* in the scenes in Naples, when a young gypsy made a spontaneous appearance in the film because he happened to cross my path. When we were shooting interiors, my friend Daniel Schmid played the piano; when we were outdoors, we made live music in every possible way, even with a tootophone, for instance. We had very slender means to create an atmosphere for the silent filming; it was all about pure movement and physicality.

Eika Katappa, then, is a collection of associations in image and sound from the world as I saw it, a freely created compendium. A dramatic concept emerged only in cutting. Very important was the confrontation between Magdalena and Carla, who stood for two opposite types: Magdalena and her innate tragedy, Carla and her dadaist humor.

I was careful to avoid anything too smooth. I wanted the film to turn out the way I envisioned it and to reflect the way other people saw me. In the course of the work, which entailed traveling from Munich by way of Heidelberg to Naples, other characters appeared in self-contained episodes . . . I was a strange, curious character myself back then, accosting strangers and asking them to work with me, but I was always ready to communicate, and so I soon overcame my shyness.

My meeting with the Neapolitan fisherman came as a surprise.

I thought the man ugly in an attractive way; he looked like a parody of someone from the sixties. We also found a handsome French gypsy. The couple had to be inseparable; that was our sole point of departure for the characters. When I put the idea to the fisherman, he said, "Si, siamo tutti autori," meaning, roughly, "Yes, we are all authors"—or it could also mean "perpetrators." Anyway, he had a natural talent and enjoyed working with us.

I went to Naples on my own for this part of the shooting. At first Rosa von Praunheim was going to be my assistant; he decided that he didn't like the idea, but in the end he did help out. I found the people who were willing to be in the film as I went along, which often happened in my films. When Magdalena and I were on a train, we spotted the blond, incredibly old-fashioned young man who appeared as Christ with his crown of thorns in a Passion play. That's absolutely the sentimental look we want, I said, and we went over and asked him. At first he was taken aback. It turned out that he was the son of the German ambassador in Moscow, but then he decided it would be fun to work with these strange filmmakers.

In my childish delight and arrogance, I didn't mind the fact that only Neapolitans understood the dialog. I knew that their gestures and tones of voice would make it possible to follow what they were saying. When the fisherman, his black-haired, tie-wearing son, and the son's boyfriend sat talking to each other, the gist of what the fisherman said was "My son, don't you see that you can't go away with this stranger? He'll abandon you, it will be the end of you, you must stay here." That basic thematic melody can be understood as you would understand it in a silent film, and so can the fisherman's lament when he finds his son's body on the Riviera di Chiaia.

Ten years later, when I was shooting my historical film *Nel regno di Napoli* [The Kingdom of Naples], the fisherman turned up again and asked me whether I remembered him. His language had the authentic Neapolitan cadence; he wasn't pretending. He told me, in distress, that five years after the making of *Eika Katappa*, his real-life son had died on the Riviera di Chiaia, and he, the young man's father, wanted to leave me his little restaurant in his will. I was to be adopted, so to speak. I was both fascinated and disturbed by such parallels, seeing them in the light of the duplication of a tragedy and illustrating the unvarying nature of death. They have always been my subject. Of course, I declined the legacy.

A sense of closeness developed among us while making the work, without any compulsion and according to no rules. We took our time shooting and didn't feel that we were wasting time. My dream has always been to present life as something light, a hovering or floating entity. People told stories and talked about themselves. I could watch them looking thoughtfully out to sea. It was never a pointless loss of time; something always came of it. The shooting itself was not expensive; all we needed was a little makeup, and sometimes a different pair of pants or another dress found in the flea market. Working with the photography and the actors lasted at the most four hours a day, and we spent the rest of the time in each other's company. For a long time, that was how I saw my work as a filmmaker.

We had put together about seven hours' worth of material for *Eika Katappa*, and in the end the film was two and a half hours long. I created a montage of it on a moviescope, a small editing machine with a tiny screen, and with the reel for thirty meters of film on one side and an empty reel on the other, both wound by hand. I had no money for a copy, so I shot on reversal film. Ektachrome Commercial and Kodachrome were my favorite materials for my next films too. I cut without sound, relying on being able to see enough on the little screen for the later enlargement with sound and music. Then I gave the film to a wonderful lady from the ARRI copying works in Munich, who stuck it together for me properly—meaning while it was still wet—and charged only half the usual price. I myself used ordinary Scotch tape. The result was a black-and-white working copy for my self-taught filming.

At the time, you could get into the Bavarian Radio building at night. When it closed down for the day, I was allowed in, and I could work on my carton full of reels of film and music there, sitting at the cutting table until eight in the morning. I spent all night experimenting with sound and music, wondering how I could do without the usual kind of narrative drama that kills the images stone dead. I wanted all the music that I used to keep its own acoustic character. I used old recordings like the aria from *La traviata* that Maria

Cebotari sang on Reich Radio in 1943. I didn't level out anything in transferring Tina Turner's "If I Dance" to tape either; every recording retained its own character, from the tinny sound of the old People's Radio of the Nazi period to the recordings of Callas in the 1950s. I connected it all up at the cutting table, so that music was followed by silent passages or carefully chosen single sounds, but no extraneous noise could ever be heard at the same time as music and language. That was my way of sabotaging normal narrative drama, a provocation to eye and ear that was, of course, meant affectionately. At the end of the film I had a picture of Callas, accompanied not by her own voice but by that of Celestina Boninsegna, a fine Italian spinto soprano. Boninsegna was singing one of Callas's showpieces, Leonora's aria from the third act of Verdi's *The Force of Destiny*. I was playing with the myth of Callas, linking her image to the sound of another voice. It was up to the viewers to gauge where the "truth" of the performers' identity lay.

To my delight, Josef von Sternberg, then an old man, whose films *The Blue Angel*, *The Devil Is a Woman*, and *The Scarlet Empress* I had admired even as a child, liked *Eika Katappa*. That I was awarded the Josef von Sternberg Prize at the 1969 Mannheim Film Festival represented a rebellion against ordinary narrative drama in the cinema. In the end, North German Radio bought the film for a wonderful ten thousand marks. But when it was transmitted on Bavarian Television, they simply cut the end. And when the film was screened again in the seventies, the reels were switched around. I was watching it with [the transsexual singer] Zazie de Paris in her apartment, and when we noticed what had happened, I called the TV station. By dint of threatening those responsible, I actually made them stop the film forty minutes into the screening and begin again at the beginning—as a result, it went on for three and a half hours.

... and what came of it

Now that we had won the Josef von Sternberg Prize we were well known. The newspapers wrote about *Eika Katappa* and about me as a maker of underground films. Wim Wenders described my work as "fantastic films about artificial characters," and the critic Wilfried Wiegand, writing in the *Frankfurter Allgemeine Zeitung*, said that my films represented "total criticism of our consciousness."

The prize showed that we had an audience in film clubs and art-house cinemas. To get into the major cinemas we would have needed distributors, but we couldn't think of that. Nor did the prize change our chaotic situation. We were behind with working out costs for the music in *Eika Katappa*, and demands for payment from filmmaking firms kept coming in. Even the work's rating as a "film of artistic value," which qualified it for tax relief, entailed bureaucratic expenses that we couldn't meet. So I went back, of all places, to the Munich University of [Television and] Film, from which I had dropped out because of sheer boredom, to earn some money by giving lectures on "the structural problems of musical films."

Magdalena was kind enough to take on the office paperwork, which I could never have dealt with. She answered the inquiries that soon came in from Brussels, Paris, New York, London, Montreal, and Rio de Janeiro and arranged for the film to be sent on from cinema to cinema. She wrote wonderfully courteous business letters, with phrases such as "Je vous prie d'agréer, cher Monsieur, l'expression de mes salutations les meilleures." She patiently coped with correspondence, freight, and the accounts while at the same time earning her living and working on our next films.

In spring 1970 *Eika Katappa* was invited to the Cannes Film Festival. Volker Schlöndorff mentioned my film to Pierre-Henri Deleau, who had come to Munich for the selection of German directors to be included in the Quinzaine des réalisateurs (Directors' fortnight) held parallel to the festival. Deleau immediately included the film in the program, although everyone knew it wouldn't be easy viewing.

Of course, I was very proud to have *Eika Katappa* shown at Cannes. I was both annoyed and amused by the violent reactions to the film, because this was the year after the 1968 riots, and most of the critics were expecting political films. I was never afraid of disapproval. Aggression arises between people, especially in an intense exchange of opinions, but personally I like to avoid conflicts. I thought it would be cineasts who assembled in Cannes, but I was concerned above all with strict form and a ritual that provoked many critics. I remember during the showing in Cannes that someone threw a shoe at the screen. Naturally I reacted to those who booed the film by calling them fascists, the preferred term of abuse at that time.

But Pierre-Henri Deleau went on showing my films, and so I was represented at Cannes by *The Death of Maria Malibran*, *The Black Angel*, *Flocons d'or*, *The Kingdom of Naples*, and others. In 1972 we were invited to the festivals in Avignon and Nancy, in 1973 to the Hyères Festival, and in the same year the first retrospective of my films took place in Paris, organized by Frédéric Mitterrand at his cinema l'Olympic. Our success abroad began early, especially in France.

In Cannes, the Argentinian documentary director Fernando Solanas paid me a compliment that pleased me very much. In 1968 he had made the famous essay in film form *La hora de los hornos* [The hour of the furnaces], which I loved. Solanas told me that this socialist film of his about Argentina and *Eika Katappa* resembled each other; I explored souls and passion, while he explored politics and polemics.

At this time the films of the Quinzaine des réalisateurs were shown frequently at the Cinémathèque française, and in 1970 Henri Langlois, the legendary head of that archival film collection, fell in love with *Eika Katappa* when he screened it at the Palais Chaillot. This "curious Monsieur," as many people called him, understood me very well. He became a dear friend, and we enjoyed many jokes together.

Henri Langlois and his partner, Mary Meerson, were very fond of Magdalena. Mary Meerson, whose eyesight was extremely poor, touched Magdalena's face and was then able to describe it perfectly. In Paris, Henri Langlois always put me up at the Hôtel de Seine. But when he traveled to the Cannes Film Festival incognito, as he often did, I was the only one he arranged to meet. We had an excellent relationship. For instance, if he wanted me to kick up a row with someone he couldn't stand, he would ask me to dinner at the best restaurants, saying, "Come on, Werner, come on! I have to meet Sergei Bondarchuk. Liven things up, won't you?" I was happy to oblige. So we would sit in a really good restaurant while I needled Bondarchuk. Henri Langlois might well come in a tuxedo, wearing slippers with it, both drunk and happy as a sandboy. I got to make digs at Bondarchuk's film of *War and Peace*, for instance, describing it as slushy, a way of raping the masses. I asked him about his aims and his opinion of Stalinism. I liked playing the clown and being accepted for what I was.

I was already cultivating a kind of punk style. I went about in ripped jeans, boots, and so forth, but I looked elegant all the same. For instance, with an outfit that might have come out of a garbage bin I would wear a beautiful cashmere jacket from Yves Saint Laurent. I think it was a present from Frédéric Mitterand, French minister of culture at the time of this writing. He was the first to get my films distributed in France. Between 1973 and 1975, he was in the distribution business and owned three very good art-house cinemas—he was brilliant at his profession. Sometimes Frédéric, André Téchiné, and I lived together.

Because all the major European newspapers had reviewed us after Mannheim and Cannes, television suddenly came our way too, offering to let me shoot improvised, low-budget films for the *Night Studio* programs. At that time the television editors, particularly of the *Little TV Theater* series on Channel Two of German television, were open to artistic experiments, and four of my films were made within a year: *The Bomber Pilot*, *Salome*, *Macbeth*, and *The Death of Maria Malibran*.

In that interesting year of 1970/71, my lifelong friendship with the photographer Digne Meller Marcovicz began. She was working as a photojournalist for *Der Spiegel*, we met in Munich, and from then on she accompanied all our productions, whether for cinema or the theater, as a friend and to photograph the set and rehearsals. For many years, I could call her and invite her to join us when I was beginning a new project, and she would be there, even though she had three children to look after and traveled a great deal as a *Spiegel* photographer. I couldn't pay her, but once, when her small children and her job were getting her down, I sent—no, I asked—Magdalena to help her, and there was Magdalena, dramatically dressed in black, standing at the ironing board. To Digne, life and work were inseparable; it was something that we had in common. She expressed it wonderfully well with her portrait photos and, above all, her photographs of stage sets and our activities. Apart from Roswitha Hecke and Elfi Mikesch, she took more pictures than anyone of my work, right up to *Malina*. Sometimes she could capture magical moments better than my film camera.

Comedies

Looking back at those intense and productive first few years, I realize that I was already inclined to experiment with very different forms. I didn't want to be lumped in with the underground filmmakers, such as the child prodigy Puppi Goldbär with his bombastic melodramas, or regarded as one of the postrealists with *The Kingdom of Naples* and *Palermo or Wolfsburg*. In a year and a half, from 1970 to 1971, I made five films with Magdalena and my other friends, both male and female. And not least, I was beginning to work in the theater. I lived in Munich with Magdalena and, later, from time to time in a commune with Ingrid Caven and Daniel Schmid, but we went from place to place, from Dossenheim to Vienna, London, Naples, and Beirut.

After *Eika Katappa* I almost had a chance to move into major cinema production with a 35 mm film. Peter Berling, a prominent producer in Munich, wanted to make a larger-than-life continuation of *Neurasia*. We shot it in a real film studio belonging to the firm of Schonger near Lake Ammer. Robert van Ackeren, my cameraman for the eighth chapter of *Eika Katappa*, worked with me, but ultimately the film turned out to be just a strange episode in my life, leading nowhere. No one has ever seen the finished version of *Nicaragua*.

The material was held by the ARRI company in Munich because of unpaid invoices for copying—Peter Berling had overdone things—and at some point it was phased out and lost. Maybe it will turn up one day in the Federal German Film Archive.

Another film of the time, titled *Anglia*, also remains unfinished and was never shown. Ulli Lommel, the ambitious actor who had worked with Fassbinder and was also a producer and director, began shooting *Anglia* with us, as well as his then wife Katrin Schaake and Mascha Rabben, until he ran out of money halfway through. After these dubious projects, I took to filming for myself again.

My relationship with Rainer Werner Fassbinder has been called "family friendly," in that it is not based on rivalry. But I wouldn't like to say too much about that. Fassbinder was a good friend, even if he did steal an idea that was very close to my heart in his last year of life. He called my *Willow Springs* his favorite film, but he also thought highly of *Eika Katappa*. He often quoted a line from it: "Life is so precious—even right now." It comes from the sequence in which Carla Aulaulu dies in the film and comes back to life again and again. In *Beware of a Holy Whore*, that blasphemous satire on filmmaking, Fassbinder put it into the mouth of the actress Hanna Schygulla. He asked me whether he could also copy the scene in *Eika Katappa* in which we see the handsome young gypsy sitting in the stern of a boat, surrounded by spray as he goes from Naples to Capri. He re-created it in *Beware of a Holy Whore* with Magdalena Montezuma, but using a Donizetti aria sung by Callas; my version, a year before, had used a Hugo Wolf song. I took it as a dedication, a tribute.

One more word about the Fassbinder family business: all the members of his group took part equally, so far as I could judge. You couldn't expect him always to be entirely benevolent. Fassbinder was an edgy, contradictory character, but he was always close to me despite a certain difference between us. He often said, "Werner, you're the white angel; I'm the black angel," referring to a play by Christopher Fry. I said, "You're dead wrong there. I just plaster on a thicker layer of white paint." That made him laugh.

Magdalena and I went to Sorrento in 1970 to meet Fassbinder's troupe. They were shooting *Beware of a Holy Whore*. They had originally planned to make a revisionist Western in Spain that spring, but it fell through for lack of funds and several other hitches. In September that atmosphere—of tense inactivity plus comical intrigues about the cast list—was transformed into a new Fassbinder film. To me, it was like a vacation and a war of nerves combined, not to be in charge but simply a member of Fassbinder's entourage. I played the tiny part, mute except at the beginning, of the photographer Dieters, lounging around and taking stills of the actual film on which we were working. The start of shooting was put off, so we were bored, trying to offend and to seduce one another—in a certain way, you could say we were our own subject.

How young we were then! When I was working, I hardly stopped to eat, I slept poorly, I smoked and drank. My friend Digne said that was how she always knew me in those years.

Incidentally, I often took advantage of small guest roles or visits to festivals to take a few days' paid leave from my obligations. In *Beware of a Holy Whore* I am sitting in the hotel lobby, looking out from under the brim of my hat with a melancholy and rather-stoned expression. A couple of times I dance with Magdalena, as we hold each other close, comforting one another. She was playing Irm, the director's rejected lover who has desperate, dramatic scenes with him. Fassbinder didn't want to have his ex-girlfriend and former leading lady Irm Hermann there in Sorrento, so Magdalena stood in for her. The final version of the film, however, features Irm Hermann speaking in Magdalena's voice.

Magdalena and I were amused by the quarreling within the troupe, but Rainer didn't hold it against us. Shortly before filming ended, he shot an extremely long sequence in which I, as the photographer Dieters, was to improvise a confused story about the cartoon character Goofy and a little orphan girl who is really a dwarf gangster named Wee Willy in disguise. I was talking about a crazy dream; that's all I remember. But the scene became the opening sequence of *Beware of a Holy Whore*.

Shortly before our trip to Italy, I had made *The Bomber Pilot* for ZDF (Channel Two of German TV). It was my only comedy—I was very fond of it—and it was about three women living through the transition from National Socialism to the Eisenhower era. Up to

Neapolitan Siblings [i.e., The Kingdom of Naples], a situation involving three different women was an established ingredient in my films; I sent them through different times, to different continents, *per aspera ad astra*—from darkness to light, from pain to vision.

In *The Bomber Pilot* I was interested in the great stress between the Nazi "Strength through Joy" organization and the postwar period, with its American understanding of culture and careers—not to mention that such postwar stories were very much in the air then. My film was not a million miles away from Robert van Ackeren's *Harlis* or Fassbinder's *The Marriage of Maria Braun*. I liked the latter apart from not being interested in its realism, which baffled me, and it always annoyed me to think of all the production methods lavished on such films, while we made our own way, filming a historical subject with almost nothing behind us.

The Bomber Pilot was also sometimes called a "not entirely serious Nazi operetta," because I had called Luchino Visconti's drama about the Krupps, *La caduta degli Dei* [The damned], a "serious Nazi operetta" in a piece that I wrote for *Filmkritik*. Our film was an absurdist comedy, perhaps partly inspired by my mother's and grandmother's bygone dreams of art. Magdalena played a conservator who was restoring a church, a teacher at an adult-education college under the Reich, and a snake dancer; Carla Aulaulu (this was the last time I worked with her) played a singer and a baker; and Mascha Rabben played a vaudeville dancer. In the film, Mascha suffers a nervous breakdown, Carla has a miscarriage, and Magdalena nearly kills herself on hearing of the führer's death. The three of them have careers appearing in small theaters and they go to America; it's all rather bizarre. We had no money; we boldly went after what we needed. My friend Daniel Schmid was the assistant director, and we thought up some good anarchical jokes between us. For instance, we shot scenes in the States by driving to the US Army post in Heidelberg, the three ladies made up to GIs who happened to be there, posed for a group photograph, and that was our fraternization scene. Or we went to the American school where I had once studied, walked into a classroom, filmed the three actresses with the jubilant children, and said in the commentary that the whole thing illustrated the women's huge success in Texas. We took it quite a long way, with comic contrasts between the images and what was said. The bomber pilot, by the way, never appeared in the film.

This comedy was followed by *Anglia* and then by our version of Oscar Wilde's *Salome*, for which we went to Lebanon. After that, *Macbeth*, although it was filmed in Frankfurt am Main as a TV program, took me to London with Rosa von Praunheim. And finally, Magdalena and I went to New York in the summer of 1971 to do some research for my film *The Death of Maria Malibran*.

Friendship

I can't really explain how friendships come into being, but affinities depend on contrasts, in my own life anyway. Daniel Schmid, who died in August 2006 of cancer, like so many close to me, was a good friend.

In December 2007 I drove to Switzerland and the Waldhaus-Schweizer Hof Hotel, a building of the belle époque where Daniel had spent his childhood. The filmmakers Pascal Hofmann and Benny Jaberg were making a portrait of him, which has now been shown in cinemas under the title of *Daniel Schmid—Le chat qui pense* [Daniel Schmid—the thinking cat]. I answered their questions in one of the comfortable lounges as we watched snow beginning to fall outside around the Flimserstein rock formations.

There is a poem describing the bond between Daniel and me. I wrote it myself and used it in my film *Black Angel*. "Yearning, a word easy to say / and yet so hard for me. / The stream is shallow as the day / but I dream of the sea."

Daniel's heart was set on mountains; I dreamed of the sea, of the Atlantic Ocean off San Sebastián or the shores of Portugal. We were different in the same way as what is rough differs from what is fluid, not that Daniel was in any way rough as a person. But the fact that he came from mountainous country gave him a different idea of life, not like the constant movement that I associate with the sea.

The friendship that we knew in life speaks for itself; it developed and then lasted for forty years.

Similar experiences in our childhood and youth reinforced our friendship. Daniel, who was almost four years older than me, talked about his grandmother a great deal, and so did I of mine. Both our grandmothers tried to construct the world in ways that differed from everyday life. But I came from a different background; my family had lost everything and had no money at all when I was a small child. Daniel's grandmother encouraged him in so many ways; she was the driving force behind his imagination and put ideas beyond the everyday life of hotel management into his head. She fueled his imagination just as my grandmother fueled mine.

He found it necessary to break with his family. I felt the same, while unfortunately, my brother, Hans-Jürgen, was never able to break the family bond, and it almost stifled him. I did not make the absolutely necessary break until I was about twenty, and Daniel did so even later. Earlier would have been better. If your personality has formed between the ages of twelve and twenty, then it is time to find your own life and live it.

I often went to Flims, and Daniel visited me at my mother's home in Dossenheim near Heidelberg. He liked her very much, and she liked him. With comic respect, he addressed her as "Frau Mother," because she was so very helpful and charming and was also a good cook. It was the beginning or the middle of the eighties—we went to amusingly gloomy clubs left over from the fifties and sixties when gays first dared to get together; we danced and then came home late in the evening. We would spend the next day planning films that were never made, or we traveled on to Avignon, where Daniel or I showed work we had been doing.

Daniel cultivated his liking for artificiality, for Marlene Dietrich and the style of the twenties, but he didn't feel it was any loss that none of that was left in Berlin. For us the city was still a magical world, rich in human and artistic developments. Daniel could revitalize his nostalgia in work; he didn't have to find it already present in Berlin. It shouldn't be forgotten that the ability to live openly in homoerotic relationships was by no means to be taken for granted.

But as in the twenties, it was possible to have such relationships in Berlin, and there was a homosexual milieu—although it wasn't just a matter of that restrictive concept—comparable to that of New York, Amsterdam, and other such cities.

I met him at a showing of my first 16 mm films. I wasn't particularly proud of the three or four short films that I had made. Daniel, however, had just finished studying at the University of [Television and] Film and was assistant on a film being made by Peter Lilienthal. Then he came in with me on *Eika Katappa* and *The Bomber Pilot*, as a pianist and assistant director, and he also helped on *The Death of Maria Malibran*. If I have to lead I am a very bad dancer, but I was able to dance wonderfully well with him. I remember countless Viennese waltzes that we danced on festive occasions, to the surprise of other guests. He led well in waltzes, and I could work happily with him, for in my films I was leading the dance. Our utopian idea was to reinvent life as art. It was all about crossing borders, filtering an artistic statement out of life or giving it a new form. We longed for the structuring of form, and on my side and his we had Magdalena Montezuma and Ingrid Caven working to help us as well.

Maria Callas was my diva, but Daniel saw divas everywhere; he even tried selling the idea of his Aunt Pinkie as the comic version of a diva. He was addicted to divas, looked for them in hiding so as to create an artificial form of survival with them.

To Daniel, Ingrid Caven was the ultimate diva and central female figure, his muse in his art and in real life his best woman friend and comrade in battle. There was much argument as they sought to convey their mutual and sometimes-contrary convictions, but for all their distinctions as individuals, working with Ingrid was a fine experience. After I had been shooting *Willow Springs*, he worked with her on the extremely melodramatic *La Paloma*, the story of a consumptive nightclub singer disappointed in love. When Ingrid has her big scene on the mountain, singing "Glück, das mir verblieb" [Love that remained to me], from Korngold's opera *The Dead City*, as if singing karaoke, it could easily have gone wrong—such ultrakitsch from the twenties, and in addition performed to the playback of the showstopping Lotte Lehmann and Richard Tauber—but that is not the effect. The elements of the performance turn into something new that not only creates an ironic distance but overcomes that distance and achieves the status of what Susan Sontag called camp. "Love that remained to me"—that operatic element with its wide-breathing effect linked us.

Daniel Schmid and I were firm friends with Rainer Werner Fassbinder. I remember being at the wedding of Fassbinder and Ingrid Caven in August 1970. The honeymoon journey, when Daniel made a threesome with them, must have been an amusing event, but you would need to hear Ingrid tell that story; I wasn't a party to it.

Fassbinder and Daniel had a vital if difficult friendship, and they sometimes even came to blows. That sort of thing had to be seen as teasing rather than taken seriously. Fassbinder knew just what a talent he had at his disposal in Daniel and was greatly taken by Daniel's adaptation of his controversial play *Der Müll, die Stadt und der Tod* [Garbage, the city, and death], filmed by Daniel under the title *Schatten der Engel* [Shadow of angels]. He played the third main role, the part of the pimp Franz, while Ingrid Caven and Klaus Löwitsch were in the other two main roles. Despite Daniel's jealousy of Ingrid, the two of them worked together, so that the film is entirely redolent of both Fassbinder and Daniel. It was the teasing element that I just mentioned: the sadomasochistic act, a kind of game that people play—maybe Fassbinder and Daniel felt it more strongly than I did.

Our mutual trust was never endangered, although of course there were instances of competition and petty jealousy. We were much inclined to jealousy and were sometimes disappointed because each would have liked to have made the kind of film that the other had done. But I took that as a charming aspect of our friendship. Daniel could be malicious, but his Swiss humor and my Polish German humor rubbed off on each other.

We were friends. Love, erotic experience, sex were to be found elsewhere. If you love men, you don't look for yourself in the object of your love—that's a cliché. The other man, who is different and strange, that's what is really attractive. At the time in Germany or, to be precise, in West Germany, paragraph 175 of the law, making homosexuality illegal, still held. If you started dancing while you held a man close in a bar or restaurant, it was something exotic, adventurous, and beautiful. The fact that one was also fighting against feelings of resentment made it a kind of underground romanticism.

Of course, we also took the liberty of experimenting with hash and other substances. When we were shooting films and among ourselves, we almost all smoked joints. It was as normal as drinking a glass of wine. Stimulants of all kinds were available, and we weren't going to be deterred from trying them. Doing so wouldn't have suited our active way of trying out something new in the cinema, the theater, and painting. In fact, all of that went hand in hand; we felt good even in difficult situations that might have looked negative from the outside. It was all about the exotic adventure of our own experiences, and we approached it fearlessly.

In 1973 I went to Paris with Daniel for the first time. He already knew Bulle Ogier, who would make *Flocons d'or* [Flakes of gold] with me two years later, and her partner Barbet Schroeder. On the first evening he introduced her to me at the famous La coupole. Funnily enough, Bulle's handbag was stolen that very evening, and Nathalie Delon and Gérard Depardieu turned up on a motorbike; he had had a slight accident just before. So that was my first impression of the world of Paris, which Daniel knew better than I did. Nathalie became a good friend, and I often met up with her in Paris. She wrote novels and only occasionally acted in films, but she did, for instance, in my own *Nuit de chien* [*Diese Nacht* in German, *This Night* in English].

I had come to Paris because my films were being shown at l'Olympic, Frédéric Mitterrand's cinema. Daniel had decided to live in Paris and found an apartment in the rue du Val de Grâce, in Montparnasse, near the hospital. It was an attractive place, where he kept open house, and was just around the corner from Ingrid's apartment in the rue Henri Barbusse. Sometimes I did the cooking, sometimes Daniel did, and we often ate with Ingrid, later including her partner Jean-Jacques Schuhl. Along with Bulle, Barbet, and many other friends we were a genial company, a little clique. Fassbinder sometimes stayed in a Paris apartment too. We had a good time together, although we were all occupied with our own projects. Ingrid was the only one who worked with all the rest of us.

For instance, after I had staged a show with her in Munich in 1976, I arranged for another at the Palace in Paris in 1980. It was Daniel who staged her show in 1978, a stunning production by Yves Saint Laurent. He rented le Pigalle, a former striptease joint, and refurbished it; the black dress he designed for Ingrid was a legend. Unique! One felt sorry for anyone who hadn't been there.

Salome in Baalbek

In January 1971 we set off for Lebanon to shoot *Salome* in the ancient city of Baalbek. After *The Bomber Pilot*, it was my second film for the *Little TV Theater* on Channel Two of German television. I wanted the film to follow Oscar Wilde's tragedy rather than Richard Strauss's opera based on it.

In fact, we had been to Beirut before the New Year to scout locations, and I immediately fell in love with that beautiful countryside—another Mediterranean land where I felt more at home than in Germany. And the Oriental cuisine! A wonderful aroma everywhere of jasmine, oranges, spices, and hash! It was before the disastrous civil war, and the Franco-Arab culture of Lebanon was flourishing in all its glory.

Salome was my first work to observe unity of place, time, and action. Oscar Wilde had written it in wonderfully musical French; I turned to the sympathetic German translation by Hedwig Lachmann-Landauer and for the first time worked with something like a real screenplay, a plot, a story. In my search for the essence of irrationality, logical content still seems to me a flat construction, a lie. In Shakespeare, Lessing, Wilde, and all the other dramatists whom I love, form, musicality, and the poetry of language reign supreme.

If I remember correctly, we left out the scene of the play with the Jews. It seemed to me out of place, because there was one particular point that I wanted to emphasize: "Ils disent que l'amour est amer, mais j'ai baisé ta bouche," says Salome after kissing the severed head of the murdered Jochanaan. "There was a bitter taste upon your lips. Was it the taste of blood? No, but perhaps it tasted of love. They say that love tastes bitter."

The Dance of the Seven Veils as a symbolic dance of death is a pure nineteenth-century subject, but the theme of Eros and Thanatos is close to my heart. Salome, Herod, and Herodias are driven by a desire that ends in the inevitable catastrophe. I was not interested in the play as a genre painting, as a dynastic, political, or psychological drama; to me, Salome, who desires Jochanaan and kills him, is innocent. I heard my own version of the theme of a *Liebestod*, love in death, in the work, infusing life into my tragic sensibility.

We found a beautiful, broad flight of steps in the Temple of Bacchus at Baalbek, in front of a monumental wall. With a few props, just a pair of torches, some lighting, and thrones for the ruling couple, it became a wonderfully credible abstract stage set. I had seen Pier Paolo Pasolini's film *Medea*, with Callas (to me a messenger from the gods) in the leading role, and was much disappointed by Pasolini's insistence on dragging it down to a naturalistic plane. I wanted *Salome* to be different. In fact, over the years I changed my mind about Pasolini's archaically Oriental films. Incidentally, in our conversations, Maria Callas later agreed with me that her special dramatic expression as a singer and an actor worked only onstage in a theater, but Pasolini wouldn't accept that. Our *Salome* was neither to be a beautiful travel film in a setting of classical antiquity nor to have anything to do with the symbolist kitsch of Aubrey Beardsley's illustrations to the work.

Because of being shot abroad, *Salome* was envisaged as a large-scale production, so Channel Two worked with a production company in Wiesbaden. My assistant director was Harry Baer, who was a member of Fassbinder's troupe, and I had engaged Robert van Ackeren as cameraman. In this film I had to concentrate on the actors, because for me, self-taught as I am, the dramatic development of the play represented a challenge. Our little German ensemble employed Lebanese extras and musicians for the court of King Herod.

In any event, I and Roberta, as I called van Ackeren, made minimal use of camera movements such as panning and zooming. What mattered to me was the monumental stone setting—the stairway as our stage. When we had decided on matters of craftsmanship, a production manager from the Wiesbaden film company came on ahead to Beirut and Baalbek to fix the technical requirements. But when our troupe arrived in Baalbek in January 1971, nothing was right.

Our editor, Christoph Holch (whom I called Frau Holle, like the character in the Grimms' fairy tale), described the adventure later: "Some of the equipment sent ahead had gone missing in Beirut, and up at Baalbek almost nothing was ready. In the temple precinct, instead of the power points we had been promised, we found only the ends of cables cut off short. And when the very fastidious sound mixer Günther Stadelmann realized that the narrow band for this o-tone production had already been used once, I had to suggest forcibly to the so-called production manager that he had better not turn up at the location, or he would probably meet with physical violence. Not to mention that funds designated for the production were at a mysteriously low ebb: might that have something to do with the production manager's visits to the Casino Liban? The first thing I and the whole team had to do was to figure out how to make shooting the film possible. As the tripods for the lighting had also vanished, I went to see the local village smith along with Magdalena Montezuma, who didn't know any Arabic but did speak excellent French. Magdalena had had her head shaved for her part as King Herod. She had a wig available, but with a regal gesture she declined to wear it. She made a great impression on the local smiths and metalworkers as a majestic, bald-headed figure, and the tripods were ready within a day."

We had to make up for lost time, because our flights home were booked and couldn't be changed. So we filmed around the clock, taking no breaks and no weekends off. A management assistant from the film company arrived, a sensible man this time. He checked the accounts, which his employee had left in a chaotic state, and helped us cope with the timetable of shooting, alarm calls, and meals, and we managed to get our quota of filming done in two and a half weeks.

As Herod, the courageous Magdalena held her shaven head high. Elfi Mikesch, my camerawoman in later films, was in charge of costumes and makeup in Lebanon. She made up Magdalena's surreal features to look like a ruler's abstract white mask. Elfi had to wake all the actors halfway through the night in order to get the time-consuming makeup done. In her hands, Ellen Umlauf, playing the part of Herodias, Salome's mother and Herod's wife, became a venomous and sinister version of Liz Taylor's Cleopatra.

Ellen was the only trained actor in my troupe; she had studied at the Max Reinhardt Seminar in Vienna. I knew her from the film *The Miracle of Father Malachia* and had also seen her onstage in the theater, but the great thing was that in parallel to our *Salome* she was also appearing in little soft-porn films like *Hausfrauen-Report* [Housewives' report], and I liked the contrast with her real life as an actress very much. When Ellen was woken in the middle of the night by the editor who had come with us, Christoph Holch, she greeted him, as he later recalled, in "a thunderous stage voice." As always, and particularly after an eighteen-hour workday, I found it difficult to get out of bed and needed a shot of cognac to get me through the next day's quota of work.

Mascha Rabben, our Salome, wore a translucent white robe that showed her slender body at every step she took, and she, too, was made up in outlines of black and white. Her fragility made her a good pendant to the strongly expressive character played by the obsessed Magdalena. It had nothing to do with the kitschy notion of a demonic femme fatale. Mascha, a well-known photographic model, a muse like Uschi Obermeier, had begun acting only a little while earlier in a *Schulmädchen-Report* [Schoolgirls' report]—that was the state of German cinema at the time. I discovered her for *The Bomber Pilot* and *Salome*, and then she acted in films by Roland Klick, Robert van Ackeren, Rainer Werner Fassbinder, and Helma Sanders-Brahms.

We filmed Salome's Dance of the Seven Veils as a kind of cold striptease act, performed very slowly, as if by a marionette. Mascha's nude scene—she looked extremely slim entirely naked—was a heroic performance, and we closed off the whole of the temple precinct when we were shooting it, to be on the safe side. The Lebanese took it all without fuss, and there were no protests against any offense to local morals; much worse was the icy cold weather that made the work of shooting more difficult every day. We were on our feet far beyond normal working hours, as indeed we always were, but here we wanted to have it all in the can before the first snow fell. It was pleasantly warm beside the sea in Beirut even in January, and all the people in my entourage who came down over the mountains sixty kilometers away, to use the telephone or to collect our film samples, were enthusiastic about the weather back in Beirut. Up in the high Beqaa Valley between the Lebanese mountain ranges, where we were, no one could even contemplate swimming or sunbathing.

But when we were invited to the homes of local people in the evening, there was not only good wine but home-grown hashish. The Beqaa plain is famous for its produce. And Harry Baer bought a gun. They warned us at the hotel not to take such things into the city on any account. "Frau Holle" clearly saw the signs of danger around the temple precincts. "The civil war was casting its shadow ahead. A tank with marksmen drove up to the hotel almost every day, checking cars for weapons. The hotelier panicked. Harry had to return the gun at once, unseen. He hadn't known that he was putting the production at risk."

The day after we left Baalbek, it began to snow, and so we missed out on the chance of a picture of Salome's bleeding feet in the snow, which of course would have delighted me. Christoph Holch, who had also worked on my films *The Kingdom of Naples*, *The Laughing Star*, *Palermo or Wolfsburg*, and *Malina* felt that the *Salome* trip with our troupe was "a wonderful horror production" that had saved him from "office mentality in the field of drama." I was touched.

With the cutter Ila von Hasperg, I produced a version that, to my great surprise, could be shown even without music. I tried that, but I didn't like it. As the film stood, it struck me as cold, and I revised it. The voices alone provided too little atmosphere for my liking, so I added music to provide another layer, setting off the images and the words. I used Rosita Serrano's "La Paloma," waltzes and organ music, frenzied passages from Strauss's opera *Salome*, and the sound of the airplanes that we could hear coming to land in Beirut.

Beautiful is ugly, ugly is beautiful

There is a photograph of Maria Callas that I carried around with me from my childhood onward, often using it in my films. It shows Callas as the messenger of truth, in a bright-red, ermine-trimmed coat with a broad-brimmed hat adorned with feathers; with her burning black gaze, she appears as a superhumanly feminine Lady Macbeth in Verdi's opera based on the play by Shakespeare. Verdi's credo of sublimity and brevity was ever present to me in that brightly colored picture. Since I first turned to opera, I had wanted to examine Shakespeare's tragedy and Verdi's courageous, "ugly" melodrama, take it apart and reassemble it. Then Hessian Radio came along and invited me to shoot *Macbeth* as an experimental TV play in their studio in Frankfurt am Main.

The same year, Rosa von Praunheim had a contract from West German Radio in Cologne to make his own version of *Macbeth*, on 16 mm film, in black and white, at outdoor locations in England and specifically in Cornwall. So we were in direct competition with each other, rivals, friends inspiring one another, and we both worked with the same Lady Macbeth, the magnificent Magdalena Montezuma.

Rosa von Praunheim shot his film of *Macbeth* in England in 1970, amid snow and ice. We went to London together and had some amusing experiences there. There are photos showing us both from that time, in which he is going for my throat in a theatrical and slightly sadomasochistic pose.

One evening we were the guests of Nigel Gosling, features editor of the *Observer*, and his wife, Maud Lloyd, a former dancer with the Ballet Rambert in London, both of them delightful people. Rudolf Nureyev was also there that evening. At that time I liked to wear my knee-high women's boots from Charles Jourdan, dark brown and made of very fine deerskin. They suited me, and surprisingly I could even walk well in them. So there I was, sitting at the feet of Maud Lloyd, the ballerina, on a white angora rug, when I suddenly noticed an unpleasant smell. I looked around and saw some dogshit sticking to the sole of my right foot. What was I to do? I turned demonstratively to the Goslings, hiding my foot under the sofa as I did so and rubbing away at it there, where the guests couldn't see me, hoping that the shit would dry and fall off, and so it did.

Rudolf Nureyev sat there the whole time. He had been drinking a lot and was in a cheerful mood when he absolutely insisted on my feeding him strawberry ice cream. He opened his mouth, and I fed him and felt as proud as Punch. I'd just been scraping dogshit off my boot, and now I was feeding strawberry ice cream to the greatest male ballet dancer since Nijinsky.

During our conversations that evening, we also met the attractive American Carl. I wasn't alone in falling in love with him, everyone did, but none of us got anywhere, because that same evening Nureyev gave Carl his address and told him, in his funny English, "You'll find me, just come whenever you want." Carl did visit him and later told us a story that had us all bursting with envy. Nureyev had laid a path of flowers a kilometer long, magnolia and rose petals, from the gate through the park to his beautiful villa. This path, ten centimeters wide, led up the steps, into the house, and to the princely bedroom where Nureyev was waiting for him on the bed, stark naked.

Rosa shot his version of *Macbeth* at Stonehenge in midwinter, at various places in Cornwall, and finally on a snowfield in Berlin. Magdalena stood up to the cold conditions as bravely as she did a year later when we were shooting *Salome* in Lebanon. Rosa didn't really like Shakespeare's tragedy; he was determined to show that he was the one who had power over the sound track of his film. He got Lynn, an acquaintance from Stratford-on-Avon, to record Lady Macbeth's lines on tape and presented them to Magdalena in shredded form, with extreme modulations. Listening to the playback out there, shivering with cold, she then gave expression to the distortion, making a strange drama of gestures.

In 1971, a good year later, I had something else in mind for my own sixty-minute version of *Macbeth*. In the early seventies, electronic recording technology was still in its infancy, particularly the montage technique of magnetic recordings. But it was good that broadcast editors were looking for material and forms to suit it and inviting film directors to explore the possibilities in experimental projects. For instance, Rainer Werner Fassbinder made a film for West German Radio, *Wie ein Vogel auf dem Draht* [Like a bird on a wire], a personality show on the American model, with Brigitte Mira.

You took the action—in color, of course—as recorded on six electronic cameras at the same time and had to cut it exactly to plan. At that time electronic cameras worked well only with lots of light, so our set on a flight of steps had to be lit much more brightly than we really wanted. Light and shade, so important to me in their interplay, couldn't define the structure of the project this time. Instead, there were interesting solar effects when we lit a flame. It put me in mind of Maria Callas wearing her regal, bright-red coat. Like that advertising photo, everything was to be a copy with madness lurking in it, bringing out the dissolution of the identity in glaring colors. Verdi's opera, our source of inspiration, was used just through the piano score. I intercut Maria Callas's magnificent mad-scene aria, "Una machia è qui tuttora" [This stain is still here], with untrained voices. The parts were played alternately by men and women. Magdalena still had very short hair after playing Herod in *Salome* the winter before with her head shaved. It was an interesting experiment, but I found that technology had more power over us than I liked for my idea of aesthetics. The course of events seemed too conventional. I have avoided electronic production ever since.

The Death of Maria Malibran

Jimi Hendrix and Janis Joplin, whom I greatly admired, died tragically early. Like Jim Morrison of The Doors, Joplin belonged to that club of twenty-seven/twenty-eight-year-olds who lose their lives upon becoming radiant, mythical idols at the peak of their artistic powers. Maria Malibran, who died just after turning twenty-eight, was another of them. I had read a great deal about the Franco-Spanish bel canto singer, the ultimate diva of divas, even greater than my Maria Callas, who died just after finishing a unique, challenging, and exhausting concert. Everything I tried to depict in my film *The Death of Maria Malibran* arose from my concern with those artists, all of whom I so admired.

Here's an account I wrote about an incident that took place when I was preparing to make the film; it may cast light on the tension that led me to the subject. I wrote it to be included in a book about Luchino Visconti and *Morte a Venezia* [Death in Venice]. Magdalena and I had seen the film on an unbearably hot summer day in 1971, at a small art-house cinema in New York, where I had gone to prepare for *Maria Malibran*. We thought the film superficial, arrogant, and incredible; my opinion was to change over time, but that's another story. "Two cognacs later," I wrote, "after an hour of lethargy: Visconti's evening twilight in stark opposition to New York's frantic, sultry, horrendous reality. Magdalena and I decided to go to a James Brown concert at the Apollo Theater. We took a taxi to Harlem, and crossing into that district we had to change taxi and driver because—as usual at that time—the borderline between white and black was as massive as a concrete block. It was invisible, yes, but as real as a razor blade in the cheek of a bicolored human being. That was *reality* as we, too, saw it. Then, in the Apollo, came four hours of the wild James Brown concert: *Sex Machine*. Magdalena and I were two white holes in a swaying black sea. We had taken on New York and scored a victory. It was all too far from the world of Visconti's arty Venetian module."

We got to know Candy Darling, the transgender diva from Andy Warhol's Factory, and we succeeded in interesting her in our hypertrophic and surreal art project, *The Death of Maria Malibran.*

Candy was a slim, tall, very blonde creature with a delicately shimmering, porcelain-like face. She took huge quantities of hormone tablets in order to rid herself of her other, earlier identity as James Lawrence Slattery from Brooklyn. With Warhol's help, she aimed to turn herself into a movie-star love goddess in the mold of Jean Harlow, Marilyn Monroe, and Rita Hayworth. That was her dream. I admired her elegance, her beauty, and her melancholy, all the result of the radical way she was changing her body, working on it as you might on a work of art. Candy's health was wrecked by the hormone treatments; she died of leukemia at the age of just twenty-nine, only three years after we were all working together.

Candy's radical self-transformation fascinated me; it was a truly pioneering act in that repressive period, although, for all her underground romanticism, she was to some extent protected by the Warhol entourage. I couldn't have been so single-minded, although androgynous and hermaphroditic ideas are staple components of my work and my imagination. From the first I wanted to present women in trouser roles and men in women's dresses, actresses and dilettantes, artificial pathos and innocent naivety, all of equal worth; wealth in diversity. Back then, I seldom met men whom I was interested in using for my films (in the theater, that was to change). The surface on which I projected my ideas was the severity and at the same time the malleability of women. Like Sigurd Salto in *Argila*, the handsome Einar Hanfstaengl, whom I cast in *Maria Malibran*, was silent, passive, rather like a toy. Starring Magdalena Montezuma, Christine Kaufmann, Ingrid Caven, Annette Tirier, Candy Darling, and Manuela Riva, a corpulent transgender singer I discovered in a gay bar in Ludwigshafen, *The Death of Maria Malibran* was to be a film about love, the death of the beloved, and lamentation for the dead—inspired by the historic cult of the diva.

Malibran was one of the greatest operatic divas of the nineteenth century. It was she who first made the operas of Bellini, Rossini, and Donizetti known in Europe and the USA. A street was named after her in Brussels, where she is buried, and a theater in Venice. She composed songs, some of which Callas sang, and she was famous for the elegance of her stage wardrobe, which she designed herself. Stendhal was one of her great admirers. How she died: we know today that Maria Malibran had not recovered from a bad riding accident and that she was also pregnant when she traveled from London to Manchester to give a private recital. At the end of the recital, she collapsed and died. Her death set the seal on the tragic intensity with which she lived, and that attracted me because it is a strong theme in my own work.

I encountered another such story of all-consuming beauty in a great bel canto diva, although I am convinced that even a woman who cleans public toilets can have such a life story if she lives intensely—in my film *Poussières d'amour* [Love's debris] the wonderful Anita Cerquetti, whom I greatly admired, sings without really sing-

64

ing, for at the height of her career she lost her divine voice, and since then has lived for music rather than performing it.

Someone wrote that *The Death of Maria Malibran* was a theater of faces with history playing around them. One could put it that way. It was a production commissioned for television, with a budget of only sixty thousand marks, so we had to be ingenious. We shot the film in the Bogenhausen district of Munich, where Digne Meller Marcovicz had arranged for the magnificent villa of Herbert Stiehler (who was also known as Consul Styler for having been a diplomat to Thailand) to be available for us, and also in Vienna and the castle park at Schwetzingen, where there was a rocky cave with a view of the landscape that was our setting for a dark, romantic mad scene. When I saw the portrait of Stiehler's dead wife, Isabella, hanging in the splendid Munich villa, it seemed to me that she was godmother to our film: that woman had really lived!

I shot the theatrical interiors so that the space was almost black and the faces shone like medallions: a procession of living images to the music of Johannes Brahms's *Alto Rhapsody*, based on Goethe's "Journey to the Harz in Winter": "Like the vulture / resting with gentle pinion / on heavy morning clouds, / looking for prey, / may my song hover." I also used Beethoven's triple concerto in C major, Stravinsky's *Rite of Spring*, Mozart, Handel, Puccini, Rossini, Marlene Dietrich's mouth-organ song, and Caterina Valente's song "Spiel noch einmal für mich, Habanero" [Play it again for me, Habanero]. There was also a slow waltz that I had found somewhere, with the words "The love of a boy can change a girl into a woman." And not least, I used a clip of Sir Laurence Olivier in which he is speaking to a picture while the women are simply present and looking at the camera, as he quotes from *Hamlet*, act 4, scene 4: "My thoughts be bloody, or be nothing worth."

My motto for this strangely structured film was Heinrich Heine's lines "Und mein Stamm sind jene Asra / Welche sterben, wenn sie lieben" [I am of the tribe of Asras / who will die when they make love]. We particularly liked the scene at dawn, when Magdalena and Candy, the competing divas, sway in the foreground of the Olympic stadium, which was only half finished. There was also a knife with which Christine Kaufmann, as Maria Malibran's father, puts out his own eye; there were tears, blood, and lipstick, and Magdalena made a fantastically evil figure of Death disguised as a wandering journeyman and demanding the eye in return for a bit of bread.

I may have gone rather far in my experiments: sometimes the connections were alien, contradictory, and paradoxical to the point of absurdity; sometimes they were deliberately arbitrary. I simply stipulated that we must have references to music, to women, to the landscape, the house, and the mirror.

What else can I say about the film? Perhaps this: Carl Rowe, a professor whom I had met, once wrote to say that he had run into some singers from the San Francisco Opera at a bar after their rehearsal and invited them to a screening of *The Death of Maria Malibran* at the Pacific Film Archive in Berkeley. Afterward, they had all gone on to Larry Blake's Pub and sat over their beers trilling and singing arias for a long time.

Emilia Galotti; or, How the theater discovered me

After my film of *Salome* had been shown on TV, Ivan Nagel, Peter Zadek, and Jean-Pierre Ponnelle called me to say, "Werner, you ought to be directing live theater too." The director Jean-Pierre Ponnelle had become a friend, Ivan Nagel was theatrical manager of the Hamburg Theater, and Peter Zadek was about to become theatrical manager of the Bochum Theater.

Ivan Nagel suggested a production of Jean Genet's *The Balcony*, which I connected to my image: the madman, the young prodigy. I was to direct in an extravagantly modern manner. I had always liked Jean Genet; he had worked his way into my imagination, and *Querelle of Brest* is a wonderful novel.

But what I don't like about Genet's plays is their demonstrably reactive attitude. What do I mean by that? A certain attitude whereby conclusions are drawn from reaction to the given facts. Genet says, "If people say I am a thief, then I will be a thief." That, to put it crudely, is a reactive attitude. I'm not condemning it, only saying that it has never interested me. Lessing, on the other hand, was what I considered a utopian in his way. I like him for that, and for his language, which always, without exception, speaks to my heart and my mind. To me, Lessing's use of language is miraculous. I said so to Herr Nagel, but he either didn't understand or thought I was being fanciful. I said I wanted to direct *Emilia Galotti* and stuck to it. He asked for time to think it over. Ultimately, I did direct Lessing's *Emilia Galotti* and not Genet's *The Balcony*.

Thus, I could get somewhere, but I had to know what I myself wanted. I was sick with kidney stones, and I was also working hard to get a decision that went against Genet. Rosa von Praunheim wrote me a concerned letter, saying that he saw my "imminent death before his eyes." We all know about our own sentimentalities. But he was right to warn me, "Our awareness of all our possibilities ruins us and makes us restless. We live as they do in East Berlin, unable to come to terms with the West, so near and yet so far." He hit the right note to encourage me in my future decisions: "Cultivate your own myth; don't destroy it by doing anything rash."

I wanted to have my two leading ladies, Magdalena Montezuma and Christine Kaufmann, onstage together for the first time in *Emilia Galotti*, along with actors of varying degrees of fame from the world of German theater, including Hans Peter Hallwachs and Wolfgang Forester.

As a former child star bullied by her mother, Christine Kaufmann didn't much want to act anymore, but with me she found she could enjoy participating in a creative project again. In fact, Emilia was her stage debut, and Countess Orsina in the play was Magdalena's. There was a certain tension in bringing them together. To German actors, Christine Kaufmann was defined by her part as a child star in *Roses-Resli* [Rose-girl Resli], or "Neuroses Resli," as malicious tongues put it, and Magdalena was an abstraction of something they had never seen before. In between them was Gisela Trowe, who had become a dear friend after our work together on the films *Argila* and *Eika Katappa*. She played the part of Claudia, Emilia's mother.

The production took interesting shape in a different way. Lessing's idea was a fine one: he rejected the elevated milieu of French tragedy in which only princes and other highborn characters have emotions and, above all, can suffer. So Lessing invented the bourgeois tragedy.

All human beings can feel—that is an important idea, but in addition, Lessing's language is devised to bear comparison with the velocity of French tragedy. I agreed with that and indeed proved the point by producing the play to be performed without any abridgment. It is said to take three hours in all, but in my hands it lasted only two and a quarter, because the actors had to speak very fast without any loss of expression. We rehearsed intensively for that effect. Take a speech like the following: "But what's this? No one coming to meet me. Only an ingrate who would rather have refused to let me in. What, are you here, Marinelli? Isn't the count here, isn't the prince here?" was delivered at incredible speed, as I still like to recite it today. Of course, it is spoken clearly and distinctly. All the expression is retained, so it is not just mechanical babbling but has the effect of a ritual. It was often my principle to perform the entire, uncut text when directing for live theater.

There were wonderful situations involving Magdalena's extravagant style of acting, inherent in her personality, and also featuring Christine Kaufmann, a great beauty, then aged twenty-five. They both wore splendidly decadent Baroque costumes.

The stage set was a black space inside a golden frame, with nothing kitschy about it. There was a way through the mirror hanging at the back. The characters came and went through this mirror, so that there was profound movement in the space, a sense of something unfathomable. The stage as an abstract, black hall of mirrors—what else would one have made it? A kitchen? *Emilia Galotti* is a great play, and only stupid people would set it in a palace. Such directors would work on the exterior, while we were concerned with the interior. As school students we were told that Lessing's *Emilia Galotti* was a foolish, dry-as-dust play, and thus unreadable. That is so only to a certain extent. Of course, the characters have their limitations and are rather-undistinguished souls whose moral philosophy is stale. We have only to think of Lessing's letter to Nicolai in which he describes the play as "The fate of a daughter who is killed by her father because he values her virtue more than her life." That problem did not interest me at all; what did interest me was the concept as a whole, the idea of crystallizing as much form as possible from the material and taking bourgeois tedium to the point of absurdity.

Christine acted with the resources at her disposal, which were few but convincing. That gave an unusually natural note to the text. Other famous actresses of the time had mastered that natural manner, for instance, Agnes Fink, Bernhard Wicki's wife, one of my mother's favorite actresses and a good friend of mine. Agnes approved of the fact that my production employed none of the usual clichés of state theaters. At the end, when Christine entered with the words "Are my father and mother not here? . . . Must we not keep calm when all is lost?" her father was already at the front of the stage, moving his head in the direction shown by the mirror. Her voice was unmoved, a linear voice speaking to itself. She was not droning, simply speaking without any insincere intonation, while her tears flowed, and she moved her head as if inwardly shaking off what had happened to her. Her tears could be seen flowing in the spotlights and in the mirror; it was an amazing effect.

In the end, opinions of the production differed a good deal. A place like the Hamburg Theater was obviously not yet ready for it. Although we were using the Painters' Hall, the theater's smaller stage, many spectators took offense. But there were some who reacted favorably to my work. One of the cleverest reviews, hitting the point exactly, was by Hellmuth Karasek in *Die Zeit*. He described *Galotti* as a sample of the "pattern for the lineup of characters in the bourgeois German drama" that could be classified as either something "already done" or something "not done yet," and our staging, he said, was obviously interested in the latter. His summary dwelt on the dialectic that I had in my mind's eye: "It is true that Schroeter's examination of Lessing's play not only understood how to bring out the only too well oiled hinges of a style of drama relying on such dialog as 'Ha! Here he comes!' but also showed how preserving a strict form is the corset enabling the play to tame the feelings it has released, as if imposing a straitjacket on them." Of course, I was also pleased that Karasek said the production ought to be moved to the main theater from the Painters' Hall, with its auditorium for only a hundred spectators. In particular, I liked the reason that he gave: "In a world adjusted to the general public, where every advertisement involving a stain left by sweat is seen by millions on television, Emilia's tears fell, as it were, into an esoteric void."

But I made myself unpopular with the theater management. There were a number of comic episodes. For instance, Hans Peter Hallwachs, playing Prince Gonzaga, was engulfed in a gorgeous brocade bathrobe at the main dress rehearsal, whereupon Herr Nagel jumped up, crying, "How can you hide such a magnificent torso?" A great argument. Whatever the rights and wrongs of the matter, harmony did not reign.

There were serious consequences. A deputation sent by Jean-Louis Barrault had seen the production and wanted to stage it at his theatrical festival in France. My first work for the live theater! I was very glad to receive a phone call inviting me. I called the theater and passed on the information that Barrault would like to stage the play. The reply was an unenthusiastic, "Yes, well, hmm, hmm." Then I had another phone call from France, this time to the effect that the Hamburg management said the sets had been dismantled and were no longer available, nor were the costumes, they couldn't discuss the matter any further, it couldn't be done and that was that. It was extremely annoying, and for once I took great exception to the attitude of the theatrical management. I felt they had misappropriated my work. Two years later, at a birthday party for Rudolf Augstein, I told Herr Nagel what I thought. Well, too bad, but I would have liked to get that production performed in France.

Incidentally, Lessing's *Emilia Galotti* is one of the few plays I have directed twice. Nineteen years after that experimental production in the Painters' Hall of the Hamburg Theater, I directed the play again at the Düsseldorf Theater, with Elisabeth Krejcir in the title role, Ernst Alisch, and Jens Berthold as Prince Gonzaga.

Fig. 1. Hans-Jürgen and Werner Schröter, ca. 1952. Courtesy Monika Keppler.

Fig. 2. Lena and Hans Otto Schröter, 1930s. Courtesy Monika Keppler.

Fig. 3. Werner Schröter with his father, ca. 1957. Courtesy Monika Keppler.

Fig. 4. Werner Schröter's grandmother Elsa Buchmann, née Baroness von Rodjow, the 1950s. Courtesy Monika Keppler.

Fig. 5. With Rosa von Praunheim, early 1970s. © bpk, Berlin/Abisag Tüllman/Art Resource, NY.

Fig. 6. Christine Kaufmann (left) and Gisela Trowe in *Emilia Galotti*, Hamburg, 1972. © bpk, Berlin/Digne Meller Marcovicz/Art Resource, NY.

Fig. 7. With Magdalena Montezuma, rehearsal for *Emilia Galotti*, Hamburg, 1972. © bpk, Berlin/Digne Meller Marcovicz/Art Resource, NY.

Fig. 8. With Candy Darling, rehearsal for *The Death of Maria Malibran*, 1971.
© bpk, Berlin/Digne Meller Marcovicz/Art Resource, NY.

Fig. 9. Magdalena Montezuma, 1975. Courtesy Christian Holzfuss Fine Arts,
Berlin.

Fig. 10. With Daniel Schmid, 1970s. © bpk, Berlin/Digne Meller Marcovicz/Art Resource, NY.

Fig. 11. With Ila von Hasperg and Daniel Schmid in the cutting room. © bpk, Berlin/Digne Meller Marcovicz/Art Resource, NY.

Fig. 12. With Ingrid Caven, 1970s. © bpk, Berlin/Digne Meller Marcovicz/Art Resource, NY.

Fig. 13. Christine Kaufmann in *Flocons d'or*, 1975. © bpk, Berlin/Digne Meller
Marcovicz/Art Resource, NY.

Fig. 14. Ingrid Caven and Wolfgang Schumacher in *Miss Julie*, Bochum, 1977. © bpk, Berlin/Digne Meller Marcovicz/Art Resource, NY.

Fig. 15. With Margareth Clémenti during the shooting of *Neapolitan Siblings*, 1978. © bpk, Berlin/Digne Meller Marcovicz/Art Resource, NY.

Fig. 16. Elisabeth Krejcir as Käthchen von Heilbronn, Bochum, 1978. © bpk,
Berlin/Digne Meller Marcovicz/Art Resource, NY.

Fig. 17. With Magdalena Montezuma rehearsing for *Käthchen von Heilbronn*, Bochum, 1978. © bpk, Berlin/Digne Meller Marcovicz/Art Resource, NY.

Fig. 18. Nicola Zarbo and Brigitte Tilg in *Palermo or Wolfsburg*, 1979. © bpk, Berlin/Digne Meller Marcovicz/Art Resource, NY.

Fig. 19. With cameraman Thomas Mauch, 1979. © bpk, Berlin/Digne Meller Marcovicz/Art Resource, NY.

Fig. 20. Golden Bear for *Palermo or Wolfsburg*, Berlin, 1980. © bpk, Berlin/Digne Meller Marcovicz/Art Resource, NY.

Willow Springs

The Death of Maria Malibran had gone over its planned budget, so I owed the TV editorial team a second film at half price. I kept having similar difficulties with production. My German director colleagues often got together several hundred thousand deutsche marks from television companies and institutions that supported the cinema, while I made my full-length films on budgets of between fifty thousand and eighty thousand marks, so I was often in financial difficulty from the first day of shooting. My films were produced with economical means that other directors would have used only for a ten-minute short film—as I was telling myself even after *Maria Malibran*. I felt perfectly justified in drawing only on my own world for making films of that sort, rather than compromising. Because I needed so little in the way of resources, I felt no scruples about taking the liberty of realizing my own ideas, and I also assumed that my audience was capable of a high degree of musical and literary association.

My Channel Two editors, Eckart Stein, Christoph Holch, and Anne Even, made it obvious that they thought I would be one of those unpredictable, difficult, and awkward directors whose projects they would have to defend to their bosses from the start. Of course, when my films were invited to the Quinzaine des réalisateurs at Cannes, despite their tiny budgets, and to many other film festivals as well, that helped me to make the next film, whatever it was to be. When I won prizes, for instance, the Television Prize and the German Film Prize for *Palermo or Wolfsburg*, the head of the station sent congratulations, but more important was the fact that the editors working there became braver. Some of them, such as Anne Even, worked with me for many years and became good friends.

None of that made much difference to my style of working. Even later, with more expensive films and with theatrical and operatic productions, I upset all the calculations. I had all kinds of tricks at the ready, some of them unfair, for putting my ideas into practice. I just don't like to see bureaucracy affecting art, and normal filmmaking bores me. I know I'm rather arrogant when it comes to expressing my own visions.

I worked for years with the editors of Channel Two on productions for their *Night Studio* and *Little TV Theater*. I threw away my chances with other TV companies, but that was all the same to me. In the seventies, Rosa von Praunheim and I once turned up at West German Radio, where many of Rainer Werner Fassbinder's films were produced. We marched up to the desk of the editor Günter Rohrbach, acting the part of the "Rohrbach Sisters," doing high kicks, and shouting, "Heil Hitler," to show what we thought of the editors and their bosses. I had to pay off my debts after the *Malibran* film, so in 1972 I suggested to ZDF a film essay about Marilyn Monroe. It was to be a kind of structuralist work based on Andy Warhol's pictures of Monroe, with music by Elvis Presley, featuring Allen Ginsberg, and I had all sorts of other ideas for it. I wrote a film treatment in which I claimed that Marilyn Monroe was an emotional myth of our time. I wanted to compare her to the "indecipherable expression of the Mona Lisa, a figure now above and outside history." I liked the idea at first, but then I lost enthusiasm for it.

Christine Kaufmann, with whom I had worked for a year and a half and who had become a good friend, got into difficulties around this time. After her days as a child star, she had gone to Hollywood, had married the star Tony Curtis, and had her daughters Alexandra and Allegra. In *The Death of Maria Malibran* the two girls can be seen standing rather sadly beside their mother. In 1968, after her divorce, Christine returned to Germany with the children, but then, five years later, the American custody laws said that Tony Curtis should have them in Los Angeles. Christine was miserably unhappy, so I said to her—*Emilia Galotti* was in the middle of its run in Hamburg—"I tell you what: we'll go over to the States and get the kids back."

And Christine, Magdalena, I, and Ila von Hasperg, who had been cutting my films since *Salome*, flew to Los Angeles, financing the flight with an advance on my next Channel Two film. (I double-crossed the editorial outfit; there's no other word for it.) We saw the sights of Los Angeles and sat around and waited while Christine negotiated with the attorneys. We spent six weeks there before we started filming, which I needed to do so I would have something to show ZDF for their money. In the end the girls did come back to Germany.

I was still planning to make a documentary about the life of Monroe, but then I began thinking mainly of myself. I passed the California driving test and drove around in the desert a good deal. I was no longer interested in the stylized story of the star, the structuralist stuff that I had brought with me from Europe. The material I wanted to develop was the story of my three aunts, and I didn't want to make it into anything else. In a sense, my friends and I were in almost the same situation as the trio of women in the fateful abstract melodrama *Willow Springs* that I now started to create.

We were staying in a small hotel, ten kilometers from the backwoods dump of Willow Springs in the Mojave Desert, and we were practically as isolated as the three protagonists in my film. The place where we were living, moreover, was run by an American fascist, so there was an unpleasant and alarming atmosphere.

We were not in a good way. Ila von Hasperg had a painful inflammation and was also suffering from a dental abscess. You have to remember that we had hardly any money and didn't know what to do next. So in October I went to Las Vegas and married Jutta, the girlfriend of my youth; she came from Oberflockenbach in the Bergstrasse district. She could help us out financially. Magdalena, not surprisingly, reacted in a very dominant and depressive way.

Then I sat down and wrote the cheapest story that we could manage to film in our reduced circumstances. In that sense, *Willow Springs* reflects our own wretchedly confused situation. To some extent it was a continuation of the story of the three women in *The Bomber Pilot*, only this time I made them into active destroyers of men: three melancholy women, in a godforsaken hole of a town, kill the men who break into their isolation.

Magdalena played the part of a kind of saint and wise woman, a lesbian and a powerful character. Someone wrote of the film that the men in *Willow Springs* were gutted and killed in what was a kind of counterpart to rape, and it could indeed be seen that way. I also like the possibility that the way the women acted as a sect was the explanation. It was said that my film had some similarity with the play *The Misunderstanding*, by Albert Camus. I hadn't read it when we were shooting the film. In the Camus play, a man comes home from abroad to the hotel run by his mother and sister, who do not recognize him and kill him. Michel Foucault said that it dealt with the theme of the uncanny inn.

We rented a suitable house in the deserted town of Willow Springs, a tumbledown kind of saloon full of dirt and cobwebs, and changed nothing about it. Later, I found similar gloomy houses veiled in cobwebs in Portugal, for my film *The Rose King*. Magdalena and Christine appeared in evening dress, with their faces made up, esoterically glamorous, not banal or vulgar. We hung a picture of Marilyn Monroe in Christine's room, in memory of the star.

I was behind the camera myself, of course; I had no alternative. Again, as in *Maria Malibran*, I used very sensitive film. In Los Angeles, we hired what little equipment we needed, along with Jack, the man responsible for the production sound. We spent only five or six days shooting, working very fast and nonstop, which may explain why the effect of *Willow Springs* is so terse and concentrated. I liked lightweight American films without any deep meaning, no psychology outside what can be seen on-screen.

"Christine," I wrote in my crazy script, "loves music and has a tenuous relationship to reality." She carries a doll about in her arms and says things like "I have never yet loved anyone but the child who died in me before being born." She was the cool aesthete; she withdraws to her room and listens to music on a battery-powered record player.

There is an introduction to Magdalena's part in the film: a man rides into the town on a motorbike, enters her house, and then we see him leaving it again, fastening his belt. Ila played the slightly simpleminded third in the trio of women, the maidservant who rebels. She falls in love with Michael, who has arrived by chance, and wants to save him from his fate. There is no love lost between the women; they are just obsessively dependent on one another.

My *Willow Springs* script was a good sort of Grimm fairy tale—my grandmother couldn't have thought up a better one. At the end, I added: "And Christine too, awoken by the shots, stands in the doorway, failing to understand the situation as she greets her dehumanized mistress, and she, too, is mowed down by gunshots. Magdalena disappears into the desert, not knowing to this day where she made her mistake."

Michael O'Daniels, playing the man on whom the women's passions center, allowed me to use parts of his diary in the film. And I found partly charred letters in the ruins of Willow Springs. At the cutting table, I divided it all up into tiny fragments of meaning and put it together again for the sound level. You can guess that the editorial department at Channel Two, which I had left believing that we were going to make a film about Marilyn Monroe, was shocked at first. But when they had seen *Willow Springs*, they were happy with it. It went around to film festivals and was screened at the Hamburg Film Show of 1973, in a whole section of programs on the topical subject "Class Struggles in West Germany." We won a Diplôme d'excellence at the Montreal Film Festival (unfortunately, no money came with the award).

I wasn't enthusiastic about Hollywood, and the way we lived at the time it was out of the question anyway. There are some American films I admire, like Charles Laughton's *Night of the Hunter*, but that wasn't a classic Hollywood film. And of course there were traces of *Whatever Happened to Baby Jane?* and *Sunset Boulevard* in *Willow Springs*. But my ideas came from Shakespeare, Bellini, Donizetti, and Verdi, not from Hollywood. Despite my travels and adventures in the USA, I consider myself a European artist. *Willow Springs* owes its music to that feeling. When Christine opens her balcony door, and we hear the theme of Micaëla's aria from Bizet's *Carmen* on the record player, the audience is expected to know that it runs "Here in the rocky ravine I said that I feel fearless." Or when Magdalena comes downstairs, goes over to the bar counter, and brings out her revolver, we hear "L'altra notte," from Arrigo Boito's *Mefistofeles*, and we place the reference to Margarete praying for mercy in her dungeon.

California

The time I spent in the US was full of incidents that didn't make it easy to return to Germany. My marriage to Jutta helped our stranded group of women out of a fix, in much the same way as Rosa's marriage to Carla Aulaulu had been a little financial coup. Jutta wanted us to marry, I didn't—or, now that I come to think of it properly, maybe I did. I had known her since she was sixteen, and I loved her, but not with passion. She wanted to get away from her bourgeois home and try all kinds of new adventures: alcohol, cigarettes, Captagon.

Five years before our wedding in Las Vegas, when Jutta was still underage, we had once run away to the South of France together, and her anxious parents had gone to see my mother. I still remember how we met Jean Genet in a dive in Nice, or maybe it was Marseille. He took an interest in us—well, mainly in Jutta. He addressed her and struck up a conversation with her—and with me too. I was very shy then. I got the impression of a very distinguished man.

I remember one good side effect of our marriage, another interesting journey. It was a visit to my brother-in-law, who was teaching at a university in the Indian city of Benares. I went for long trips up into the Himalayas, where we visited the old town of Manali in the state of Himachal Pradesh, at a height of almost two thousand meters above sea level, a mythical place where the legendary figure of Manu is said to have landed in his ark after the great deluge to create human life anew. Today, this former British expeditionary station is a rather-overcrowded base camp for mountaineers. But at that time I brought back from my visit to India a deep impression of what life in poverty is like, and I was moved by the way the sick, frail, and deformed live in the streets there, whereas in our culture they are hidden away.

Two years after the wedding, Jutta and I were divorced in Germany. Jutta had petitioned for divorce; we had never lived in the same place, and directly after the wedding I had returned to Los Angeles, moving on later to Munich and elsewhere, while Jutta went on traveling in her job as an air hostess. Being the free spirits that we were, we went to the divorce court together hand in hand. Or maybe I wasn't there for the proceedings at all? The grounds for divorce were that we hadn't had marital intercourse since November 1972, which was obvious.

After Las Vegas and *Willow Springs*, I was to spend Christmas in Dossenheim. My parents, my brother, and Jutta, whom after all I had married, were waiting to see me. Peace, joy, pancakes, it all turned my stomach. It was like having one's nerves under a magnifying glass. I went out of the house, through the vineyards, and up into the forest, where snow had settled on the ground. I lay down under a tree and wished for nothing more ardently than to fall asleep. It wasn't a death wish, just weariness.

But back to *Willow Springs* and my first visit to the USA: the part of the blond young man in the film was to have been played by Rosa von Praunheim. However, he was being difficult about it, so Michael O'Daniels took it on, which was much better. He had been introduced to me by acquaintances in Los Angeles. I thought him erotically very attractive and spent a good deal of time with him. He was an American beauty from the southern states, a dreamer who drifted when he had been taking drugs. His father had been governor of a state. When Ila von Hasperg sees him in the doorway for the first time in *Willow Springs*, she says in that murderous bar in the Gallows Inn: "Oh, you must have been born on Christmas Eve." That was just what he looked like.

Later, when I saw Michael during my Californian travels, we went around Los Angeles by night doing crazy, delightful things. I didn't come any closer to him erotically, although others did, including Herr von Praunheim, which I didn't like, because I had become very fond of Michael. But he saw me, the German in black leather pants, as something of a demonic figure.

I encouraged Michael to go on adventurous manhunting trips in Mafia clubs. Once I met a pockmarked guy who carried me off to his little house. It was risky but exciting. Okay, so I was thirty years old, my balls itched, my heart beat fast. I was addicted; I knew the kind of obsession with another man's body that one has at the height of erotic male potency. Women know what that's like too.

I also had another lover, a musician who had friends who dealt in cocaine on a grand scale. It was pink and uncut, top quality. I got a real taste for it—very nice.

Michael O'Daniels drove a convertible and kept a live fox as a pet. The fox wasn't very tame and kept trying to bite our noses off. When Michael, slightly drunk, met me once at the airport—I was totally jet-lagged and drunk myself—he took me to a Josephine Baker concert at the Beverly Hills Hotel. That concert was a real hoot! Josephine Baker had four ancient gospel boys as a backup chorus, and she sang, "I see God, I see God, I see God!" Then she fell on her knees, the gospel boys sang, a huge slit opened up at the front of her dress, and you could see her pubic hair going up to her navel. I'd never seen anything like it before. It was probably a pubic hair toupee. We were sitting right in front, where she could see me laughing. She came over, with her little Sarotti Moor on its cable behind her. I controlled myself, because Michael was there, with his fox under the table. She stared at me furiously, sang and stared, sang and went back up on the stage. That woman had a strange aura, but the pubic hair toupee was great—"I see God!" I couldn't resist it, I built the gospel singers into *Flocons d'or*, and then I included the fox and the Josephine Baker scene in *Two*, when Tim Fischer sings, "In the upper room with Jesus."

Another good story connected with Michael was the Easter service in Watts, in the black ghetto. At the time, thirty-four or more years ago, it was very run-down; it'll probably have been cleaned up today. We were two flecks of white among the black congregation in that Gospel church. And oh, the pastor and the people! They grabbed our arms, carrying us along with them. That atmosphere, that steamy vapor, that smell! And the singing—"Leaning, leaning, leaning on God!" I looked at the central aisle out of the corner of my eye and trod on Michael's foot. A man came racing into the church, seized the collection, and raced out again. It made me laugh so much. "Leaning, leaning on God!"

I saw Michael whenever I was in California; we didn't lose touch until 1976. By then he was married and had kids. It was sad to see how poorly he coped with life.

I heard from Tom Luddy, head of the Documentary Film Institute in San Francisco, that Michael had shown him a forged letter, supposedly from me, so as to get his hands on my only subtitled copy of *Willow Springs*. He probably wanted it in order to ingratiate himself with a producer. After that, he disappeared from the scene. Tom Luddy felt very awkward about the loss of that copy. In the end, the institute managed to offer me a replacement—Liza Minnelli, of all people, had made them a donation of a large sum of money.

Passion

Around 1974 *Willow Springs*, along with *The Death of Maria Malibran*, found an appreciative audience in France. French intellectuals also took notice of me, and that filled me with pride. For instance, I met Gilles Deleuze and was inspired by his interpretation of Nietzsche. I was able to make productive use of it later in the plays that I directed for live theater. Whenever possible, I also exchanged ideas about art and its significance with the writer Jean-Jacques Schuhl. He wrote about his wife, Ingrid Caven, Rainer Werner Fassbinder, and the artistic scene in Germany in a book to which our anecdotes, challenges, and moments of self-expression contributed. Another personality in Parisian circles was Jack Lang, later French minister of culture. I still remember him writing down his phone number for me on a notepad with a letterhead that depicted a pencil sharpener with a pencil shaving in the form of a furled flower bud. Jack Lang offered me French citizenship, and these days I tell myself it was stupid of me not to accept.

I knew hardly any literary salons in Germany, where I mixed more with film and theatrical people, at first in Berlin and Munich, later at the Bochum Theater, and everywhere else I worked. In Berlin, I sometimes mingled with a circle around Ulrike Ottinger: people who met in the seventies to eat together and show samples of their work or put on spontaneous performances.

In Paris, as I mentioned earlier, Frédéric Mitterand, François Mitterand's nephew, showed my films with other art films in his theaters and distributed them. That must be how the philosopher Michel Foucault happened to see them. The journal *Cinématographe* published an interview with him at the turn of the year 1975/76, in which he paid particular attention to *The Death of Maria Malibran*.

At the time there was much talk about Pier Paolo Pasolini's *Salò; or, The 120 Days of Sodom*, Liliana Cavani's *The Night Porter*, and sadism on-screen in general. I happened to like Pasolini's *Salò*, but that's another story. Foucault explained why he thought de Sade was incompatible with cinema. As he saw it, de Sade was a kind of drill sergeant, a pedant, a master of ceremonies in the field of sexuality who was obsessed with ideas of hierarchy, allowing no space for images, no overt fantasy, no erotic play. In my film, however, Foucault saw something new that, in his eyes, made the body itself and squandering its powers sing. I felt that he had understood my basic theme, since Foucault spoke of turning the body to anarchical purposes and found poetic metaphors for that. Bodies, he thought, would then be entirely three-dimensional in their effect and would, so to speak, put out buds; the kisses, lips, teeth, and cheeks of the women in *Malibran* were not subject to any hierarchy, as the sexualized parts of the body are in de Sade.

Today, when I am asked about Foucault's poetic images for *Maria Malibran*, I usually go back to my own craftsmanship. I am glad that, in Foucault's opinion, its physicality has a formal, aesthetic aspect, for in the close-ups, in particular the close-ups of Christine Kaufmann, I was working with low-sensitivity color film, the kind of thing not generally found today; the effect was of a documentary film in color, and those were the effects I wanted to achieve. Indeed, the cherry-red lips in the close-ups where she is holding a silver knife in front of her chin look sculptural. I was experimenting with the material to create an illusory impression of physicality. Getting that sculptural look mattered to me; one might call it a false three-dimensionality inherent in the color. These days, incidentally, the optical effect leading to Foucault's impression can be achieved only by digital processing. The philosopher saw the explicitly strong three-dimensionality of the color as a moment of intentional aggression, a challenge, and that was just what I meant, right from my heart.

When I read his article in *Cinématographe*, I wanted to meet the man who so clearly described what I myself saw in the film. But only years later did I get the chance for the meeting that he records in his article "Passion et Amour—Leidenschaft und Liebe, a Conversation with Werner Schroeter." It was all about the driving force of the principles of love and passion, and not least about the way we lived at that time.

The young film critic Gérard Courant brought us together in Paris in December 1981. He was working on a book, a companion to my work that would describe my productions of films and live theater in essays and interviews, so a conversation with Foucault fitted into it neatly. The slim volume was published to accompany a retrospective of my work, arranged by the Goethe Institute in Paris at the Cinémathèque française the following year. My conversation with Foucault was also published in his posthumous writings, but when I reread it, I could no longer summon up the strong impression that our meeting had originally made on me.

The great philosopher didn't think it beneath him to talk to me at length about the basic themes of my work, to search them out and mull over them—our conversation ought really to have been continued. I imagined it in the form of an intensive exchange of opinions conducted over several weeks, but no publisher was interested, nor did either of us have the time for it, and Michel Foucault's death in 1984 put an end to my idea.

When I think back to our meeting today, it mingles with my memory of the poetic associations that Foucault saw in *The Death of Maria Malibran* and that still interest many cinema enthusiasts. You could say that in his first article he expressed what he thought of the physicality of my work, whereas our later conversation was about ideas and feelings. Theory is not my field. My friend Wolf Wondratschek once wrote of my approach: "The code word replaces theory."

Gérard Courant, who had arranged my meeting with Foucault, sat in on the whole of it with his recorder, keeping discreetly in the background. Picture it: the stern, bald-headed intellectual with his glasses and roll-neck sweater sitting opposite me, a German film-maker fifteen years his junior, clad in black, with long hair and a small beard. I felt very proud, and I rather think that I talked non-stop. He sat down on the carpeted floor and took a friendly interest in the exotic character sitting in front of him, chain-smoking—in any case, he went along with my ideas and made some very acute comments about them.

I knew his book *The Order of Things*, and I was also well informed about his history of sexuality and systems of surveillance and pun-ishment, although I have always been more fascinated by poetry and experiment than by academic discourse. To take just one example: on my travels in the USA, I visited prisoners in the high-security prison of San Luis Obispo because I had always been interested in the figure of the criminal. Foucault and I did not discuss anything controversial, but we talked, with reference to *Willow Springs* and *The Death of Maria Malibran*, about what we understood by passion and love, and how passion can help make oneself into a work of art.

Foucault avoided saying anything about his homosexuality in public. I am open about mine and more or less challenged him to celebrate it as the more attractive option in life. Even after his death in 1984, I was surprised to find that his friends wanted to keep his AIDS secret. There was more of a stigma attached to the sickness then than there is today, but we all knew about each other—all of us who followed in the footsteps of Oscar Wilde, Jean Genet, Paul Bowles, William Burroughs, and the rest, who traveled to Marrakesh and visited the saunas of San Francisco to experience living as a ho-mosexual there.

In many interviews, I have described my own homosexuality as the form of life close to my heart, and I was saying so at least a year before I met Michel Foucault, in response to my friend Daniel Schmid's questions about the societal function of art. In everything I did, as I said, the poetic substance of an outsider's existence was important to me. Homosexuality goes against the norm, against sexuality functionalized in a way acceptable to society, and that is just what made it attractive to me and still does. In addition, as I said then and I say today, it is beautiful.

Foucault gave me a little lecture on the difference between love and passion, and I asked him about his own passions. From today's vantage point, those are just vague anecdotes; more important, maybe, is that at that time we couldn't deal with the concept of love. During our conversation I quoted my friend Ingrid Caven, who once said, pertinently, that love transfers one's own feelings to the other person and, because of the inequality of the situation, begins to make demands on that person. Love makes you lonelier, puts more distance between those involved; I called it a spent force, a fantasy in isolation. We felt that violent passion, openly aggressive and not hidden in clichés about love, was the more intense way of experiencing life, was communicative and creative.

Foucault compared *Willow Springs* to the depiction of women in Ingmar Bergman's films. Bergman, he said, had always wanted to know what happened between them and why. But plain evidence without psychological depth, my way of leaving the mainstream cinema behind, was more appealing to him. We understood each other, for if I am asked, I say to this day that I am against psychology. At the time I called it a dangerous system that plays people off against one another, and I still think it an instrument for encouraging conformity—though it is quite capable of presenting human behavior pleasantly in the form of knowledge of human nature and wit. I refused, and still do, to distort my relationships with Maria Callas and with my mother by means of psychological hairsplitting.

Although my films take life from the evidence of the images in them, never from logical narrative and symbolism, they do disclose inner experience. I once received a letter from the psychiatrist Ernest Holmes, who wanted to borrow a copy of *The Death of Maria Malibran* because he felt sure the film could act as a therapeutic tool in treating the psychiatric patients in his hospital.

Michel Foucault and I agreed that we did not seek passion with women, although we both valued our friendships with them. Love that does not coincide with desire was always very important to me. The kind of love that exists between brothers and sisters, in friendship and joint creativity, is something that I have found in the women in my life. If desire does not get between me and the other person, then the woman, the actress who is my friend, is a better surface on which to project the eternal and insuperable conflict between love and passion.

Gods in decline

Peter Zadek had been appointed theatrical manager of the Bochum Theater in 1971. When he invited me to direct a production for him, we agreed that I would return to *Salome*, and having directed it as a film I would direct it again for the theater, only in an entirely different style. It was a play that Zadek loved; he had chosen it for his own first production in London in 1947.

I was not the only director recruited for Bochum by Peter Zadek; also invited were Rainer Werner Fassbinder, Augusto Fernándes, Rosa von Praunheim, Fernando Arrabal, and others. Each was allowed to bring his own troupe, so that there would be no danger of the productions resembling the usual routine fare of a city repertory theater.

While we were rehearsing *Salome*, Fassbinder was working on Franz Molnár's *Liliom* in Bochum. He and I were both convinced that Zadek was equipping his own productions with everything he needed, while the rest of us were kept on a rather-tight budget. Fassbinder, who enjoyed giving expression to his contradictory character and his sadism, bought a dog that he called Zadek and ostentatiously ordered it around. I criticized the great director myself, and I wasn't happy with the situation at the theater, but on the whole, looking back at it later, Peter Zadek and I liked and valued one another.

Since the publication in the summer of 1972, in *Filmkritik* magazine, of my draft for a film to be called *The Sailors of This World*, I had been obsessed by the idea that it was time I made a large, 35 mm cinema film. But I made no more progress with that than with a project about the English poet Thomas Chatterton, a genius who had taken his own life in 1770 at the age of only eighteen. I couldn't drum up the money for it anywhere. Another of the films that I never made.

When I arrived in Bochum and was beginning on the stage rehearsals, I felt like going away again. The whole system wasn't in my line, or the way it worked. I shrank from it, even though my engagement by Zadek meant that I would be earning a steady income for a while, after the financial debacle of *Willow Springs* and the productions that followed it. There was a point when I really did walk out, but Peter Zadek sent a Rolls Royce after me to fetch me back.

We began rehearsing *Salome* when *Willow Springs* was finished, and its première was on 16 April 1973. Magdalena played the part of Jochanaan, Fred Williams was Herod Antipas, Ingrid Caven played Herodias, and Christine Kaufmann, in a see-through floor-length robe, was Salome. Rainer Will, an enthusiastic beginner who helped out with everything, played the part of Herodias's page, and after that he was in many of my films and stage productions, for instance, in *Palermo or Wolfsburg*, *The Soldiers*, and *Le prix Martin*.

In Bochum at that time, Ingrid swept across the stage in her white fin-de-siècle dress, delivering her harsh monologs in a voice like thunder that was in great contrast to her outward appearance. The critics called it roaring and howling, as if she were speaking into a watering can, but it wasn't like that. I sensed her musicality; I had wanted her to sing. Three years later, we staged her first big show as a singer of chansons in Munich.

Peer Raben was of great importance for Ingrid's career as a vocalist. I knew him from Munich as a musician, composer, and man of the theater; he had been friends with Ingrid for a long time. Now we were working in the Bochum Theater together. He composed the incidental music for *Salome* and *Lucrezia Borgia* and for the productions of other directors. Peer wrote beautiful cryptic chansons, and later he also set poems by Hans Magnus Enzensberger, performed by Ingrid in Munich, Paris, and over half the rest of the world.

The stage set that Magdalena and I had designed, in collaboration with the technically experienced Jan Moewes, was an enormous stairway curving inward, mounted on the large Bochum stage. The heights of its tiers had been worked out by computer, and were painted all over with mother-of-pearl nail lacquer. It glittered and sparkled, but the effect wasn't kitschy; the set looked like the inside of a seashell. Down below, in the orchestra pit, there was a landscape of black coal. Magdalena as Jochanaan stood down there, long-haired and naked except for a loincloth, like a figure of Atlas bracing himself to raise the world out of the black pit below.

The play ended with a chorus of children wrapped in muslin bandages; after Herod's final order, "Kill that woman!" they struck up an a cappella song from *Faust*. "Judged—saved!" The children drew Salome up the stairway, the red sun rose, and ten thousand liters of pigs' blood flowed toward them.

The pigs' blood was to be forbidden on grounds of health, which of course was nonsense. I mean, we eat blood sausage. The blood for the production was to have come fresh from the abattoir every evening and wouldn't have harmed anyone. The management wanted to use artificial blood, but I turned that idea down because it really was too risky; artificial blood is poisonous. Naked kids in artificial blood—no. I think there was some idea of forgiving Salome instead of killing her, but I forget now how I solved the problem; all I remember is that Magdalena as the murdered prophet, equipped with a crown of thorns and a crucifix, emerged from the dungeon again.

Anyway, the production was a hit. At the time you could be accused of pornography just for having two half-naked boys standing onstage and singing the aria "Ruhe sanft" from Mozart's *Zaide*, let alone showing Salome's Dance of the Seven Veils mechanically performed to the accompaniment of fairground music. At the dress rehearsal, I had to turn photographers from *Bild-Zeitung* out of the wings and the backstage area. They wanted to take pictures of Christine Kaufmann in her see-through chiffon dress; after all, this was 1973. Then *Bild-Zeitung* published a review saying the production featured "the least talented actress and the dimmest director in Germany." I thought that was funny; Peter Zadek thought it even funnier. He had a facsimile of the review blown up and hung outside the theater. But after a while it had to be taken down again because of car accidents in the street; all the drivers were staring at Christine's picture.

My production was invited to the Nancy Festival, and in an interview in *Le monde* I told the paper how I had imagined it before coming up against the restrictions imposed by the Bochum Theater. Salome, Herod, and Herodias would all have appeared naked but covered in body paint, like a nightmare family of heathen gods in decline.

The next year, when I was just back from Mexico, I was supposed to take the Bochum production of *Salome* on tour. It was Peter Zadek's idea; he wanted to introduce his theater to provincial audiences. But I protested vigorously. In the end I fell sick, or at least I got a medical certificate confirming that the tour would be too much of a strain for me.

The year 1974 was also when I directed Victor Hugo's *Lucrezia Borgia* in Bochum. It was billed as the version translated and adapted by Georg Büchner, but in fact both were my own work. Büchner had dashed off the translation quickly and carelessly, a run-of-the-mill job. He also did a translation of Victor Hugo's *Mary Tudor*, which is not very good either, as well as writing his own play *Danton's Death*. But his name brings people into the theater. Zadek had a running ad outside the theater promoting *Lucrezia Borgia* as "a romantic drama by Victor Hugo, translated by Georg Büchner."

Magdalena, Katharina Schüssler, and I had designed stage sets involving blue-gray travel brochures of Venice and a gloomy crypt, surrounded by a three-dimensional gilded frame. We depicted the society of the court as nocturnal marionettes. Magdalena was playing Lucrezia Borgia, the wife of Duke Alfonso d'Este of Ferrara; Lucrezia was the pope's daughter, and in that degenerate society, out of touch with the real world, disposed of anyone who got in her way by poisoning them. Fritz Schediwy played her husband, Alfonso d'Este; Siemen Rühaak, her twenty-year-old son Gennaro, who knows nothing about his mother. He receives a letter from her every month and dreams of maternal love but hates the Borgias because of their monstrous way of life. He insults her, and she demands his death without knowing that he is her son. In the end, with his dagger transfixing her, she reveals her identity to him just as he is about to die of poison himself.

We were successful with this production of *Lucrezia Borgia*. The performance was good, Magdalena was excellent, although some accused her of playing the title role as the wicked witch from Christmastime fairy tales. Audiences didn't always understand that I liked rough-hewn, edgy dialog on stage, rather than something too smooth. But the newspaper reviewers described it as a fine production, and it was well received—much better received, in fact, than *Salome*.

El Angel

The Black Angel was my Mexican disaster. It began when I was invited to a retrospective at the Goethe Institute in Mexico City. Dr. Christian Schmitt, director of the institute there, also wanted to encourage Mexican culture, and so he had initiated a number of coproductions involving both native Mexican and German artists. I thought it was an excellent idea to give Mexican culture a voice at the Goethe Institute, although many of Dr. Schmitt's colleagues saw things differently.

So I went to Mexico for the first time on that mission, with Magdalena Montezuma, and Ellen Umlauf was also with us. She had played Herodias in our Lebanese film of *Salome*, and was now a good friend of mine. I had thought up a crazy story about a whimsical blonde American woman with kitschy ideas and kitschy pink costumes. She gets together with dark-haired Magdalena, who plays the part of an uptight woman from Göttingen who is a devotee of the Mayan cult. These two highly strung characters in stiletto heels, the blonde a tourist, the brunette an idealist with a hint of tragedy about her, set off to see the ruins at Palenque and Uxmal. The American is disappointed because no one loves her just as she is; the woman from Göttingen, who has misunderstood everything, sacrifices herself to the gods, longing nostalgically for the old myths. Originally, the whole thing was to have been called *El aeropuerto de las lacrimas* [The airport of tears].

So we arrived to see Dr. Schmitt, and I wanted to visit the Mayan sites at Palenque, Uxmal, Chichén Itzá, and Mérida at long last. For a long time I had yearned to see Mexico, a country of which I dreamed; it was not by chance that I had given my friend Erika Kluge the stage name Magdalena Montezuma. My poem "Yearning, a word easy to say / and yet so hard for me . . ." was written on that trip, and in the end one of Caterina Valente's remarkable songs to the dance rhythm of the bolero gave the film its title:

> All you artists, let me say
> If you have so much insight,
> I will ask you, if I may,
> why you paint all angels white?
> Down they float from skies above
> But there must be some other kind
> of these small messengers of love.
> Does it never cross your mind,
> Does it not enter your head,
> an angel can be black instead?

Caterina Valente still exerted a strong magical effect on me. High art and triviality can combine in a film, with images elevating and reinforcing both. Valente occupied an in-between area, where there were both hits *and* outstanding jazz disks by her and Chet Baker. She sang with wit and humor, rising to the point of ecstasy in "Island in the Sun," and I was enthusiastic about her. I endow the trivial with emotion in my films too, and that leads to life-giving contradictions. You enrich the spectrum with a wonderful system like that. In a film, you have to deal with all kinds of sounds, music, and language, and the combination enables them to take on a new form.

So we wanted to film in Mexico, but first we had to look around, and that was possible. As usual we were short of money; this was one of my programs for Channel Two's nighttime transmissions. Eighty thousand marks had been made available to us, the largest sum possible for the editorial department at the end of the annual budget that November. The Goethe Institute helped to assemble a small Mexican film crew and got the permits to shoot film, as well as coping with the Mexican censors, who wanted to know all about everything. I got to know Arcibaldo Trueblood-Burns, half Scottish, half Mexican, and he became a good friend. It was through him that we came by Paul Helfer as an assistant director, and Helfer was indeed extremely useful, as well as Louis O'Keedy, who told me that he had worked with Luis Buñuel in Buñuel's Mexican phase. Louis could make gold out of a pile of shit—for instance, he covered a photography light box with silver foil to make it look like a candelabra. That was the way we worked.

One day, while the two women were at the Hotel Luma in Mexico City, I decided to join the Cruz verde, the Mexican equivalent of the Red Cross. I was sent off to assist some paramedics and spent a lot of time sitting around the hospital waiting for the ambulance to be called out. I was nicknamed El Angel, the Angel, because there was a general feeling that fewer emergencies happened when I was around. I did go out to some calls, the run-of-the-mill sort—for instance, to a woman who had been knocked down. But then one day there was a mass catastrophe in a football stadium, with many dead and some incredible stories. At that point I stopped working for the ambulance service, realizing that it was beyond me. I can only quote the old proverb: cobbler, stick to your last. Or say, like the actress Marianne Hoppe, that stupidity and pride grow on the same rootstock.

I was dealing with every aspect of the film: the sound, the camera. I was author, director, and producer. Of course, I also shot some film while I waited about in the hospital and in the ambulance, because joining the Cruz verde meant that I came into contact with the real Mexico. I assembled images and facts, all kinds of material about the social situation and the injustice rife in the country, which was dependent on the USA. I also found a deaf-mute boy in a hut somewhere in a poor part of the city when I was going around with the Cruz verde people. I worked him into the film as a silent observer, as a contrast to the highly strung foreign women. Back in Germany, when I was cutting, I mixed all this with music, poetry, and aphorisms—for instance, quotations from Hölderlin, Nietzsche, and Hans Henny Jahnn.

To cut a long story short, I filmed the actresses in the markets of Mexico City. Our Mexican photographer, Rodolfo Alcaraz, shot some beautiful footage. Then we went to Palenque and Uxmal. We saw some amazing things at the Fiesta de la muerte, the Day of the

Dead, the crazy Halloween festival that is really a kind of carnival. The "black angel" of the title of my film is Magdalena, playing the fake Mayan priestess in an extremely long black wig and the black dress from the Boutique Daisy in Munich that Hartmut Rathmayer had given me.

All the same, the film was only partly successful; it was amusing but not exactly what I had wanted to create. Nostalgic fun, but rather rubbishy. I never include it in the more obvious selections from my work for retrospectives, although that may be stupid of me. It was an amusing failure to film my subject and now seems to me like something strange from the past, although it is not without humor.

A sense of the world— journeys in Latin America

In Latin America I found that I always developed a sense of the world in general that overturned my former tragic feeling toward it. To name just one example: in 1975 I had a friend in Paris who came from the Dominican Republic, a filmmaker called Juan-Luis, whom I was very fond of. I moved into his little Paris apartment with him, and we lived together there. One day he said he had to go back to Santo Domingo de Guzmán. That was the capital of the country, where the crazy dictator Trujillo painted his face pink so as not to look so black.

Juan-Luis and I made a date to meet on the day exactly two and a half months after our last day in Paris. I would never have thought of writing or phoning him; I didn't do that sort of thing. I was busy, I was on the road a good deal, and in those days communications weren't as universal as they are today. I set off to go by air to the USA, but the Lufthansa plane developed a problem, and I had to spend a night at Miami airport. I had no money; I stole some chocolate by way of dinner and drank water from the faucets, always keeping one step ahead of the security men. And I had no way of getting in touch with Juan-Luis. I finally arrived in Santo Domingo, and there he was, expecting me as if it were the most natural thing in the world. He knew he could trust me and that I would be there. That's what I mean by having a sense of the world in general.

In the 1970s I felt at home in Mexico for a while. I could imagine staying there forever. I spent several weeks in Las Ánimas Jalisco on the Pacific coast, with Wolf Wondratschek, a good friend in life as well as work, to write a screenplay, although unfortunately nothing came of it. We were living in very simple conditions on a lagoon, staying with an extremely poor family, a couple with fourteen children, who had no work except what little came their way in the bay there. I felt so close to them that the mother of the family would have liked to adopt me. When I left, she burst into tears. At the time my own mother had just died.

In the eighties I dreamed of living entirely in Mexico again—if only I could afford it. I was feeling good because I was to stage a production of Richard Strauss's opera *Salome* there, something that had been impossible in Augsburg, where there was a great political sensation, but I will return to that another time.

My third *Salome*, after the film and then the stage play in Bochum, was my first production in Mexico, at the Palacio de bellas artes in Mexico City, and was a delightful task. The opera was staged in German, of course. I was working once again with my close friend the mezzo-soprano Kristine Ciesinski. This was our third production together, after Alfredo Catalani's opera *La Wally* in Bremen and Luigi Cherubini's *Medea* in Freiburg. Kristine sang the part of Salome; the rest of the cast consisted of excellent Mexican singers. The Herodias was Estrella Ramírez, no raging Fury but a beautiful woman in her early thirties with an outstandingly well-trained voice. She sang the part in what was almost the bel canto style. The Herod, sung by Ignacio Clapés, a Mozartian tenor, and the very young Jochanaan of Armando Mora were both very good too. And as for the gigantic orchestra—we played the score in its large-scale setting for 110 or 120 instrumentalists, so that the music seemed to be coming from every nook and cranny, from the boxes, from the orchestra pit, and it still sounded a little like Mexican mariachi music. It was a dream.

The concept of the stage set was different from what we had in Bochum. It was to resemble the shape of a glass bell, placed in the desert, as if a spaceship had landed, a transparent dome such as you put over a cheese board, only in the art deco style, enormous, and open at the front. There was to be a view of fellaheen, Bedouin, children, and camels in the desert around it, all going about their normal lives, maybe throwing something into the dome from time to time or peeing against it. The idea was for the audience to become involuntary observers of the tragedy of Salome's failure to achieve emancipation or, if you like, a child's experience of horror, nightmare, and the frenzy of love.

This production of *Salome* cost the Palace of Fine Arts 75 million pesos, the equivalent of about 125 thousand euros, making it the most expensive Mexican operatic production of that year, although I asked only a quarter of the director's normal fee. We spent a year preparing for the production; they wanted it to be *Salome* because of the film that I had directed at Baalbek. But then, when I came to Mexico two months before the opening, the staging had to be altered as Mexican bureaucracy dictated. The sand that had been ordered did not arrive at the opera house, the camels I wanted also fell by the wayside, and so we had to change the original idea of the set and make it something unreal. The theater curtains of the Palace of Fine Arts were taken down, and the stage itself became Herod's glass palace, open on all sides.

Kristine Ciesinski, our Salome, was a great sensation. Unlike the Mexican singers, both men and women, she is tall and slender, so as well as her wonderful voice and capacity for expression, it was partly her sheer height that made audiences see her as a diva. We staged the Dance of the Seven Veils to be athletic, almost a gymnastic display; I think she even did the splits. I told the journalists about my first operatic experiences and how I had seen *Carmen* in Bielefeld with a tenor who was only a meter and a half tall, while the American Carmen towered a head above him. Beauty by accident—it was an idea that pleased me.

South America has been close to me all my life, providing both delightful and terrible experiences. In Manaus in Brazil, I staged the operatic scenes for *Fitzcarraldo*, directed by Werner Herzog, my old acquaintance from my Munich days. In Buenos Aires, I taught, I directed and made a film, and I met my beloved Marcelo Uriona, as well as my friend Marie Louise Alemann; I also experienced firsthand what it is like to be exposed to a dictatorship. And my latest film, *Nuit de chien—This Night*, a parable about terror, is based, although it was made in Portugal, on a novel by the Uruguayan-Argentinian writer Juan Carlos Onetti.

My sense of the world is very much at home in Latin and Latin American cultures. As well as English, French, and Italian, I also learned Spanish and Portuguese. Today I speak those languages naturally and feel more at home in the countries where they are spoken than in Germany, because people take life more easily there. I don't want to transfigure realities; in Europe, particularly Germany, violence is internalized, in Mexico and elsewhere in Latin America, it is on the outside, palpable and close enough to touch. To my mind, there is no doubt that what goes on in Germany is ultimately more destructive.

However, we also had trouble with the Argentinian military dictatorship. Just that once, I gave way to fear; I say just that once because life is all about not being afraid. In the seventies, at the time of *The Black Angel*, in spite of my punk behavior I was mainly, to my friends, just "the puppy" who talked about operas. To Mexicans I was El Angel, and my presence meant that nothing too bad would happen in the streets. I loved the rent boys, who looked divine, as Wolf Wondratschek put it, but I was generally out and about with my dramatically impressive women actors and was adopted almost everywhere by kind motherly women. Such a strange phenomenon arouses curiosity and hatred in equal measure. With my love of opera, my Jesus hairstyle, my rings, necklaces, and brooches, the scarves and hats that I loved to wear, I was *poco hombre*, not the ideal macho man.

Today, Mexico City has made marriage between same-sex partners legal, but it is still the Latin American metropolis where more gays are murdered than any other. Homophobia is rife; hatred for everything that doesn't conform to the rigid stereotypes of sexual roles is considered normal. People think homosexuality is infectious, that men and women are opposites, not simply different human beings of equal rank.

One of the best books I know got to the heart of that lingering discrepancy between humanity and violence. Maryse Holder was a New York professor of literature, about thirty years old, who decided at a certain moment in her life to go to Mexico and find out what life was like there. Her book *Give Sorrow Words* consists of the letters she sent to a woman friend in New York. She was looking for better sex, real passion, and recklessly exposed herself to the brutal side of Mexican gigolos. In the end she was killed by one of the men whom she met in discos. I wasn't interested in the film made of that book, which is a total failure. It unfairly judges her by suggesting that Holder was delusional, and it stigmatizes her, interpreting her as having both a beautiful and an ugly side.

Today, of those countries on which Latin, South American, and African cultures have left their mark, Portugal is where I would most like to live. Since making *The Rose King*, *Two*, and *This Night*, I dream of its warmth, the kindness and physicality of people there, and I long in particular for the Atlantic. I ought to be able to make another film or, rather, two to realize that wish: *Gender: Ways into Reality* and *Gender: Ways out of Reality*. They would study the question of why the emancipation of women and gays has not taken place in Portugal. I ask myself why women take less part in their liberation there than in the rest of Europe, and I ask the same question with regard to Portuguese gays. What does that remarkable imbalance have to do with the imperialist past and the dictatorship of Salazar? I would like to go to Portugal and find people in the streets, at work, and in the theater who would tell me, speaking to the camera about themselves—the way I always work when a country interests me.

Adventures

How did we live? The more of a foothold Magdalena got in the theater, the more often she was away on her own for performances or stayed in Bochum. We had an apartment in Kraepelinstrasse in Munich (the street was named after Emil Kraepelin, the famous psychiatrist). I was constantly traveling too, staying with friends, in hotels or temporary accommodation, or with my mother. I used Kraepelinstrasse as an official address, but the people who were familiar with me usually got in touch through my mother in Dossenheim. In the midseventies Cheryl Carlesino and Marion Kroner of Munich did my correspondence for me, particularly about the distribution of my films. I needed someone to cope with the paperwork; using a typewriter was not in my line.

To this day I draft film summaries, ideas for productions, and articles in a few handwritten notes scribbled on used envelopes, paper napkins, and other oddments of paper. In the end it can all be thrown away, because I don't stick to any written draft even during the work of directing; I depend on friends to note down what I have in my head and keep it ready. I admire artists who can work in some other way, like my friend Ulrike Ottinger. She puts all her preparatory work, photographs, texts, background materials, and sketches together to make beautiful books. I can't do the same—I myself, so to speak, am the concept.

Magdalena sometimes sent me letters that she wrote on long rail journeys. If she had been horrified during rehearsals by one of my rare outbreaks of rage, she put her cautious criticisms down on paper only after she had done justice to her boring companions in the compartment, the railroad officials, and the landscape going past outside the window, and when she had struggled to find the right way to express what she thought. Ultimately, she was asking me to stop upsetting other people. That was typical of my friend Magdalena in everyday life.

In his book *Die weisse Reise* [The white journey], Wolf Wondratschek describes a scene showing that Magdalena's theatrical way of life isn't my own invention. On vacation in Greece once, he says, he was going to teach her to swim. "She was perfectly willing to try but couldn't be persuaded that it would be better not to immerse herself in water wearing a summer dress and a bucolic straw hat." He concluded that Magdalena didn't in fact want to stay above water but "was studying the opposite: how to sink into it—without becoming a carbon copy of Ophelia."

In the 1970s I went to Italy many times without Magdalena, often traveling to Rome with Daniel Schmid. By day we visited friends; by night we wandered around in search of sexual adventure and danced waltzes.

In the company of Daniel, an attractive young Italian, and his American boyfriend, who loved him dearly, I remember once climbing into the Trevi Fountain, in imitation of Anita Ekberg in *La dolce vita*. After that we must have looked hilariously funny, marching into the Via Veneto grand hotel, to which an elderly gentleman had invited us, like a bunch of wet frogs. That was a good adventure. Living it up like that, in search of vitality and beauty, was part of the life we led. Our experimentation gave us clarity of vision, and creativity arose from the longing for life and overcoming fear.

In 1975 my travels took me back to the USA, to the Goethe Institute in San Francisco and the University of California, Berkeley. You crossed the enormous Bay Bridge and found yourself on the university campus. The Pacific Film Archive, under its then director Tom Luddy, was an attractive little *cinematheque*, a very nice institution. Later, Tom Luddy became Francis Ford Coppola's manager in chief in San Francisco.

My first journey to the States in the midseventies was for a retrospective, and in addition I was professor of modern French literature, theater, and film at Berkeley for a while. The head of the department, a specialist in Romance languages and literature, had invited me. The plan was for me to speak French to advanced students. It was clear, however, that the students were not in the least interested. After ten minutes, I realized that no one understood anything except *bonjour*, so I went on in English. Only eight years after the 1967 student riots at Berkeley, the students were once again privileged kids whose rich parents were paying for their studies.

Admittedly, there were exceptions. In the street, I met what they called among themselves a real black nigger, a great guy with a wild black-power hairstyle. I was alarmed at first when he addressed me—"Hey, man." He was not a student, but he asked if he could attend my seminar. I told him I'd fix it. There was some objection from the predominantly white moneybags in the class, but apart from one other student he was the only one to ask intelligent questions and come up with good ideas.

On another occasion, I was staying in San Francisco with Mabel Sacharow, a good friend of mine and of Rosa von Praunheim's. In 1977 we were all lecturers at the Arts Center. Mabel Sacharow had taken in a dark-skinned man who had killed his girlfriend in a fit of fury and had just been released from prison. At night I had to go along an eerie, dark passageway, where he used to lie in wait for me, presumably just to scare me. A silly thing happened at the San Francisco Opera House. I was to meet Jean-Pierre Ponnelle, who was directing a production of *Otello* there. The huge marble building lay right on what at that time was the dividing line between wealth and poverty in the city. I got out of my taxi with Magdalena, who happened to be with me, and went up a flight of steps to a large door. Magdalena was waiting for the taxi driver to give her our change, but I called back to her, "Come on, hurry up!" And out of the corner of my eye, I saw a bunch of black men approaching on foot from the other side of the street, clearly not well disposed to us. I ran on, Magdalena was still waiting for our change when one of them kicked her in the rear end, and she came flying toward me. Luckily the door was open, so she wasn't hurt. There we all were: Jean-Pierre Ponnelle, Plácido Domingo, Mirella Freni, Magdalena, and I, all of us calm but still on edge. We could have expected violence at any moment. I don't remember now who it was who said, "Onstage, get onstage!" And we ran; the building was full of nooks and crannies, so they couldn't find us, but they did come into the opera house, five or seven men, and it was some time before they went away again. I could understand them; after all, the luxurious opera house right opposite a slum, bel canto next door to the ghetto, amounted to an ugly provocation.

I was once staying at a luxury hotel with the great pianist Christoph Eschenbach. I was spending the night in the city and didn't go back to Berkeley. Eschenbach closed all the windows tightly and drew the draperies. He didn't want so much as a glimmer of light to come in. I myself was used to sleeping in a room with a dim light on, because I don't like losing my sense of direction, and it was strange to spend a night in total darkness. Eschenbach, on the other hand, needed it so that he could concentrate, and there was no arguing with him. The next day I heard him playing Beethoven's Fifth Piano Concerto, with Seiji Ozawa conducting. Christoph and I had had a long conversation before the performance about the timpanist, the best percussionist I had ever heard in a symphony orchestra; she was also a beautiful woman and the only black instrumentalist in the orchestra, but she was about to be fired. In the slow movement of the concerto, there is a dialog between piano and percussion that she performed beautifully with him. I had told him in advance that I would never speak to him again if he didn't bring her forward at the end to take the applause with him; the idea of firing her must have been pure racism. And he did indeed bring her to the front of the stage to receive applause.

I stayed for a while with Viva, Andy Warhol's muse, who had acted in Agnès Varda's film *Lion's Love*, and her lover the French filmmaker Michel Auder. I had met Agnès Varda in Paris and we met again in California. At Viva's place I also lived with Sammy, a rent boy of Mexican origin—a delightful, dear boy I liked very much, but he just couldn't stop stealing things.

There were also unpleasant incidents with the remnants of the Charles Manson group, who had set eyes on me once when I was in Los Angeles and staying at the dilapidated Hotel Château Marmont on Sunset Boulevard. Several young men and women had approached me, maybe thinking I was their new leader and savior. They were all high on drugs, the situation became uncomfortable, and so I returned to San Francisco. At first they left me in peace there, but then I saw them again. They simply turned up at the hotel and sat around. I was supposed to cook for them, while the women knitted. They always wore berets on their heads to conceal their sign of the ax tattoo. One of the men, a horny guy, who was certainly on the elephant tranquilizer known as Angel Dust, wanted to swim

99

in the dirty hotel pool with me. I thought, why not, but he was a muscular man and pressed me against him so hard that he almost choked me. I got away only by breathing out underwater, making myself as small as I could and wriggling away. It wasn't attempted murder, just a state of drugged frenzy, but it was a risky thing to do.

It may have been that all this happened because, at their request, I had visited Tex Watson, a member of the Manson Family and one of the murderers of Sharon Tate, in San Luis Obispo High Security Male Prison, Main Section. He was called Tex because he came from Texas, and he had fled there after the murders. I did visit him, because he interested me. He has been in that prison for forty years and is a fascinating character. Watson married and had four children as a result of his wife's marital visits to him in prison. He wrote me one letter saying, "Come back to Jesus, Werner." He meant it seriously; he was devoted to God and described himself as a born-again Christian. I can only admire his extraordinary development.

I attended some remarkable events with Daniel Schmid during those years. Once we were meeting Ava Gardner at a hotel. She told the waiter, "My breakfast, please," and he passed on the message. "Miss Gardner wants her breakfast." And then they brought her a bottle of Scotch. Very logical! It hurt no one; she was simply doing her own thing.

At the time, Daniel and I dreamed of making films with Ava Gardner or Rita Hayworth. I once met Rita Hayworth at the casino in Cannes, but unfortunately, I couldn't scrape together the money for my film project. Daniel and I went to a concert given by Marlene Dietrich in Los Angeles. Daniel was a Marlene fan; what had interested me most about her for a long time was the sheer amount she could eat. If she cooked asparagus, she added half a pound of butter to every serving, yet she never got fat. I also met her family and was to have opened an exhibition about her later in Rome, but it never came off because I asked for too much money. On that occasion in Los Angeles, Miss Dietrich was very drunk and sang, "Frag nicht warum ich gehe, frag nicht warum" [Don't ask me why I'm going, don't ask why], and trailed off into babbling the way you do when singing while you are tipsy. Then she stumbled and fell into the orchestra pit. There was a loud sound—it was the plaster cast that she was wearing under her dress splitting. The audience was horrified, and Daniel, the lover of divas, succumbed to emotion, but I was shaking with laughter when Dietrich's voice emerged from the pit. The fall had obviously sobered her up, and she said, in her inimitably cool way, "Miss Dietrich won't leave the orchestra pit before the audience has left."

Flocons d'or

When I was living in Mexico and California, in order to finance my stay there I needed invitations to a retrospective or a university seminar or the prospect of making a film that had a reasonable chance of being realized. In Germany I could earn money by directing for the live theater and from advances for my films, none of which had so far made a profit. *The Death of Maria Malibran* had been made for around seventy-five thousand deutsche marks, and we had kept ourselves as a group on that for several months; it had been the same with *Willow Springs* and *The Black Angel*.

I would happily have moved to Mexico, the country of my dreams, particularly as my films were appreciated more there than in Germany, but the fact was that I had to earn money in Europe with my various projects.

So I prepared to make my last super-underground film, *Flocons d'or* [Flakes of gold]. It happened like this: I had won the main prize at the Avant-Garde Festival in Toulon in 1974 with *Willow Springs*. The prize didn't bring in much money, about the equivalent of three thousand euros in today's terms. It happened that I crossed Chantal Akerman's path; she was showing her *Je, tu, il, elle* [I, you, he, she]. "How come you won the prize?" she asked. "Because you didn't," I said. We have been friends ever since.

Anyway, with the prize money I began making a film without defining its subject yet. I was used to working in financial chaos, and I was still doing so, although the state Institut de l'audiovisuel (INA) in Paris, the production company Les filmes du Losange, Channel Two of German TV, and I were producing *Flocons d'or* together ourselves.

The cast included Andréa Ferréol, who had become well known from *La grande bouffe* [The big feast] and to whom *Bild-Zeitung* claimed I was engaged; Magdalena (of course); and Irene, a beautiful prostitute from Zurich. My friend Roswitha Hecke had published her legendary photo-book *Liebes Leben* [Dear life] about Irene. Also in my film were Udo Kier, Ellen Umlauf, Christine Kaufmann, Ingrid Caven, Isolde Barth, Ila von Hasperg, and Rainer Will, and not least the enchanting Bulle Ogier, my friend from Paris, whom I had liked so much in Luis Buñuel's *The Discreet Charm of the Bourgeoisie* and Jacques Rivette's *Céline et Julie vont en bateau* [Céline and Julie go boating]. They had all waived any fee, and Andréa and Bulle even paid their own travel expenses.

We shot one episode in an abandoned railroad station in Bochum when we were working in the theater there; another was shot in Avignon, where the director of the Avignon Festival, Jacques Robert, invited me to give a presentation of my films and put me up in his own villa. I wanted to take advantage of both that city and the invitation to get some work done on my film, not knowing whether I would find anyone else to come in on the production.

It was to be the third part of a trilogy that had begun with *The Death of Maria Malibran* and *Willow Springs* and fitted together episodes illustrating human tragedy and comedy. The piecemeal work done on *Flocons d'or* gave me the idea of telling the story in four independent short narratives, like novellas, bracketed by a prolog and an epilog with the overriding theme of death. Viewers would see Christine Kaufmann, Udo Kier, and Magdalena, their gestures and games with falling Mikado sticks and a card house, and would hear the fading sounds of an old recording of the trio in Bizet's *Carmen* when the title character and her two friends are reading fortunes in the cards—"Toujours la mort" [Always death], a disk by the marvelous Spanish mezzo-soprano Conchita Supervía that I had found in Mexico.

To the horror of the Channel Two editorial department, *Flocons d'or* was ultimately two hours fifty minutes long, but at least I delivered it complete. It was my farewell to my career as a filmmaker so far, before I began on something entirely new in principle by writing *The Kingdom of Naples*. *Flocons d'or* was to arouse a sense of tragedy achieved through kitsch, without shrinking from triviality. In my outline I wrote: "*Willow Springs* would have nothing to do with love; *Flocons d'or* resurrects it." The first episode, entitled "En Cuba" [In Cuba], was my answer to cinematic melodrama on the grand scale, in the style of Ava Gardner and Rita Hayworth. Five characters and their love intrigues are set in Cuba in the 1940s, the ambience is that of a Caterina Valente fantasy, and Magdalena plays the French wife of a large estate proprietor who is a heroin addict. We shot the second episode, "Un drame de rail" [A railroad drama], as a naturalistic drama set in the Bochum freight rail station. It was about a woman whose mother tries to prevent her from loving an immigrant worker. In the end she throws herself in front of the next train in despair. The third episode, "Tag der Idioten" [Day of the idiots], was shot in Avignon and anticipated my fascination with madness. Andréa Ferréol, wearing a tarty black negligee that she imagines is her wedding dress, is grieving for the loss of her lover. In confusion, she haunts her house in the country, looking after four dogs. The mysterious Bulle Ogier appears to her, an oracular figure, and so does Magdalena as the messenger of death, looking for "living victims for her hungry soul." I shot this summertime ghost story in top-lit black and white, which made the characters, faces, and spaces seem curiously transparent. Bulle Ogier, who had great difficulty at first in coming to terms with my style, improvisation, and the blurring of borders between work and real life, opened up when she didn't know exactly what she had to do in the next moment, and in the end she was very enthusiastic.

The crazed dog-loving woman played by Andréa may have been suggested by *Les chants de Maldoror* or maybe by our actress colleague Tana Schanzara in Bochum, who shared her little house with forty dogs and sometimes slept on the coffee table so as not to shoo the animals off the bed.

In the film treatment, which the television editorial team accepted with amusement and expectantly, I sketched out the fate of Andréa's character thus: "Only one of the four parts of the film has a kind of glimmer of ironic hope about it. The story concerns the beautiful but feebleminded woman played by Andréa Ferréol, who is not going to be cornered by the alleged messenger of death and, although she seems to have been drowned, reappears from the muddy waters of a stream instead of obeying a mystic command. She moves on to new and unknown shores." That was just how the self-confident Andréa played it: climbing out of a shallow brook with head held high, after a failed scene of rustic suicide, takes some doing. The fourth episode, "Réalité–vérité!" [Reality–truth!], was a parody of the new style of German *Heimat* [homeland] cinema (films with outdoor settings in the rural areas of the German-speaking countries), in the manner of *Pioniere in Ingolstadt* [Pioneers in Ingolstadt] and *Jagdszenen aus Niederbayern* [Hunting scenes from Lower Bavaria]. Udo Kier, in a German army tunic, played the part of Franzl, a simpleminded rapist and murderer on the run, and is pursued by the black angel of death personified by Magdalena until he comes to a bad end.

Once again I was the author, director, and cameraman rolled into one. My two French stars had to be prepared for rehearsals and recordings almost around the clock. I showed them everything they were to do, because as usual I was developing my concept on location and as we went along. And of course they helped with the décor and costumes. Even some of the music was created between us: for instance, Andréa played the mouth organ, Magdalena sang the Cuban national anthem, and Peter van Hornbeck and I made music when music boxes and glockenspiels were called for. It was while making *Flocons d'or* that I discovered Mozart's music for glass harmonica, and I returned to it in 2009 with my theatrical project for *Antigone/Electra* at the People's Theater in Berlin.

I could have gone on along the same lines, but when the film was finished in 1976, I knew that I must set off in a new direction. I couldn't take my form of underground cinema any farther.

The Death of Maria Malibran had appealed to an intellectual public made up entirely of thoughtful, open-minded viewers, particularly in France and Mexico. But you can't survive on audiences of that kind. Filmmaking is very expensive. I spent a year paying off debts to a copying firm in Munich for *Flocons d'or*, amounting to an enormous sum for me. I had about a hundred thousand euros available for the production, but the film cost one-third more. None of the actors were paid; no one was paid. It was difficult to work on such terms with friends who had helped in so many ways. I found it intolerable and didn't want to go on like that.

I had tried cocaine in the USA and developed a taste for it; it was the only hard drug that interested me. If I could get hold of good coke, it brought me to positive ecstasy. In Paris, even the headmaster of the English lycée for girls handed it out once at a school festive occasion when there was very good coke available in the city. After more than thirty years, I feel sure I am not harming anyone's reputation by saying so. The headmaster was a distinguished and highly educated gentleman. Women friends of mine were there too, and they celebrated by snorting cocaine while the English parents and their English children strolled around the English lycée. It was the kind of fun that appealed to me.

Then, one day, I stopped taking cocaine, and that was that. In working on *Flocons d'or*, I became aware of the shadow side. If I had taken it at night during the montage, when I returned the next day, I didn't recognize the rhythm of cutting because my criteria had shifted. Once you have been taking coke for too long, the effect stops being euphoric. You get used to planes of perception and times mingling and shifting. Sometimes I felt as if something were crawling over my skin. So I told myself: okay, time to stop! I spent two days in bed, drinking peppermint tea with lemon and ice cubes, and that did the trick.

One must leave so as to understand

When *Flocons d'or* was finished and was transmitted on German television soon afterward, in May 1976, I would have liked to travel to Mexico to think over my next step in peace. In Munich, I met Ingrid Caven and Daniel Schmid to prepare for Ingrid's première as a singer of chansons. Then my brother and I heard that our mother was very sick and would soon die. We took her home to our little house in Dossenheim, but there was nothing we could do to help her.

My mother, who had been a great help to us as head of production during the making of *Flocons d'or*, had often felt unwell that summer. The doctors, suspecting trouble with her circulation at first, sent her much too late to a specialist, who diagnosed liver cancer that could no longer be treated. She was a strong-willed woman who hated being sick and going to hospitals. So my brother and I nursed her at home as best we could, shattered as we felt by the inevitability of her death.

In those four weeks when she was dying, I came closer to my brother again. Hans-Jürgen had never been able to break free from the loving embrace of the parental home and had gone on living there even after studying physics. There had often been angry confrontations between us, usually inflamed by me, because I wanted to get my brother, who is four years my senior, out of the hole he was in. But was I to blame my mother? Was I to dig about in her life for reasons why my brother and I had turned out the way we had? Maybe it was odd that our mother still liked to wash us, even long after we had grown up. But I saw us all as curious, special people, gifted with humor, and in that self-confidence I told stories of such scenes, even to journalists, to make them sound endearing. As I have said, I don't like psychologizing.

My brother had more difficulty in accepting me than vice versa; after all, I had left the family and gone my own way. But back then, there with our dying mother; we talked to one another again. Hans-Jürgen dabbled in the esoteric; he had written a book about astrophysics and astrology and told me about it, and for the first time I understood what made him tick. Incidentally, he has never published it; it seems to have gone missing.

My brother lived in Dossenheim with our mother. Our parents had separated, but a formal divorce was out of the question for a married couple of their generation. My father, Hans, moved to Munich, my brother followed him after our mother's death, and I made their address my cover address in Germany. My father built a little house in Geretsried near Munich and had a small factory there for making mechanical brakes; my cousin runs it today.

When my mother died, something came to an irrevocable end. I grieved for a long time. With my mother, I had lost a home to which I could always return. Until then, I had always imagined death as an ecstatic merging with everything that would be around my bed, and I myself lying in it. In my films, I depicted death as something sublime, and when Maria Callas died, I wrote, in my obituary of her, that she could stop time with her voice and raise the certainty of death to a moment of beauty. As if I had foreseen what lay ahead, *Flocons d'or* had been an ironic exaggeration of theatrical posing and the yearning for death, bringing a kind of closure. For sitting beside my mother's deathbed, I suddenly realized that dying is a very lonely thing. My mother lay upstairs in our little house, drugged with morphine, and then fell into a coma and perceived nothing anymore. Her body still defended itself, like a reflex action, against the total extinction of vitality. It was unbearable, and very sad. For a long time I was unable to talk about it.

Magdalena, too, died a difficult death, and so did my father and my brother, my life's partner Marcelo, my beloved Arpad and Jens, and many friends, both men and women. I was aware that many who were close to me felt that I had abandoned them when they fell sick, but I never undertook nursing duties again. Magdalena, to whom I was so close, was cared for by her women friends, and I kept away from the deathbeds of my other friends as well. When Marcelo was in the hospital in Düsseldorf, I was directing a play in Cologne. I called it "the AIDS shuttle" as I traveled between the two cities, but for weeks on end I had no time for hospital visits. I have known quite enough cases of death and suicide in the course of my life. I had to try living with that; the belief in God and the positive thinking that are part of me helped there.

I took on my mother's love of aquamarine, and since her death I have worn aquamarine rings on all my fingers and aquamarine pendants around my neck, a way of remembering her that means more to me than the rituals of mourning. Recently, I had a present of one from Arielle Dombasle, the crazy actress and singer who was in *Two*.

After my mother's death, I took *Flocons d'or* to the Locarno Film Festival, where I met Detlev Sierck, known as Douglas Sirk in Hollywood and famous for his melodramas. I spent a wonderful night with him; we got into conversation about old age and death, and he sensed how sad I was feeling. Douglas Sirk from Lübeck, who had fled from the Nazis to Hollywood, was a fine human being, an old gentleman of eighty then. Of course, I admired his lavish style and the sophisticated expression of feelings in his films. In my youth I had been horrified by *Imitation of Life*, with Lana Turner, because I thought it kitschy; only later did I take a certain pleasure in it on another level. But I was far more interested in the great humanist who chose his own path by leaving Germany. We sat together for a long time that evening, and he comforted me for the death of my mother.

In the fall of that year, I met my friend Alberte, and she became my set and costume designer for many years. So life went on. Udo Kier, who had been in *Flocons d'or* and was a friend of mine, invited me to Paris. He was shooting *Spermula*, a terrible film directed by Charles Matton, and when I was having dinner with the team one evening, I met Alberte, who had designed the set for the film.

The year after that I nearly expanded our family by adding a foster son. Balthazar Clémenti was the son of Pierre and Margareth Clémenti and was eight years old. His father, Pierre, was very good-looking and was a famous actor who had been in films by Pasolini, Buñuel, Rivette, Visconti, and Philippe Garrel. But drugs had taken their toll on him.

Balthazar had been expelled from school, no doubt for doing stupid things. His mother, Margareth Clémenti, who had appeared in Pasolini's *Medea*, Fellini's *Casanova*, and my own film *The Kingdom of Naples*, had just had a baby by another man and was living with him. Balthazar was probably jealous. When I met him in Rome, he suddenly said, "Take me with you." I was surprised that his mother immediately agreed and gave me letters of permission to take the child traveling. So Balthazar traveled around Europe with me.

At first it was difficult, because he spoke only French. I took him to Dossenheim, where my father tried out his schoolboy French and played badminton and table football with him in the garden. I would have adopted the boy; you have the strength for that kind of thing when you are young. However, I wasn't actually quite sure about it. Not long before, I had made a woman friend pregnant. It was a fact that, even though I am gay, women kept wanting to get me into bed with them. It bothered me, although it was pleasant all the same. So I sensibly said no to the boy. I'd have acted differently today, now that I see how difficult young people make things for a child with their decisions.

In 1977, when I went into the famous Grand Hotel in Locarno, where all the film festival guests had gathered, I took Balthazar along. At the time he was refusing point-blank to wash, so I used to take his underpants and socks away surreptitiously by night and give them a quick wash so that he wouldn't notice anything. There were two English gays there, in the circle around Derek Jarman, who was directing his film *Sebastiane* in Latin. To them, I was nothing but a queen, a fag, a pederast. Okay, but people gave me odd looks in the hotel; I was persona non grata. When I noticed that, I took Balthazar aside and told him he had better think something up. So he acted all cute to the pair of them and fooled around in the swimming pool until they offered to let him have a rest in their room. He went up there, found their shaving foam, and sprayed it into all their pockets and shoes. Then he came downstairs again, saying, "We showed them!" Sad to say, after the summer vacation Balthazar's parents decided to send him to another school, so I lost sight of him, and to this day, unfortunately, I have no idea what became of him. When I reached the age of forty, I once again felt the wish to have a son, but the young actress whom I could imagine as the mother of my child fell in love with someone else.

Madness, the key to all hearts

The theater is closer to life; films are closer to vanity. It's wonderful to have made a film that can be shown over and over again. All artists are vain enough to feel that. The live theater is transitory; the cinema is a manifesto, something that you can take with you, so to speak. That's not by any means contradictory.

When Peter Zadek, Jean-Pierre Ponnelle, and Ivan Nagel urged me to direct stage plays, I took some convincing at first. I didn't like the bureaucratic aspect of live theater, and I didn't feel comfortable with it until I was directing *Salome* in Bochum, where Peter Zadek was the manager. That eventually made me feel part of a theatrical family, and then, in the usual way of families, it's difficult to wriggle out again. One production followed another, and since 1972 I have directed almost eighty for the stage. Given that every production takes two to four months of a director's life, you can work out how many months I spent in the theater. My friend Ingrid Caven coined a witty phrase to describe the constant state of suspension in which we live, oscillating between rehearsals and performances: days of twilight, nights of frenzy.

Work is the wrong way to describe the concept; my life lies in it. I regard expressing myself as a huge strain but also as an inner necessity. I don't think of the work itself as strenuous, since it is extremely pleasant, but it does put a physical strain on me. However, that is how I choose to live. I believe that if we were all truthful, we would consider our lives fulfilled only if we worked as creatively as we love. I don't see the borderline between the two. I have always lived only with people who were involved in the theater or films; I have only ever seduced actors and singers. I have loved people in such careers whose personalities are very different from mine. I wouldn't have had the time to look around anywhere else.

As it was, I didn't have enough time to immerse myself entirely in the world of films, but I don't regret it. There were always more friends of both sexes coming along—actors, people on the production side. Wonderful and inspiring. So for a long time, I didn't miss the world of films at all. The theater calls for a great deal of energy, and I went along with that, because I could realize my idea that there is no difference between art and life better on the stage of live theater. Conversely, the fact that I knew about complex situations in the theater helped me in making films. Look at my friend Fassbinder's film *I Only Want You to Love Me*. In that sense, trying to express yourself in art is also, always, an attempt to be loved. As primus inter pares in the sphere of work in the theater and the cinema, the director is the one who most wants to be loved but makes it most impossible. That is true of me and, ultimately, of all directors. In what I call a cocreative group, so much is contributed by all involved that I no longer know which visual, artistic, or dramatic idea was whose. The result is a joint creation, although it is steered by one person: that director who wants to be loved most.

Art cannot be achieved collectively. That's not what I mean by a cocreative group; nor is it the same as my deep friendship with Magdalena. I don't know how collective art is supposed to function—even socialists like Brecht couldn't manage it. Brecht had help from his wife, whom he failed to credit. Maybe that's all part of it. My own women friends have sometimes accused me, too, of imposing on them.

But how could a collective work? With several directors at once? I can't imagine it. The more of an individualist someone is, the better he can work with others. Peter Zadek had enough money available in Bochum for everyone to bring their own people along. Fassbinder, Jiří Menzel, Augusto Fernándes, directors of different nationalities, all brought actors, set designers, and musicians with them. That was a very good idea. Variety in the same place without group ideology. Once I acted in the production of *Atlantis* directed by Augusto Fernándes, and on another occasion Magdalena took the part of one of the daughters in Zadek's production of *King Lear*.

Magdalena blossomed in Bochum. Peter Zadek made very good use of her talent and her intelligence and wasn't bothered by stupid criticism of her amateurism, far from it. She was a dream as the Ghost in *Hamlet* and danced like Valeska Gert in *Professor Unrat*, both productions directed by Peter Zadek. Working in the theater gave her more freedom; she got to know other directors who eventually worked with her. She was able to emancipate herself from me, and our relationship gained by it.

We spent almost all our time in the theater in Bochum, and there was almost nothing entertaining to do outside it. Peter Zadek had opened the Bo Bar in the cellar, and we met there. He described the club of which it was a part in his memoirs, making fun of my entourage as "tall, good-looking, slender people who strode slowly around the place like some kind of sect." It was a fact that I looked thin and amusingly gloomy in my black leather pants; we did seem different from the other groups. Even our coffee and cake sessions with Traute Eichhorn, who mothered us and was prompter at the evening performances, didn't change that. Zadek liked us, you could sense that through the mockery. And he really had no reason to do so; he was deeply hurt when I began an affair with his partner Roswitha Hecke. Roswitha and Zadek separated, and then she became the lover and companion of my friend Wolf Wondratschek, who contributed a fine foreword to her book *Liebes Leben* [Dear life], about the beautiful lady of the night Irene in Zurich.

Speaking of vain and voyeuristic theatrical managers, Claus Peymann always hailed me by saying, "Ah, here's His Majesty again!" It wasn't meant maliciously or cynically. When I was directing the première of Georg Kreisler's *Adam Schaf hat Angst* [Adam Schaf is afraid], with Tim Fischer at the Berlin Ensemble, the work was in a terrible crisis because I was part of a love tangle around Fischer. One day I simply disappeared, and thereupon Claus Peymann sat up at night until three in the morning trying to reach me on the phone. If he could help, he said, he would come over at once. "Herr Peymann," I told him, "you don't need to help me. It'll be better in the morning." He proved very loyal, without really noticing it. Maybe he thought there was something exciting about a gay man in such amorous difficulty. The only criticism I have to make of him is his poorly chosen program. The Berlin Ensemble is the only German theatrical company known all over the world, definitely the most famous. But its program is pathetic compared with what it ought to be.

Myself, I often spent my time at the Bochum Theater with classic plays featuring women characters. When Peter Zadek was manager there, I directed *Salome*, *Lucrezia Borgia*, *Miss Julie*, and *Käthchen von Heilbronn*. If we add *Emilia Galotti*, my first production in the Painters' Hall at the Hamburg Theater in 1972, and *Miss Sara Sampson* at the Kassel State Theater in 1977, both by my beloved Lessing, you can see that I had a strong liking for dramas prominently featuring women.

Lucrezia Borgia was one of Magdalena's finest performances. I was determined to direct the play. I also suggested *Miss Julie*, as well as *Miss Sara Sampson* because I wanted to direct the precursor of *Emilia Galotti*, the entire uncut text performed at high speed. But it went on for three hours after all, because the tempo of the play got out of hand. They were all wonderful works that I was keen to direct. I had chosen *Käthchen von Heilbronn* myself, and also my first opera, *Lohengrin*, which I directed at the Kassel State Theater in 1979. Then, when I began working on a regular basis at the Düsseldorf Theater, it was the theatrical manager Volker Canaris who suggested Federico García Lorca's *Doña Rosita*. Wagner's *Lohengrin* could also be regarded as a confrontation between man and woman, with different characters and personalities setting out from different premises—for instance, when Elsa cannot bring herself to keep her lover's secret. To me, the woman has always been the lucid model for real life in theatrical and cinematic work, although in the course of time my perception was enormously extended by Jules Massenet's *Werther*, *Caligula* by Albert Camus, Shakespeare's *Othello* and *King Lear*, *Die Soldaten* [The soldiers] by Jakob Michael Reinhold Lenz, and *Don Carlos* as written by Friedrich Schiller and set as an opera by Giuseppe Verdi.

A good theory could be constructed to explain why I directed works involving so many women, but apart from saying that I thought them more interesting than men in their social role, and as a surface on which to project my imagination, I can't cast any light on it. What mattered to me was finding good parts for Magdalena, Ingrid Caven, Tamara Kafka, Elisabeth Krejcir, Traute Hoess, and the many other actresses in my theatrical family.

I lodged with Tamara Kafka for a while in Bochum. She was in the cast of *Miss Julie*, *Lucrezia Borgia*, and *Käthchen von Heilbronn* and was also in my film *Day of the Idiots*, and other productions. Later she became a literary consultant in the theater, an author, and a director herself. Once she lent me a hundred and eighty deutsche marks for a rail journey—a large sum for her, in view of her salary then. She had to ask my father to return the money, because I simply couldn't scrape it together. Since *Emilia Galotti*, my own fee had risen from three thousand to eight thousand deutsche marks, especially when work on the sets and on textual revisions was involved. I would have been paid fifteen thousand marks for Shakespeare's *As You Like It*, but I backed out; it was during the year my mother died. However that may be, I always had debts from my films to be paid off, traveling as much as my way of life called for cost money, and I have never been good at saving.

But back to *Miss Julie*. The production I had directed was invited to Persepolis in 1977, to be staged in Shah Reza Pahlavi's Metropolitan Palace. I declined the invitation on ideological grounds. Today I would agree to take it there—given that the identical production could be staged, without any changes.

Anyway, for us at the Bochum Theater what mattered was to oppose the mistaken assumption that the gulf between serious art and entertainment cannot be bridged. I wanted to attack the German lack of a sense of humor with my productions of Lessing and with Kleist's *Käthchen*. Heinrich Kleist's play had been downgraded to a sentimentally Romantic mystery drama; we brushed it against the grain to let what had previously been missing show through. I saw the play as much crazier than normal productions make it appear. The unconditional fervor with which the heroine pursues her man! Her inner strength, although he inflicts sadistic torments on her! I interpreted Kleist's play to show that its subject was the author's secret fear of such strength in a woman.

With Hans Peter Schubert, I created a wonderful set, consisting of metal rods hanging down, and we used them to create fantastically simple effects: the walls of a knight's castle, a landscape in a storm. Magdalena's Kunigunde von Thurneck was just as Kleist described her: a bald-headed puppet, naked under a chiffon gown, suggesting a water nymph. In our production she was no Undine but a more grotesque figure. Elisabeth Krejcir played Käthchen as a victim of the knight Wetter von Strahl—we couldn't interpret her submission to the torments that he inflicts on her as love. We took the melancholy words of Käthchen's father—"Madness, the skeleton key to unlock all hearts"—as our motto. And in my ironic contribution to the program notes I wished the pompous knights a terrible death in "their metal baby rompers, thanks to their chauvinistic lack of insight."

Maria

I was proud of it when *Bild-Zeitung* wrote unpleasant things about me. But I thought German criticism of Maria Schell disgraceful. It's a German phenomenon. French journalists keep asking me why we are so often unkind to artists in Germany. Romy Schneider bridged the gap; Maria Schell didn't. By the gap, I don't mean the gulf between Germany and France but between Germany and Hollywood. In fact, Maria could have stayed there, since after all, she made three Hollywood films.

I knew Maria very well. We were close friends, and it was a really good friendship. Maria was a fine person, intelligent, sensitive, and staunchly loyal. But the younger generation in Germany hated her, regarding her as a kitschy star who acted in slushy tearjerkers. When I was rehearsing *Miss Julie* in Bochum, with Ingrid Caven, she was in *The Tower of Babel*, by Fernando Arrabal, directed by that splendid little Spanish Moroccan master of the absurd himself. When he dipped his pecker into Schell's coffee cup in the canteen, she was surprised but decided in the end to take it as a joke and laughed.

In Bochum on that occasion, I asked Maria, "You know that film of yours *Le notti bianche* [White nights]?" No, she said, as a matter of fact she had never watched the film that she had made with Luchino Visconti. We didn't continue the conversation, but in secret I organized a screening in the Chamber Cinema, so that she could see how well she had acted for Visconti. I told her, "Maria, they're about to show a film of mine," sat her down in the cinema, and *White Nights* began running. So she did see herself on the screen, and said, "I'm not so bad after all." I knew she lacked confidence in her own talent.

Good directors could make something of her: Wolfgang Staudte, Robert Siodmak, Luchino Visconti, and René Clément. With Clément she made *Gervaise*, a film that I liked a lot in my childhood. In *The Brothers Karamazov* she was better than Yul Brynner. A sensitive woman. I shall never forget how she consoled me after the death of Maria Callas. I liked her honesty.

We had met in Berlin in 1969. I was in the artists' bar Der Diener with Rosa von Praunheim, who was my lover at the time, and my fiancée Jutta. Maria was sitting at the other end of the bar with her husband, Veit Relin, and she sent the waiter over with a billet-doux: could they offer the charming young people a glass of wine? After some hesitation, we went to join them. I got the impression that Maria, who was forty-three then, fancied my fiancée. In fact, it was a wonder she didn't fall on Jutta then and there in the bar. Later we went over the Kurfürstendamm to another bar, and people gaped. "That's Maria Schell—is she lesbian or what?" She had linked arms with my fiancée, and I told her, "That's a real compliment, Frau Schell." That made her laugh.

In his book *50 Jahre pervers* [Gay for fifty years], Rosa von Praunheim told a similar anecdote about Maria Schell. Then he got cold feet, expecting her lawyers to call on him. He sent me a witness statement prepared in advance, in which I was to confirm that I had heard the story with my own ears. I was supposed to sign it and send it back to him, but I didn't.

The friendship between Maria and me began with that meeting and lasted for years. Once Maria practically saved my life. I had a date to meet her at the Free People's Theater in West Berlin, where she was playing Mary Queen of Scots in Ferdinand Bruckner's *Elizabeth of England*, directed by Rudolf Noelte. I collected her and her assistant at the stage door, and we went off to eat oysters together; she had invited me and the young man. Afterward, I just made it to the door of the oyster bar before throwing up and soiling her mink coat. It went on and on, terrible, and she looked after me. We went back to the theater, where I found plastic bags so that I could go on vomiting in her Mercedes. Then she drove me home. By now I was on all fours, and surviving the journey was a trial. Shellfish poisoning is horrible. At four in the morning she managed to find a doctor. She filled wine bottles with hot water and put them under me. She was still there with me when day dawned, waiting to make sure I had survived the doctor's injection. She left me an autographed card from a touring company of earlier times, with her as the Lady of the Camellias on the front, and on the back she had written, in English, "Anyway, Werner, I've always loved vomiting men.

Cheers, Maria." She had a sense of humor—and that evening she was onstage in the play again.

Naples in winter

The idea for *The Kingdom of Naples* came to me in 1975/76, after I had exhausted all my stylistic mannerisms and fought all my battles with myself and my personal genius in *Flocons d'or*. That period was over, and I was in search of a new departure. When I felt that I could go no farther in the underground cinema, I thought of Naples. I wanted a period that I could confidently survey and the elements of a family saga reaching from 1945 to 1972. I wrote the scenario and created an extended version with the beautiful photographs I had taken in Naples and its surroundings.

For once, I actually put together a well-constructed screenplay to be shot in various possible locations, also adding some associative factors, such as the veiled figures of the Virgin Mary and Christ that appear at the end of the film.

I found an incredible place: the chapel of the prince of San Severo, no longer consecrated these days. The prince must have been an unusually cruel if ingenious character who did crazy things. For instance, he forced his sculptor, who was working in marble, to produce a veiled figure of Christ and another of the Virgin. Try carving a veil out of a block of marble! How can you capture the effect of a veiled face? It can be done, but you really need to see the statue. We got the effect in the film, but that wasn't three-dimensional; the sculptor must have toiled for ages to create the illusion. And there were two such blocks of marble, one for *Christo velato* and another for *Maria velata*.

I put all this together in the scenario and then phoned my friend Wolf Wondratschek. Wolf dropped by one evening, we discussed it all for a while, and I said, "Put your name to it, and we'll get somewhere more easily." Right, so now I had my treatment, and I talked to the cameraman Thomas Mauch, whom I had known for a long time. He waxed enthusiastic about the idea and agreed to be behind the camera. Christoph Holch of Channel Two came in on the project, and so did my old friend Peter Berling, who was keen on fostering coproductions between Italy and Germany and brought in partners from Rome. The film was produced on a very small budget, I think about three hundred thousand marks, an incredibly low sum for a feature film. We shot it in Super 16 format and then blew it up to 35 mm, a method that made it less expensive.

We arrived in Naples with our team at Christmas of 1977 and celebrated New Year's Eve in the usual local way, with something resembling an air raid. At midnight people set their trash cans alight with Swiss firecrackers and threw everything they didn't want anymore out of their windows: radios, refrigerators, sofas, armchairs. You had to go carefully crossing the road. Thomas Mauch and I stood behind the net curtains in the hotel, looking at the street, which was bathed in smoke and color, with young Neapolitans leaping about like beautiful ghosts. There was something that I can only call erotic in the air.

I was looking for a male protagonist to take the part of the young man in the family saga, an attractive little Neapolitan aged around twenty-two to play Massimo, the son of the Pagano family, as a youth. There were a number of amateurs in the film, because just about everyone in Naples was convinced they would be ideally cast in the role, whether or not they could act. I had a comically pompous assistant director called Gerardo D'Andrea, who did the casting with me. We had an endless procession of young men applying, until Gerardo couldn't take any more of it—the scene I had chosen for the auditions was one where the boy talks to Rosario à Frances, the prostitute played in the film by Margareth Clémenti. Poor fat, pompous Neapolitan Gerardo had to take the part of the whore while the boys auditioned as her customer. We saw all sorts, a few with talent but spots, others with no spots but no talent either.

Then, one day, along came Antonio Orlando. I noticed at once that he had better than basic acting ability, along with intelligence and serenity. He played the scene—to Gerardo's horror I had summoned him to stand in for the tart again—the same dialog came up, and I told Mauch, "Get closer! *Più vicino, più vicino!*" When Antonio had left, I told Gerardo, "That's him—*è lui.*" At which Gerardo flung open the door of the room in our wonderful hotel right by the Santa Lucia yacht harbor and ran along the corridors and down the stairs shouting, "Heurika, heurika, l'abiamo trovato! Il cazzo del maestro ha parlato finalmente!" [Eureka, we've found the boy for the part! The master's prick has finally spoken!].

Gerardo had a talent for comedy. In the film, he appears as the fat, dim-witted mama's boy who becomes a rich but still dim-witted property owner. As for Antonio with his irresistible charm, a liking developed between us, leading to erotic contact a good year later.

The other parts were also cast, by dint of people coming along and introducing themselves. They included the great diva Ida Di Benedetto, who plays the part of Pupetta Ferrante, a coldhearted theatrical climber and factory owner. Our first meeting was amusing. Ida was wearing a large hat and looked wonderful, very elegant and as Neapolitan as you could wish for. She almost got wedged in the doorway of the Hotel Santa Lucia because stout Peter Berling was just going through it and collided with her. I merely said, drily, "*Que incontro*—what a meeting!" and we had made contact. Ida was hired and became a good friend of mine. Liana Trouche, who plays the impoverished, calculating single mother in the film, was also quickly found—without any collision. That meant we had filled the parts of the main characters, and we began shooting.

I took care to avoid the folksy approach. I had been well advised not to rely solely on my own ear for language and my knowledge of the authentic Neapolitan dialect, which has countless linguistic facets, differing from one part of the city to the next. We didn't want it to feel like a German film in which Neapolitans just happen to appear; I went to a great deal of trouble to preserve its authenticity. *Una cronica familiare* [a family chronicle]—that was the story of the Pagano family from the war, the American occupation, and the subsequent string-pulling, going on to depict the establishment of Christian Democracy and the Communist Party and showing how the poor were losers all along the line. That chronicle was the story's point of departure, but I wanted to reconcile it with my own sense of what goes on in the world.

I had no difficulties at all with the Neapolitans themselves. The producers in Rome made themselves ridiculous with their fears; they obstinately refused to find us locations in the slums. So I went off myself with my assistant, found the right sort of tumbledown buildings, and no one gave us any problems. The Romans thought it would be dangerous to shoot such scenes in Naples, but that was so only if you assumed that the local people were idiots. They wouldn't put up with arrogance. When we were shooting *The Kingdom of Naples*, I recognized the warmth and frankness of the Neapolitans as I had known them since my youth, and I felt even more familiar with them after making *Eika Katappa*.

In spring we finished shooting in the harbor of Naples, with the scene in which Michelangelo's famous *Pietà* is put on board a ship. I had it shown twice its real size; I was after the impression—well, this was a film—rather than academic accuracy. After that we moved to Rome and cut the film at the Fune roma, an old, established firm that, unfortunately, went bankrupt some time ago. It was a good firm; it had stills from the classic Italian cinema hanging on the walls. The cutter Ursula West and I sat together during the montage, which was to follow the course of the historical events in the film. When it was all done, the film was blown up, and I had a surprising experience: a young woman with a slight physical disability was working in the lab of the Fune roma in the old-fashioned way—she had the Super 16 material in one hand, the 35 mm material in the other, and she cut them in parallel. How on earth did she do it? I asked her if she really could, and she replied, with the courteous pride of an expert, "*Io mi spaliero mai*—I never go wrong." And she didn't; not a single frame was misplaced in the whole enormous film. When we came to the mixing, I used music especially composed for me by Roberto Pregadio for part of it, and the rest of the music, as usual, came from my own repertoire.

The Kingdom of Naples was invited to the Taormina Festival, a wonderful film festival at that time, with an amphitheater overlooking the sea. Ida Di Benedetto had come, with my friend Giuseppe Fava, a Sicilian writer and journalist with whom I was discussing another Italian project; the outcome of that was *Palermo or Wolfsburg*. After the screening I went back to Naples from Sicily because I had a dental abscess. I didn't think I stood any chance of a prize at the festival. There were so many proud figures in the world of cinema walking around in Taormina, including a famous Czech director who was sure he would get the prize. Finally, a phone call from the festival organizers reached me, telling me to come back to the island at once. I was so happy! So back I went to Taormina, where the Czech maestro looked at me with deep suspicion, as if to say, "How come this guy is here on the day when the prize is awarded?" And that was how I won the wonderful prize at the Taormina Festival!

The Italians were critical of a German director telling the story of Naples, complete with the aftermath of the war and the American occupation, revealing the destructive economic upturn brought about by consumer interests. There was a certain perceptible chauvinism in the air. The entire left-wing press, from *Lotta continua* to *Il manifesto*, protested against my film, because it showed up the Italian Communists as a band of comrades out to enrich themselves. Some people made out that they knew better than me, because in my excitement I had made a couple of grammatical mistakes in Italian at the festival. It was very petty, as if they thought, How can someone too stupid to speak Italian make a film about Italy? But who doesn't make a mistake now and then when he is in an excited mood?

As it happened, my friend Peter Berling brought off a clever PR coup. Originally, the German producer Hanns Eckelkamp had been going to enter Rainer Werner Fassbinder's film *The Marriage of Maria Braun* for the Taormina Festival, but then he decided to keep it for the Berlinale. However, he had already paid the Sicilian press representatives and advertising firms, and at Peter Berling's request he transferred the benefit of this preliminary outlay to our *Kingdom of Naples*. So we were able to come up with the right ads and special press issues, in which I gave a serious account of my film. In the past, I had always talked ironically about the films I directed, as if they were pulp fiction. Peter Berling suspects that this new form of advertising may also have made an impression on the jury: "The period from 1944 to 1976 is shown in sixteen characteristic sequences, to some extent following the Brechtian theatrical principle, seminaturalistic but also with something of the political pamphlet about it." In fact, if anything can be seen as a model for the poetic construction of my film, it is Buñuel's early film about

Mexico City, *Los olvidados*, and for factual precision, films like *Titicut Follies*, a documentary about an American mental hospital for the criminally insane. I fulminated against what I thought intolerable in modern Italy, taking Naples as my example: "Like the entire communal life of the city of Naples, the personal development of its individual inhabitants has been unable to withstand the constant, violent infiltration by foreign powers, consumer interests, and tourists. Present-day Naples presents a picture of desperate dissolution, a phenomenon inimical to life and even worse than the social decline of such a Latin American metropolis as Mexico City. The criminal form of anarchy that has taken hold in southern Italy prefigures the development of the whole European continent."

In short, a few critics did take my cultural criticism seriously, backed up as it was by the ideas of Buñuel and Pasolini, and they praised *The Kingdom of Naples*. But it was also clear that people didn't much like to see a German making a film about the sacred city of Naples and its language when that film went on to win the main prize awarded by an international jury at a festival in Italy itself. In the course of time, *The Kingdom of Naples* became a myth, and today it is cited in the history of Italian cinema as a late masterpiece of neorealism in the tradition of Roberto Rossellini. Naturally I felt flattered. It gave me the courage to go on working. And it made Thomas Mauch want to produce the next film himself.

Champagne Schroeter

As well as the prize of the Taormina Festival, I won the Italian State Prize and the prize of the Chicago Film Festival for *The Kingdom of Naples* and the German Film Prize and the Grimme Prize for the best TV film.

With these awards, I could go to branches of the Goethe Institute and film festivals in many countries. I took the film to Cannes, Brussels, Orléans, and to India as well—all of them wonderful invitations to see the world, rest, and relax. I was more and more attracted by Asia; I felt that it was comparable to Mexico. People weren't shy, and life was lived in public. I realized that I was changing.

But my personal life was only one side of the story.

Maybe I ought to add that the Italian production company went broke in the summer of 1978, and it was months before I received any payment. I had no money at all for the Cannes Festival, and the company wasn't coming up with a penny to promote the film. Without posters or press material, my film was lost in all the hurly-burly there. Soon after that, in June 1978, Channel Two showed *The Kingdom of Naples* on television, not under that name but as *The Neapolitan Siblings*, with reference to a novel by Franz Werfel that no one read anymore. Since people in Austria and Switzerland also watched the German TV channel, my chances of selling the film to distributors in the German-language area sank to zero. However, I couldn't really complain, since Channel Two had borne 90 percent of the production costs and had always been fair and honest with me, but it prevented me from getting a good start on the regular film circuit.

And that was what I really wanted. That was why I'd insisted, all along, on Super 16 material. The trick was to be able to make copies of the film for regular cinema screening, despite the low budget for a TV production. Because if you shot on Super 16 film, there was no room on the film strips for the sound track, so you necessarily had to blow it up to 35 mm for mixing, and working on that basis I hoped we would be able to make a few copies for screening in normal cinemas.

The problem with my films to date had always been that I could show them only as examples of "alternative cinema" or on TV. I wasn't earning money, even if I worked like a Trojan. Now, with *The Kingdom of Naples*, I had made a film that had a linear narrative but still took my themes of love and death farther. I stuck to those ideas and wanted to get the film shown in mainstream cinemas; I was tired of merely being complimented by cinema enthusiasts on my unprofitable art. After all, my friends Wim Wenders, Werner Herzog, and Volker Schlöndorff were all shooting films abroad at this time, and they were all being screened in mainstream cinemas. So were the films of Rainer Werner Fassbinder.

After my mother's death, I looked back on my films, taking stock. I couldn't stop at that, fond as I was of them all. *The Kingdom of Naples* was more accessible, less subversive, but I felt good about it because the people in Naples had confirmed my own feelings. Previously, I had been more absorbed in myself, but I couldn't go on identifying with youth forever. Ten years after 1968, I was looking for a new way to ask the basic questions by which I stand to this day: How can the power of death be broken? How can we love human beings with all their contradictions?

Many who were close to me could not accept the way I linked these questions with criticism of political circumstances. The team working on *The Kingdom of Naples* confirmed my belief that I had understood the situation and mentality of the Neapolitans surprisingly well, and that approval seemed to me more valuable than all the outspoken criticisms of my style.

I saw the political events of the year 1977, during what is known as the German Autumn, from the Italian point of view. My friends and I saw the role of the artist at that time through the eyes of critical outsiders. We considered ourselves anarchists or, at least, radical free spirits. I knew Holger Meins of the Red Army Faction, because he attended the Film and Television Academy in Berlin at the same time as my friend Daniel Schmid. There were many artists who helped the RAF, and some of them gave its members temporary accommodation. They saw nothing criminal about it. We and Holger Meins lived together from time to time, and I lent him my clothes. Irmgard Möller, who survived the RAF suicide pact in Stammheim Prison, is another of them I know well, a very intelligent and sensitive woman. Incidentally, she was the only person to ask me a good question after the première of *This Night* in Hamburg.

But at the time I was more concerned with the situation in Italy. The Red Brigades who were operating in that country might call themselves anarchists, but we had every reason to regard them as modern fascists. The former prime minister of Italy, Aldo Moro, was abducted and murdered in the spring of 1978, when *The Kingdom of Naples* came out. Moro was a right-wing politician of the Democrazia Cristiana party, in favor of a "historic compromise" with the Italian Communists, and had wanted to involve them in government in order to surmount the economic crisis. Today we can be fairly sure of what was rumored then, that the secret services, with the help of the CIA, had taken part in his murder in order to discredit the Communists and destabilize the country. We were all discussing it openly at the première of *The Kingdom of Naples* in Cannes.

The Italian Communist Party seemed to me like a loudmouthed outfit, the party of fatty livers and paternalism, and that was when Italy was in chaos and couldn't organize any opposition to it. I refer to that, for instance, in the scene where Antonio Orlando's character, who helps the Communist Party out for ten years, believing that it represents the hopes of the poor, is finally fobbed off with a job as a cleaner and garbage man.

That scene made trouble for me. The people at the production company in Rome had the nerve to say I ought to cut the film again, give it a more high-minded tone, and eliminate the political side. I argued with them vigorously, but I was also afraid they would censor it themselves, since they had the negatives in their hands. In the end the prizes it had won, and the attention they attracted, came to my rescue.

In January 1979, Herr von Praunheim wrote an article, "With Regards from Rosa von Praunheim to Champagne Schroeter," about my film in which he tried to crush me. He offered it first to *Bild-Zeitung*, which turned it down, and then to *Filmkritik*, which had the effrontery to publish it. "The film," he said, "is without humor, unlike Schroeter's other films, and takes itself terribly seriously. It is about suffering and death in Italian families, the hearse keeps turning up, one character dies to the sound of operatic arias, others are shot, a mother loses her mind. In the end the character of the prostitute dies; her scream is Schroeter's message to us. It is highly reminiscent of Fassbinder: there's no point in anything, we're all done for." Fassbinder wrote an article countering him in the *Frankfurter Rundschau*, entitled "Letting Your Best Friend Down," and read it aloud to me over the phone first to see if I could accept it. He felt he needed to show his friendship and good opinion of me in that way.

The White Journey

Rosa von Praunheim and I went our different ways. To this day, he is deeply committed to the pro-gay movement and has done great things for it. It was only natural for him to expect me to participate too, and he kept appealing to me to do so. I'm in favor of it, that goes without saying, but when I was asked to put my signature to declarations, I usually said I couldn't sign a protest about the oppression of gays because, personally, I didn't feel oppressed. You can take that however you like, but I have my own difficulties with associations, organizations, and activists, and I don't see "career gays" as any big deal. I always regard my own sexual inclinations as giving me a chance to do unconventional work. I was in more conflict with myself than with straight people and had to be prepared for more opposition, but I guess that is the case with all outsiders.

The White Journey was my first film on a gay subject in twelve years. In between the main shooting of *The Kingdom of Naples* and the final work on it in the spring of 1978, I was in fact preparing part 2 of my planned Italian trilogy, *Palermo or Wolfsburg*, but I also had with me a script that had already been published in *Filmkritik* in 1972, *Die Matrosen dieser Welt* [The sailors of this world]. My story about two sailors in love had also appeared under the title of *Tous les marins du monde* in the French journal *L'énergumène*.

With the painter Harald Vogl, I had left Italy for Lucerne in Switzerland, where we met Daniel Schmid and Eric Franck, a Swiss gallerist and film producer who now lives in London. At the time, Franck happened to be producing Daniel's film *Violante*, in which Maria Schneider appeared. After the shooting of *The Kingdom of Naples*, Margareth Clémenti was also passing through Switzerland, and naturally we all met up. I really hadn't meant to stay in Switzerland for long, because after *The Kingdom of Naples*, I was busy working on *Palermo or Wolfsburg*, but then my obsession with liberation came over me—I wanted to beat the drum again.

Originally, *The Sailors of This World* was a synopsis of my first large-scale 35 mm film. It was to tell the story of the love between two sailors and their adventures in the great seaports of the world. Over five years, however, my plan for filming on a large budget in genuine locations such as Genoa, La Spezia, San Francisco, Hong Kong, and other ports had always come up against a lack of financing.

I simply wasn't trusted, and the time for a radically tender love story between gays wasn't ripe yet either. Back in 1972, I really laid the pathos on thickly. The story was to immunize viewers against banal consumerism. Here's an example: before the apotheosis when Thomas, the fair-complexioned German American, and Fausto, the brown-skinned Italian American, lose themselves in the dangerous streets of Hong Kong, I describe Thomas's search just before their love-in-death scene together: "Close to tears, Thomas wanders through the city in search of his friend, down the now hostile streets, seeing the terrifying poverty of his surroundings, their abnormality in the early morning light, addressed in incomprehensible Chinese by police officers who are supposed to be directing the morning traffic, insulted by prostitutes whose heavy makeup is flaking off and who haven't done any good business that night. He goes from hospital to hospital, from police precinct to police precinct, asking for Fausto, racing past flower stalls stained with the dirt of the streets and garbage, breathing in the sudden stink of thousands of unfortunates, taking it into his lungs."

When I met Eric Franck while he was shooting Daniel's melodrama *Violante*, I persuaded him to produce my film very quickly. He made about twenty thousand euros available, and on that budget we shot *White Journey* in a Zurich villa, in just seven days. Maria Schneider was in it, so were Margareth Clémenti, Harald Vogl, Jim Auwae, the dancer Tilly Soffing, and Trudeliese Schmidt, a mezzosoprano who was Ingrid Caven's sister.

As for the locations in the world's great seaports, they were simply backdrops painted by my brilliant Austrian friend and lover Harald and hung on the walls. We amused ourselves enormously with our "home movie." All the cast gesticulated like opera singers, playing several parts each and improvising like crazy. I was behind the camera myself. It was a punk film, shot with humor and tomfoolery.

Dietrich Kuhlbrodt wrote an essay giving a delightful description of what happened during the fifty minutes of our journey through the world: "However much talk there is of foreign lands and seas, no one actually leaves the country. The journey takes place on a home-movie stage, and the title comes from a railroad journey. On the way to Zurich, Schroeter held the camera out of the train window and filmed the very white snow with the very dark shadows of the landscape falling on it. The autobiographical trail of snow follows the trail of the sailor lovers. The rails of the line to Zurich turn, so to speak, into the long, white, foaming wake of the ship carrying the lovers to their deaths in the dark distance. The film is enriched by biographical and documentary elements, by the director's experience of the cinema, literature, and the theater. It moves on many different levels. Like a deranged elevator, it travels vertically up and down at the same time. Along with Hölderlin's 'Aber silbern an reinen Tagen' [But silvery is the light on clear days], rock and pop texts are quoted—'By the time you get this letter' and 'Should I tell him?'"

A year later, I met Bulle Ogier again at the Montreal Film Festival and asked her whether she would like to synchronize the film. She said yes, and we spent two days in a studio, while she spoke all the parts in the film, without thinking very hard about it, simply as if it were a game. She was Maria Schneider, Margareth Clémenti, Tilly Soffing. I cut the whole thing again with associations in mind, just as I had done in *Willow Springs*. Then it was ready and had been great fun for all of us. One more amusing example of Schroeter's work in his first phase. Afterward, I finished with that phase.

It was a crazy, punk film anyway. Maria Schneider was in a terrible state, severely sick with her drug addiction. Luckily, she is better these days, living happily with her girlfriend [Schneider died in 2011]. With that film, my last spasms as *regina del underground*—as I was called in a book about the German cinema—were finally over. Although something of the underground always clung to me.

Abroad in Germany and Italy

It was obvious, immediately after we had made *The Kingdom of Naples*, that Thomas Mauch and I wanted to make the second film of what turned out to be my Italian "duology" together. Mauch is not only a cameraman but also a filmmaker, and he has his own small production company. He went to see Eric Franck, who was producing Daniel Schmid's film and had helped to get *White Journey* made so quickly. So *Palermo or Wolfsburg* was created, with a small amount of Swiss participation, and Channel Two TV came in on the act again.

I knew the Sicilian journalist and writer Giuseppe Fava, who opposed the Mafia in his native Sicily in the seventies with his articles, books, and theater plays. Fava was a charismatic figure, an impressive man twenty years my senior, whose books—for instance, *Violence: The Fifth Power*—I devoured. In January 1984, a few years after our film was made, he was shot by the Mafia outside the Teatro Bellini, the opera house of Catania. A very sad fate. In *La passione di Michele*, he wrote about a young Sicilian immigrant worker, and that book was one of my points of departure for the film. I met him in Rome and Munich, and also in Sicily, to work on the idea.

But apart from my connection with Italy, and my sense of having roots there, I had another source of inspiration. While I was directing a play in Bochum, I had gone for a walk and found a torn newspaper, a local Ruhrland publication, lying around. I read the headline, picked up the newspaper, and read on. It was the story of a boy from Greece, or maybe Italy or Spain—those details were missing from the torn paper. What happened to him in Germany was the story as we told it in the film: he killed a German girl's friends because they had been laughing at him. The clarity and simplicity of that story fascinated me. With Giuseppe Fava, I expanded it to take in the whole of the boy's social environment. I wanted to find the kind of place that would reflect my concept of the origins of a young immigrant worker here in Germany. With a young assistant, I traveled through the south of Italy, Apulia, Calabria, and Sicily, and finally we reached Palma di Montechiaro on Sicily. "This is ideal," I said. "Well, we've certainly picked a fine spot," said my assistant sarcastically. "The Mafia runs this place." "That's exactly the ambience I want," I said. "Look at those buildings!"

We began shooting in Palma di Montechiaro, known locally as *il chesso di la Sicilia*—the toilet of Sicily—at the end of 1979. It was already the run-down village that you see in the film. Not a single house was complete; the local people had gone to Germany to earn money so they could finish building. But then they lost their jobs there and never could put together enough to complete their houses. It was the miserable situation typical of what was called the "exchange of labor" between northern and southern Europe.

Even if I described it poetically, the conditions to which people living in the workers' hostels in Germany had to adjust were terrible. They tried to keep some of the culture of their homeland going by gambling and throwing parties—fueled by plenty of alcohol, of course. What else were they to do? Although they wore ear protectors, their hearing was damaged by the noise of the conveyor belts and the incredibly loud machinery. Their jobs sometimes took them from the cradle to the grave—a wretched life.

In Sicily I was relaxed about possible trouble with the Mafia. Once, when Alberte Barsacq, who was designing the sets and costumes, stepped out of the aircraft with me on reaching Sicily, two ferocious-looking characters came over, claiming that they were to act as our chauffeurs. I went along with that as if it were normal. They wanted to see if we could be intimidated and whether we were dangerous. They sat around in the hotel lobby for a few days and then disappeared. Of course, they looked alarming; that was the whole point. I thought theirs was a centuries-old system that I could neither understand nor alter. To this day I'm not sure whether it is a good idea to goad the Mafia into armed resistance by waging fierce war on them. I can only say that they didn't scare me while we were shooting the film. Alberte, however, saw things differently.

One day, toward the end of the filming, I was sitting in our hotel by the sea a little way from Palma when a production assistant asked, "Would you come down, please, Herr Schroeter? There's a lady here to see you." It was very early, we had worked late into the small hours the night before, I hadn't had enough sleep, and I had a hangover. However, I went down to the hotel lobby, where a lady in black was sitting, clutching her handbag, and looking like a dark bird. I asked, in a friendly tone, how could I help her? She sat there as if frozen, then trembled and said, "Why are you doing this to my son?" "Why am I doing what to your son?" It turned out that the story I had read in the tattered newspaper in Bochum was about a boy who really did come from Palma di Montechiaro. I was speechless. Out of a thousand villages in Greece, Spain, and Italy, I had picked the authentic scene of the young man's origin! I like such coincidences—they remind me of something out of a fairy tale.

I tried to explain that it was all meant in defense of her son and to make people understand his position. Suddenly she took a pistol out of her bag. No one else happened to be with us at the table—very funny, I'm sure. The production team didn't fancy exposing themselves to a situation like this—we even had to set up the cameras at night, under cover of darkness, so that they wouldn't be stolen.

Finally, I managed to placate the lady. Others came along to calm her down. We took her home to Palma, and in the car she said, in a heavy Sicilian accent, "Lui ha fatto bene" [My son did well]. Extraordinary things do happen.

When people accuse me of being melodramatic, I always say that to me, melodrama is first and foremost a form of opera, a *Singspiel* with spoken dialog. The operas of my emotions come from life itself, if also from the garbage of newspaper reports jumbled up together. I never took Douglas Sirk's *Imitation of Life* as my inspiration; if I drew on anything, it was *Il Cristo proibito* [The forbidden Christ], the only film made by the writer Curzio Malaparte. That was high art and at the same time surreal, grandiose kitsch, a tale of two brothers involved in the betrayal of their village's resistance group to the Nazis. There is a scene in which one of the brothers comes home after the war to find the other, the traitor, waiting for him. They meet in a white room with walls that reflect the light, making them resemble supernatural figures. One brother approaches the other, and they embrace in that eerie light. Then the home-comer steps back, and we see that he has a knife in his heart. The blood flows black in the white light.

Visconti could never have made *Rocco and His Brothers* if that film by Malaparte had not come first. On the other hand, all the melodramatic filmmakers of Hollywood could be dismissed. I was scared of genuine melodramas, yes, but not of a vengeful Sicilian woman.

Nicola Zarbo, playing the sixteen-year-old boy in *Palermo or Wolfsburg*, seemed to me to come from a totally corrupt family, semi-illiterate, not that he could be blamed for that. We all had the impression that his family were trying to blackmail both the production team and me. I got on well with him, but even our Italian colleagues couldn't understand him because of the heavy dialect he spoke. The wonderful letters that his character writes in the film are by Giuseppe Fava. Incidentally, I altered the script as we went along, as usual. If you are working with amateurs in a semidocumentary atmosphere, you have to enter into the spirit of the situation in order to do it justice.

For instance, the strange baron who keeps saying, "Marlborough, Marlborough!" was a genuine aristocrat from an old Palma di Montechiaro family. We changed nothing about his curious way of life; he really did live, surrounded by china figurines, in the crazy mountain village shown in the film, thought himself widely traveled, and gave Nicola advice. And what advice! I improvised the character of the priest who warns the boy against going abroad.

In the two months we spent on the road for the film, Nicola grew fatter and fatter. In the end I had to apply his makeup myself, because anyone could see that he was stuffing himself with food. Suggesting muesli and lettuce got us nowhere. Then I gave Antonio Orlando, playing his friend in *Palermo or Wolfsburg*, a good supply of five-mark coins, and pointed them both in the direction of the Wolfsburg peepshows. From then on Nicola lost weight again.

Everywhere, we worked with authentic local amateurs, and that includes the Wolfsburg scenes. You can see, in the film, how life there rubbed off on them. The German amateurs we found in Wolfsburg acted as if they were in a soap opera—an amateur soap opera. Whereas the melancholy Sicilians and Greeks maintained their authenticity. The wife of one of the immigrant workers, a blonde German Fury, acted exactly like the woman she was in real life, convinced that it is right and just to turn away someone looking for help. She had a topsy-turvy idea of hospitality. In Nicola's masculine world, no one understood the way German women behaved.

We shot the closing sequence of the film, a courtroom scene, in Berlin. Our location, the building on the Reichpietschufer, had been the Nazi People's Court. The scene we were shooting took place on the very spot where the fanatical Nazi judge Roland Freisler passed death sentences. At the time, the building still radiated that atmosphere; today the historical effect seems to have been blotted out by modern renovation.

From the juridical point of view, the trial that we show in the film is authentic, and the actors with whom I was working here—Otto Sander, Tamara Kafka, Ula Stöckl, and many others—performed realistically, but at the end I allowed the trial scene to tip over into absurdity. I have always thought judging other human beings a grotesque process, reminding me of the biblical injunction "Let him who is without sin cast the first stone." I directed the trial as a piece of exaggerated grotesquerie, until at the end it falls into a more relaxed tempo as Magdalena Montezuma, in the role of Nicola's attorney, gets him acquitted. At that moment the light falls on his face like an artificial sun, he gets to his feet, and confesses: "I did it, I wanted to do it." His affirmation of his existence is naive but honest. It all depended on that tragic realism.

At the end of the film I speak to the viewers, off-camera, appealing to them: "Touch one another, touch one another."

I had a feeling that, in Germany, personal contact was unthinkable. Today, when everyone moves around in virtual space, the sheer oddity of it, our inability to make physical contact with other people, seems even greater.

In the end we had material for a film five hours long. I had to make cuts; whole sequences were jettisoned, including one with Christine Kaufmann. In 1980 *Palermo or Wolfsburg* won the Golden Bear award at the Berlin Film Festival. It was a great artistic success, and I was very happy about it. Sad to say, my producer Thomas Mauch didn't have much luck in selling the film. It was still three hours long, and finding audiences for such a film was difficult.

My third film in the trilogy was to have been titled *Italia—speranza del futuro?* [Italy—hope for the future?]. At the time I believed in the

133

utopian idea that, because of its people, its quality of life, and its sense of liberty, Italy could still be a model for Europe as a whole. I gave that hope up long ago, and as a result the third film in what would have been a trilogy, a journey through Italy in the style of the commedia dell'arte, was never made. I cleaned the makeup off the subject's face, so to speak, and forgot Italy. Only in September 2008, when I was honored for my lifetime achievement at the Venice Film Festival, did I say what I thought about Italy again in interviews. I was being dragged around from midday to evening, facing cameras and microphones until I felt sick and feverish, so great was the interest in hearing what I thought of Berlusconi's Italy. I haven't been able to think of anything poetic to say about it since then, but the subject is still a sore point. Even at the festival itself, I could hear the harsh tone of voice in discussions, the emotional barriers that went up. If you love a country, you see the unfortunate cultural changes in it with particular clarity.

The Bavarian Sausage Conspiracy

In 1980 posters went up in the city of Augsburg giving an idea of me that I didn't recognize at first. The message conveyed by placards on the advertising pillars was roughly to the effect that Bavarians like the good folk of Augsburg should vote CSU [Christian Social Union] if they didn't want people of my kind producing works of art in their city. It was all about the extraordinary campaign for election to the Bundestag in which Franz Josef Strauss aimed to become chancellor of the Federal Republic.

I had just won the Golden Bear at the Berlin Film Festival for *Palermo or Wolfsburg* and had been engaged by the Augsburg City Theater to direct *Salome*, with the première to take place on 4 October that year. After the film of *Salome* and the live theater production at Bochum, I now wanted to direct Richard Strauss's opera on the same subject.

But in March a long interview that I had given the journalist André Müller appeared in *Die Zeit*. We talked about events in my life and turning points in my work leading up to *Palermo or Wolfsburg*, also the death of my mother, my love for Maria Callas, and my attitude to Germany. Toward the end of the interview, André Müller asked me about Franz Josef Strauss. In *Palermo or Wolfsburg*, which had just been launched in German cinemas at this time, I had imagined his potential election to the office of chancellor as a kind of horror scenario. Müller's question was whether my last hope for Germany was that Strauss would *not* become chancellor. My answer, on the spur of the moment, was that my last hope was "for him to burst, because he's so fat. Someone ought to feed him a little bomb in the form of a Bavarian *Weisswurst* [white sausage]. But I don't really want to talk about it. I don't feel any wish to confront such a mediocrity." Müller went on to ask questions about Hitler, and I said Hitler had worn his potency for outward show by oppressing others, but impotent as he physically was, he had lusted for power. He couldn't fuck properly and thought, as it were, "If I can't get it up, then everyone else is to blame for it." Finally, I commented on my self-liberation from my own guilt feelings. As an example, I described how, in my youth, I used to give back music records that I had stolen because I suffered pangs of conscience, except for Callas records, because she had been stronger than any moral sentiments. Then I added, "Today I could kill without thinking anything of it, because I have a sensuous feeling for such an anarchic attitude. It excites me enormously, above, below, and everywhere in between."

The interview set off an avalanche, an ideological tremor, as *Der Spiegel* wrote. There was an enormous quantity of press reports, including outraged comments. Readers' letters were printed in the local Augsburg papers, denouncing me as a gay, a degenerate artist, and a capitalist. Horror was expressed at the idea of using animal blood in a production of *Salome*. I was called an exhibitionist and accused of making a "direct attack on the existence of moral laws in the West" (*Der Spiegel*). One CSU politician turned on another: "If you think it's normal to be gay, that's your business!" (*Der Spiegel* again). One man wrote a letter to the local paper saying that I ought not to be allowed in the city, since who could guarantee that Schroeter, as a gay, might not make improper advances to him, the letter writer, and kill him in order to satisfy his lusts on the dead body?

The *Frankfurter Rundschau* printed this curious epistle on the front page, because they thought it as ridiculous as I did. I think that the caption was adapted from Spielberg's famous film: "A Strange Encounter of the Augsburg Kind." Only it was not supernatural and friendly but parochial and unpleasant, with a touch of unintentional Satanic comedy about it too. If I remember correctly, the man who put forward such views was a teacher, which added an extra crazy dimension to the whole thing.

I am a pacifist, not a terrorist, as everyone who knows me is aware. Naturally, I regarded the interview as blackly satirical. But Franz Josef Strauss, who had distinguished himself by pronouncing, "Better a cold warrior than a well-intentioned poofter," took it all personally and said that what with my lack of any sense of shame, and the public incitement to murder that I promoted, I had no right to direct a production in the Bavarian city of Augsburg, on the grounds that the theater was financed by Bavarian taxes. I had been offered twenty-five thousand deutsche marks for *Salome*, ten thousand more than usual in Augsburg. The money had been raised by donations, which annoyed the verbal arsonists even more. My provocation, they said, might be seen as a faux pas—and admittedly it could be considered that—but on the whole it was claimed that I lacked any qualification for my job, and the letter writers were foaming at the mouth with malice: "In his interview in *Die Zeit*, this gentleman has shown himself to be perverse, shameless in his demands (25,000 DM!!!), dishonorable, and abhorrent in his means of expression. Where such persons are at work, how are we to go on believing in the sublimity of art?"

The Bavarian minister of the interior, Gerold Tandler, acting as his master's voice, now intervened and called on the mayor of Augsburg, by order of the authorities, to annul my contract with the City Theater, although neither of them had the right to do so. Someone even laid charges against me for the "glorification of violence." The charge was actually accepted, and the matter went back and forth between Hamburg, where the newspaper was published, and Augsburg, where the idea was to get rid of me. Only in June did the courts throw it out again. The Catholic bishop of Augsburg, Stimpfle by name, joined in the witch-hunt and gave as his reason that the city would be to blame "if we put up with this sort of thing."

I had the honor of appearing in a splendid cartoon in the *Süddeutscher Zeitung*, in which the portly Strauss sat on Herod's throne, Interior Minister Tandler performed Salome's Dance of the Seven Veils, and my severed head was served up on a platter, complete with black hat, long hair, mustache, and sunglasses, as I looked at the time.

The theater manager, Rudolf Stromberg, and his general music director, Gabor Ötvös, thought my interview was adolescent, silly, and irresponsible and told me so publicly, but they still wanted to stick to our agreement. Then the composer's heirs protested. Richard Strauss junior, executor of the estate and a stamp dealer by profession, was not going along with any of it, not even when the theater administrators offered to send him the designs for the set. "The *Salome* that I love entails a precarious balancing act," he said by way of explaining his distrust, which was running ahead of the facts, "and if someone puts a foot wrong, it ruins everything."

The major newspapers published long articles expressing support for me. Benjamin Henreich, whom I admire to this day as a writer and a theater critic, wrote in *Die Zeit* about the "hysterical local farce," although his article did seem to me ambiguous. He condemned my interview with André Müller as an act of self-exposure, but he also condemned the reactions to it. However, I thought it questionable that he did not criticize the ideological scandal behind it clearly. Where would we be if stamp dealers who happen to be the heirs of composers declare a director heretical and intervene in the principle that art is free?

Benjamin Henreich also quoted Oscar Wilde, who said that the "moral people, as they are called, are simple beasts." Augsburg certainly showed that homophobia has hardly changed much since Oscar Wilde suffered from it. I love Wilde's comment that he "would rather have fifty unnatural vices than one unnatural virtue." Maybe all that annoyed me about the Henreich article was that it printed a particularly unattractive photograph of me. Or that was how I saw it after drinking hard for three days. And beside it there was another photo, in which Franz Josef Strauss looked almost human.

The situation became even more complicated. The Augsburg cinemas refused to screen *Palermo or Wolfsburg*. The film *The Candidate*, made by the *Spiegel* journalist Stefan Aust and his colleague Alexander von Eschwege, with Alexander Kluge and Volker Schlöndorff, as propaganda against Franz Josef Strauss, was not on the local cinema programs either. However, *The Candidate* was finally screened at the Komödie, a stage in the City Theater, and Volker Schlöndorff, Alexander Kluge, Rainer Werner Fassbinder, Alf Brustellin, Christian Rischert, and other filmmakers used the occasion to show solidarity with me, in which they were joined by the entire Federal German Film Association. The live theater also expressed solidarity via an announcement from the Cologne Theater, signed by actors in Hamburg, Berlin, Bremen, Stuttgart, Ulm, Mannheim, Kassel, Cologne, and Bochum.

"And Augsburg tomorrow!" is the groan uttered by the circus manager in Thomas Bernhard's comedy *Die Macht von Gewohnheit* [The power of custom]. Bernhard, too, had incurred the anger of that city, because his character expresses horror of its cold nature. He is said to have apologized for showing the city that can boast of Bertolt Brecht and Leopold Mozart in such a poor light purely for the sake of onomatopoeia. I wasn't about to do the same thing: on 1 July, when I had definitively been fired, I fled forward, as the saying goes, and had placards put up in the city showing me in long underwear. With the picture there was a quotation from the Germany Report of the underground Socialist Party in the Nazi year of 1936: "The filth of the police and the military apparatus in Augsburg is perceptible at every turn. The whole atmosphere of the city is redolent of oppression and the penitentiary."

One evening that summer I received a phone call: would I be ready to accept the Bavarian Film Prize for *Palermo or Wolfsburg*—a prize that brought money with it this time! Obviously, this was an instruction from the very highest quarters, indicating that I ought to be magnanimous. And then the message would have been: aha, this artist sees his mistake and will graciously take what he's given. I was silly enough to say no. It was plain stupid: a sin of my young age.

I told Herbert Achternbusch—my Bavarian fiancé, as I called him—what I had done. "You idiot, Werner, you could have handled it differently," he said. "Yes, but how?" I objected. "In your place, I'd have smartened myself up and collected a lot of old cat shit. I'd have put that in my right pocket, lining the pocket with plastic, I'd have accepted the check with my left hand, then I'd have dug my right hand in the cat shit, I'd have shaken hands heartily with Strauss, and then I'd have left." Herbert ought to have told me that earlier. Ha!

So how did the story end? The theater and I weighed up possible alternative productions, operas such as Umberto Giordano's *Fedora* or Luigi Cherubini's *Medea*, but the quarrel had become a matter of principle by this time. When the theater management said they wanted to present my concept of *Salome* to the stamp dealer, to get his approval, that was another scandal in the affair of the Bavarian Sausage Conspiracy. It turned into a tragedy: I was booted out, and when it came to the question of compensation, the management was suddenly on my enemies' side. They insinuated that I had wanted to remodel *Salome* as a manifesto of social criticism and claimed that I had "anarchist tendencies." A year after that interview in *Die Zeit* the court of arbitration admitted that I should receive the agreed fee for directing the opera—and not a penny more.

La patrie de l'âme

Being called a rat and vermin in the Bavarian Conspiracy affair naturally depressed me, but I wanted to move on. I never spent much time thinking about a project I had left behind me, particularly when it had ended in failure. Sentiment is an essential force; sentimentality does nothing but damage.

Despite the award of the Golden Bear—which was the first time it had ever gone to a German director at that festival—*Palermo or Wolfsburg* was passed over at the awarding of the German Film Prize, which meant that I had no financial backing for the production of my next film.

While the Bavarian campaign against me was going on, I had been in France, then in the fall I was in Italy, then I went to Brazil, and back to Italy. If I couldn't direct a production in Augsburg, then I could in Florence and Venice. My crisis left its mark on the film that I directed in May, *Die Generalprobe* [The dress rehearsal], a documentary essay about the Festival mondial du théâtre in Nancy and at the same time the first of my documentaries about artists. Added to it later were *Á la recherche du soleil* [In search of the sun], about Ariane Mnouchkine; *Poussières d'amour* [Love's debris], about my favorite singers; and *Die Königin* [The queen], about Marianne Hoppe.

I shot *The Dress Rehearsal* with the help of Thomas Schühly, formerly assistant director at the Bochum Theater and now an ambitious film producer. My friend Colette Godard, a French theatrical and film critic who had seen all my work in Paris and Avignon, and when writing in *Le monde* had made me known in France as an "underground superstar," advised us about the preparation. Mostefa Djadjam, a friend with whom I was in love, was working as an actor in Paris, but he was my assistant director for *The Dress Rehearsal*. But the thought of the campaign of rejection and detraction going on against me in Germany was ever present. I never felt part of the community in the country where my mother tongue was spoken, and that campaign made it clear to me once again that, for me, it was the *patrie de l'âme*, the homeland of the soul, only in a utopian sense.

Wonderful dancers, mimes, puppeteers, and performers met at Nancy in that Rococo dollhouse, held wild discussions about the future of the theatrical art, and performed choreographed dances, sketches, and scenes that had never been seen elsewhere. It was wonderful to be close to them, watch them rehearsing, or simply be able to film them, seeing how they included the city itself in their art. Those in Nancy on that occasion included Pina Bausch; the old Japanese dancer Kazuo Ohno, who conjured up memories of Maria Callas with a flower in his hair; Reinhild Hoffmann, who danced without ever leaving an enormous sofa; and the white-powdered Japanese male couple Sankai Juku, who looked to me like twin Maldorors. There was also a dignified old tramp from Nancy who looked like a Russian prince down on his luck and told us what he thought about love. Life itself, and our mood as we shot the film, mingled with the theater. You had to have seen those faces, those bodies—there was something light, hovering, and melancholy about us all, something that Colette Godard interpreted as "life hand in hand with death."

In Paris, my friend Catherine Brasier-Snopko—she was my cutter for this and my two following films, before she died in 1990, much too young—helped me to track down the theme of the film. *Parle-moi d'amour*—our conversations, scenes, dialogs, and the music we made were all about love, commitment, and transience. We worked it all out in countless night shifts together; I cut all the material into tiny fragments and reassembled it to make that poetic message visible—just how I can't really describe.

When *The Dress Rehearsal* had its première at the Venice Film Festival, in parallel, incidentally, with the screening of the fourteen episodes of Fassbinder's miniseries *Berlin Alexanderplatz*, the critics were complimentary.

But the tiresome campaign against me went on, and I was always being asked about it. In the press release for *The Dress Rehearsal* I quoted the beginning of the fourth song from the *Songs of Maldoror*: "If your foot slips on a frog, you feel disgust; but if you touch the human body only lightly with your hand, the skin of your fingers reacts like the scales of a mica block struck by a hammer; and as the heart of a shark that has been dead for an hour still twitches as it lies on the bridge, with the tough force of life, so our guts are moved, to their last fiber, for a long time after that touch. So great is the horror that a human being can inspire in his fellow men!"

I gave many interviews in which I went back to the basic questions that mattered to me: whether I was welcome at the City Theater or whether I should go on working elsewhere. I simply insisted on my own eccentricity, to encourage other people. I was aware of the unfavorable image that clings to someone who allows himself a certain amount of freedom. People who try to act fearlessly are necessarily regarded with hostility by a society that values order. But if, as an artist and with my access to the general public, I did not try it, then who would? Back in 1973, long before the Bavarian contretemps, I had read in critical reviews of my production of *Salome* in Bochum that measures other than those merely linguistic ought to be taken against me. Peter Zadek, my group, and I made light of it, and mocked it, but what kind of hostility was hidden behind it? You never read theatrical criticism of that kind abroad. In France, conflicts of a very different kind would have been necessary to have a director fired from working on an operatic production and branded a heretic. In Germany, on the other hand, an artist could quickly be regarded as surplus to requirements.

I wasn't much troubled by the stamp dealer's emotional condemnation of me; I didn't even hold anything against Franz Josef Strauss, who, incidentally, did not win the election. His candidacy had been accompanied by vehement protests and police operations, and shortly before election day there was a terrorist attack at the Munich Oktoberfest, which was blamed—overhastily—on the Red Army Faction. The atmosphere was heated, and Strauss made use of that, but with his complex-laden energy I felt he was closer to me in human terms than other German politicians—only in human terms, nothing else. Basically, in his ugly monstrosity the man touched hearts more than other politicians because he was more like people who were trying to live. Not that I wanted to see him as an active politician and a head of state. It was depressing to find that the emotions could be manipulated and inflated in that way, and hostile images were built up against people's better judgment. We saw that as the threat of fascism, and I commented on the situation from that viewpoint in the interviews that I gave the German newspapers when I was in France and Italy. Fascism always begins by seeing extremes painted in black and white, with an image of an enemy deriving from a pietistically unattractive idea of human nature: those on one side are pure, while those on the other personify the depths of wickedness. The most alarming outcome of the Augsburg affair, to me, was the use of false assumptions, such as the mixture of anarchism, murderous impulses, homosexuality, and capitalism imputed to me. The sacred values of capitalism—my alleged merit when it came to the production of *Salome*—were coupled with the femme fatale of homosexuality, and my unwelcome political attitude was linked to the murderous anarchism of opponents of the Bavarian Sausage-throwing persuasion. All that came from people who never thought of anything in their lives but earning as much as possible, in line with the norms of our meritocracy. In principle, they were blaming me for their own aims.

I also criticized the fact that Germany would not confront its past under the Third Reich in a credible and serious manner but was playing a negative game involving complexes and emotions that were an obstacle to historical analysis. The Hitler films of Joachim Fest and Hans-Jürgen Syberberg made money out of the subject and inflated the figure of Hitler more and more, instead of explaining it. To connect me with Syberberg's filmed monstrosities was an entirely inadmissible parallel and annoyed me very much. My films set dream and reality against one another; I could never have gone in for German realism, or indeed for the historical films that suddenly came into fashion.

Failure makes you human

We were never really political people, but insofar as individualists can bring something to honest political commitment, we were on the side of those who try to alter the intolerable everyday life of society. At least, we supported their ideas. When Kemal Altun, a young Turkish asylum seeker, fell to his death from a window of the building where the Berlin social welfare tribunal met, fearing that he would be sent back to the military dictatorship of Turkey, I had to make use of my public profile as an artist to raise my voice against the terrible measures taken by the German authorities. I was directing a production of Shakespeare's *Comedy of Errors* at the Freie Volksbühne [Free People's Theater] in Berlin, and after the première I came out in front of the curtain and appealed to the audience to protest.

But first and foremost, as artists we wanted to destroy the dominant structures; think of television, for instance, and its smooth psychologizing designed to create form or, rather, the simulation of life without any real innovative form at all. We wanted to go far where content was concerned, and even farther aesthetically. I was thinking along the lines of Alain Resnais in *L'année dernière à Marienbad* [Last year in Marienbad], but the bold approach was my own.

Herbert Achternbusch showed us how to approach the subject of Germany and, more particularly, Bavaria in dramatic form. His sense of humor was like my own, as expressed in my artificially Bavarian episode in *Flocons d'or*, so I felt honored to play the bishop in his blasphemous farce *Das Gespenst* [The ghost]. It is a splendid story in which Jesus, having come down from the cross, stumbles through Bavaria doing everything wrong. Annamirl Bierbichler, Sepp Bierbichler's sister, who was living with Herbert Achternbusch, was in the film as well. What a wonderful woman she was! Beautiful, really great; she died young of cancer. Her lover Achternbusch is a real grouch, but she was the one who had her feet on the ground. Not anymore, sad to say, now that the ground itself has swallowed her up.

Be that as it may, when *The Ghost* was finished in 1982, the self-appointed censors of the Freiwillige Selbstkontrolle der Filmwirtschaft, the voluntary self-regulation branch of the German movie industry, decided that the film was blasphemous, a campaign began, and the CSU [Christian Social Union] parliamentary deputy Alois Zimmermann, recently appointed federal German interior minister and top man for policy on the cinema, punished Achternbusch by withdrawing the final installment of financial support owed to him for the film. I might have been an oddity, with my fantasy about the murderous Bavarian sausage blowing up Strauss, but I was not alone. Of course, I joined the ranks of German artists protesting against Christian cultural policy.

Meanwhile, I was preparing for a new project; I wanted to film Jean Genet's brilliant novel *Querelle de Brest*. Jean Genet, thief and rent boy, who began writing in prison, was one of our domestic gods. To me, he seemed particularly close, a family member in the spirit of Lautréamont, Oscar Wilde, Antonin Arnaud, and William Burroughs. Since deciding to go on developing new forms of style, I had been busy adapting *Querelle de Brest* in my own way. It would have been the black version of my love story *The Sailors of This World*, a necessary sequel, and an intensive look at evil and the beauty of evil. Only criminals and artists still have scope of their own in bourgeois society. My basic idea is that everyone cherishes a wish "to let longing unfold in his existence," that this original wish aims for a sense of joy in life and contact with other people, and that life in this sense is very much something social, a cataclysm of longings so far unrealized. Art, I say, concerns social life as well as crime, because it is also an expression of frustration, and braver than buying three Mercedes cars or anything of that kind.

The artist, as a radical outsider, holds the mirror of society's negativity up to it in an embarrassingly provocative way—that was our attitude. For me homosexuality was and still is attractive as the design of an artist's life, if you reject the social norms of materialism and consumerism. Being gay, being an artist, opposing the system and thus, logically, heterosexuality as the prescribed form of sex have more poetic substance than doing something socially acceptable that one doesn't really understand, because the society in which you live formulates that social enforcement as a repressive claim.

I had already cast actors with attractive pricks as the sailors in *Querelle de Brest* and had found a ship's cemetery belonging to the Italian army in Sardinia, where I had even been given permission to shoot the film—an incredible coup. The producers in Munich, who had signed the contract with me, met the depreciation experts and got cold feet because of the political opposition to me—the *Salome* campaign was in full swing at this point. They were afraid that they wouldn't be able to pilot *Querelle*, with its apocalyptic plot featuring gays and criminals, past the committees giving financial support to films, because members of political parties had a finger in every pie. They did issue a press release in January 1981, stating that I had been engaged as director, and shooting was to begin in the fall. What followed can be described only as a grotesque tale of villainy—at least, I was dropped, and my friend Rainer Werner Fassbinder couldn't take the opportunity of directing the film himself.

Other projects that I was thinking about that year also came to nothing. I was in touch with Romy Schneider, thinking that we might perhaps film the life story of the Swiss world traveler and adventurer Isabelle Eberhardt. Romy Schneider had secured an option on it, and she knew my *Flocons d'or* and *Day of the Idiots*, but she died in May 1982, before any concrete discussions could take place. Other projects never got beyond the idea stage: for instance, an adaptation of Gabriele D'Annunzio's *La contessa d'Amalfi* and a film essay about the Stalinist judge and GDR minister of justice Hilde Benjamin. *Im dunklen Herz des Nachmittags* [In the dark heart of the afternoon] was to be a film about a young man who discovers his love for books and his homosexuality in the company of two considerably older women. James Baldwin's novel *Giovanni's Room* would have been another film in which a young man finds that he is homosexual. All I was able to salvage of *Hochzeit mit Gott* [Wedding to God], a project for a film about the dancer Vaclav Nijinsky and his descent into madness, was a page of the script, written with Meir Dohnal and published in *Cahiers du cinéma* when Wim Wenders was guest editor of the journal's two hundredth edition in 1987. In the end all these plans fell through.

My chances were slim in the complicated deals between private financiers, committees deciding on the award of grants to promote films, and television channels. And yet I was working almost all the time. The Augsburg *Salome* would not have been my première as a director of opera. In 1979, even before *Palermo or Wolfsburg*, I had already accepted an invitation from the Kassel State Theater to direct a production of Richard Wagner's *Lohengrin*. At the time, I was so ebulliently delighted to be able to work in a house with a good budget that I designed a set with a pyramid and a starry sky above it. That set alone would have cost three hundred thousand deutsche marks. In the end I was able to realize only a less expensive variant, but it was a fine début, and I greatly enjoyed working with the conductor James Lockhart. Here, music was no longer an elevated or contrasting element of the montage, as in my films, it was *the* means of expression to which everything else was subordinate. I was so happy with this new experience and my teamwork with the conductor that, with childlike delight, I emphasized the romantic heart of Wagner's opera. I wanted to bring out the naive, fairy-tale aspect of *Lohengrin* rather than dissect it with a critical scalpel. Although the critics often didn't believe me, on principle I never staged a work using the weapons of deconstruction against it.

My Italian films had the welcome side effect of getting me invited to stage works in the Italian theater. Thus, I was working in January 1980 at the Teatro Niccolini in Florence, with the stage star Piera Degli Esposti, on Corrado Alvaro's modern adaptation of the Medea story, *Lunga notte di Medea*. And in October of the same year I was lucky enough to direct another opera with a theme derived from Oscar Wilde at the famous Teatro La Fenice in Venice, not *Salome* but Alexander von Zemlinsky's one-act *A Florentine Tragedy*.

Another project for a film that also remained only an idea in the early eighties would have taken me back to South America. In Rome, Peter Berling came upon the story of an eccentric ballet company about which we could make a historical film, sending it on tour to nouveau riche postcolonialists in the Amazon area. Toward the end of the year 1981, I made use of a retrospective of my films in Brazil to meet Peter Berling and explore parts of the Pan-American Highway with him; its building was a cultural shock, showing us that the exploitation of the country around the Amazon was no longer a mythical and romantic subject. But in Manaus, where of course we had wanted to shoot scenes in the legendary opera house, Werner Herzog's brother and coproducer Lucki Stipetic had already prepared to shoot *Fitzcarraldo*. Peter Berling's film would have been on a subject too close to Herzog's project and as a result couldn't have found financial support.

As it turned out, we ourselves were engaged for *Fitzcarraldo*: Peter Berling to play the opera director who makes a brief appearance in Manaus, proudly showing off the rubber barons' extravagant building to Klaus Kinski as Fitzcarraldo, while I was to stage the opening sequence of Werner Herzog's film, depicting the appearance of Caruso and Sarah Bernhardt at the opera house in the jungle.

Fitzcarraldo, wrote the film critic Wolfram Schütte, shows that, basically, opera as an art form is a jungle in itself, and he is exactly right. In March 1982 I directed the scene of the opera-in-the-film in Manaus for Werner Herzog. Unfortunately, the montage made it look, far too frequently, like part of the opening credits. At the time

Werner Herzog had no idea how to build up an operatic scene himself, although later he directed over twenty-five operas, not least because of *Fitzcarraldo*.

In the opening scene, Klaus Kinski and Claudia Cardinale arrive in Manaus in a rowboat, after traveling along the river for a thousand kilometers from Iquitos so that for once in their lives they can see a performance by Caruso and Sarah Bernhardt in the Manaus opera house, but they arrive too late. Caruso has just died a hero's death; his stage bride is wringing her hands in despair; the curtain falls. I chose Giuseppe Verdi's *Ernani*, described by the composer as an *opera lirica*, from which I had quoted in *The Death of Maria Malibran*. It hinges on the murderous and grotesque ideas of honor and vengeance expressed by Spanish aristocrats, notions that had been exported to the colonies in South America.

In reality, Enrico Caruso never appeared onstage in Manaus, but the tragic actress Sarah Bernhardt did, wooden leg and all. The rubber millionaires insisted on engaging her, although she couldn't sing a note. We had Jean-Claude Dreyfus, whom I knew from Daniel Schmid's *Shadows of Angels*, with his striking face, miming Bernhardt, while Mietta Sighele sang the part from the orchestra pit. Jean-Claude came limping down the spiral staircase in a terrifying wig and the diva's puff-sleeved gown, reaching out his arms in melodramatic despair. What Fitzcarraldo had admired as a monstrous figment of European opera was extremely comic.

After that we gave ourselves a treat; by "we" I mean Peter Berling, Magdalena (who had come with us), and me. We went down the Amazon by steamer, like members of the leisured class on the Grand Tour, complete with tropical suits, cognac, and hammocks. Peter Berling was spreading the bons mots of a Roman journalist about the Werners of German cinema: Rainer Werner Fassbinder looked like a thug in the red-light district; Werner Herzog, like a madman on leave; Werner Schroeter, like a wandering prophet.

Fig. 21. Antonio Orlando. Courtesy Christian Holzfuss Fine Arts, Berlin.

Fig. 22. With producer Peter Berling. © bpk, Berlin/Digne Meller Marcovicz/Art Resource, NY.

Fig. 23. Alberte Barsacq. Courtesy Christian Holzfuss Fine Arts, Berlin.

Fig. 24. With Carole Bouquet during the shooting of *Day of the Idiots*, 1981. © bpk, Berlin/Digne Meller Marcovicz/Art Resource, NY.

Fig. 25. During the shooting of *Day of the Idiots*, 1981. © bpk, Berlin/Digne Meller Marcovicz/Art Resource, NY.

Fig. 26. With Mostefa Djadjam. © bpk, Berlin/Digne Meller Marcovicz/Art Resource, NY.

Fig. 27. Elisabeth Krejcir, Peter Kern, and Karina Fallenstein in *The Tropical Tree*, Düsseldorf, 1987. Photo: Lore Bermbach. Courtesy Theatermuseum Düsseldorf.

Fig. 28. Traute Hoess and Martin Reinke in *Intoxication*, Bremen Theater, 1987.
Photo: Elfi Mikesch.

Fig. 29. Marcelo Uriona and Sandra Kunz in *Grief, Longing, Rebellion*, Düsseldorf, 1987. Photo: Lore Bermbach. Courtesy Theatermuseum Düsseldorf.

Fig. 30. Elisabeth Krejcir and Barbara Nüsse in *Medea*, Düsseldorf, 1989. Photo: Lore Bermbach. Courtesy Theatermuseum Düsseldorf.

Fig. 31. Zdzislaw Ryczko, Eva Schuckardt, and Christiane Lemm in *King Lear*, Düsseldorf, 1990 Photo: Elfi Mikesch.

Fig. 32. With Isabelle Huppert shooting *Malina*, 1991. © bpk, Berlin/Digne Meller Marcovicz/Art Resource, NY.

Fig. 33. Isabelle Huppert, Martha Mödl, and Elizabeth Cooper (from left) in *Love's Debris*, 1996 (screenshot).

Fig. 34. With Anita Cerquetti in *Love's Debris*, 1996 (screenshot).

Fig. 35. Marianne Hoppe and Martin Wuttke in *Monsieur Verdoux*, Berlin, 1997.
© bpk, Berlin/Digne Meller Marcovicz/Art Resource, NY.

Fig. 36. Isabelle Huppert and Zazie de Paris in *Two*, 2002 (screenshot).

Fig. 37. Pascal Greggory and Amira Casar in *This Night*, 2008. Photo: Cinetext.

Fig. 38. With Wolf Wondratschek, Vienna, 2008. Courtesy Starpix GmbH/ Alexander Tuma.

Fig. 39. Elfi Mikesch, Vienna, 2008. Courtesy Starpix GmbH/Alexander Tuma.

Fig. 40. Dörte Lyssewski, Anne Ratte-Polle, Almut Zilcher, and Pascale Schiller in *Antigone/Electra*, Berlin, 2009. Courtesy Thomas Aurin.

Fig. 41. Wim Wenders presenting Werner Schroeter with the Golden Lion of the International Film Festival, Venice, 2008. © epa european pressphoto agency b.v./Alamy Stock Photo.

Day of the Idiots

I met Carole Bouquet in the summer of 1980, when I was recuperating from the stress of directing *Salome* in Augsburg at a friend's house in Saint-Tropez. She was twenty-three years old and well known in France since making her début in Luis Buñuel's *That Obscure Object of Desire* and appearing in Bertrand Blier's *Buffet froid*. I liked both films very much. If you appeared on the street with Carole in Italy, she caused traffic accidents, and jealous men almost killed me several times. They had every reason to feel jealous; I thought Carole incredibly beautiful, *aigre* as one might say, with a gray, sharp, tremendous erotic charge. After her parents' divorce, she had grown up with her taciturn, strict father. Without a mother, she hadn't known for a long time what femininity is or how to live. She was extremely shy, very serious, could hardly make conversation or look in the mirror. She hated it when people stared at her.

At that time the exiled Czech Karel Dirka approached me about shooting a film coproduced by him, Veith von Fürstenberg, and Peter Genée. Dirka, that sly fox, as my friend Peter Berling called him, had fled from the Communist regime in 1968, had spent some time working as a stills photographer, and then had set up a production company in Munich that by some mysterious means got the job, despite his background, of making a coproduction with the state Barandov studios in Prague. The script was by Dana Horáková; she was a journalist on *Bild-Zeitung* and later became senator for culture in the Hamburg city-state Council.

Dana Horáková came up with the idea for the film, I revised the script, and in February 1981 we began shooting in Prague: in the studio, in cafés, and on the street. Carole Bouquet played Carole Schneider, a woman who wants to be committed to a psychiatric hospital because she is afraid of life. Many of my women friends and other actors were in the cast: Magdalena Montezuma, Ingrid Caven, Ida Di Benedetto, Christine Kaufmann, Ellen Umlauf, and also Carola Regnier, Fritz Schediwy, Hermann Killmeyer, Tamara Kafka, and Marie-Luise Marjan, whom I had met in Bochum. Later,

Marie-Luise Marjan took on a regular part in the long-running TV soap opera *Lindenstrasse*, which I have never watched.

Prague itself is a theatrical place, and in line with that, the psychiatric hospital that we built in the studio was an ancient setting outside real time—I wanted everything to be surrealistically strange and unreal, but we had only a tenth of the budget that I really needed.

I have always felt very close to the psychological inner worlds of the deranged; they are the kind of transgression, lived out in reality, that has always been my subject and a source of inspiration to me. The idea of *Day of the Idiots* was to depict madness in such a way that it connected up with the world outside the hospital.

Dana Horáková had written a political plea, and I had long been interested in Michel Foucault's *Madness and Civilization*, the *Anti-Oedipus* of Deleuze and Guattari, as well as the antipsychiatry writing of R. D. Laing, David Cooper, and Franco Basaglia. In Italy, the last named had succeeded in his demand to have mental hospitals opened and schizophrenics let out into the world. The philosophy and politics of that policy of opening such institutions interested me greatly, since homosexuals had also been defined as sick, people to be shut away and treated therapeutically—that repression, sanctioned by authority, was one reason why I rejected psychology, psychoanalysis, and psychiatry.

But most interesting of all are the individual patients: the question of how they stand up to being let out of institutions, and how they overcome their fears.

Day of the Idiots was full of ideas, and with the women we staged the inside of the hospital, the manias and fears, and the special sense of humor of the sick.

Carole's character in the film does all she can to get sent to the closed asylum, so as to escape from her madness into regulated constraint, into the world described by one of the women patients in an improvised rhyme that she keeps repeating: "I go around and mewl, I feel a fool; I go in a circle and feel all whimsical; I go all about and I want to get out . . ." It ran something like that. She gets where she wants to be by denouncing another woman to the police, claiming that she is a terrorist.

I wanted to include the witch-hunting of terrorists that was going on at the time, without implying any moral condemnation. The theme appears in the hospital we depicted in connection with all sorts of characters: with women in a large hall who are all close to their obsessions, sometimes too close. Magdalena Montezuma demands the soap she has lost; Ellen Umlauf boasts forty-nine times a day of her prowess in the Eros Center; Christine Kaufmann bites her nails; Ula Stöckl proudly urinates standing, like a man, something I had always imagined Maria Callas doing. But the hospital doctor Laura, played by Ingrid Caven, and a male nurse doubt that Carole is really deranged. The outcome depends on deciding whether she can satisfy her needs in the outside world, indeed whether she will venture to find out what those needs are. The hospital doctor says plainly, "I believe in open psychiatric hospitals." And we see the studio set being literally taken apart. But once Carole is outside, dressed as a boy, she can't manage and throws herself in front of a car. It is always up to individuals whether or not they can find freedom for themselves.

I thought Carole perfect in *Day of the Idiots*, in her own way. In 1982 the film won the gold award of the German Film Prize. But I was persona non grata in Germany as a director of major feature films, so there was no follow-up to the production. I would have liked to choose the music myself; the score composed by Peer Raben seemed to me like muttering. The film was called *Jamais la vie* when we took it to the Cannes Film Festival, and perhaps that was the better title.

Carole was going on adventures now. I remember that after the shooting I drove to Italy with her. I was thirty-five; she was twenty-four. We were traveling in her wonderful car, but we had no money, although no one could believe it when they saw that car. So I said to her, "Time to take your acting exam," and sent her into a café in Florence, where the proprietor grabbed his balls at the sight of her—that typical Italian gesture indicating that a man has all the equipment a girl could want. That was always happening to Carole. I told her to say she was madly in love with her husband out there, but unfortunately, he also needed young men, so could the proprietor tell her the best bars to find gays? The poor man almost fell over with the shock of it. I could read from her lips that she was telling him to get a move on and answer her. He scribbled down an address. "Good, you pass your exam," I praised her. So we drove to a gay bar, not that there are many of them in Italy, where gays and lesbians sat together. After a while an Italian in the prime of life spoke to us. He was driving a Jaguar, either black or silver, and invited us to his house up in the hills above Florence. The other guests warned us that it was dangerous, but they all just wanted to get their hands on Carole; some of them there were also happy to have it off with women.

So we went to the man's beautiful villa with him. He actually had a swimming pool lit from the inside; it was summer, mild air, warm water. He gave us a wonderful bed with pink champagne in an ice bucket. "This is the life!" said Carole. It was terrific—she was a great traveling companion.

In the same year as we made *Day of the Idiots*, she was the James Bond girl in *For Your Eyes Only*. From then on she was a star, and a few years later she also appeared in Daniel Schmid's *Jenatsch*.

Carole married the eccentric film producer Jean-Pierre Rassam, a Lebanese who had found fame and fortune with Marco Ferreri's *La grande bouffe* [The big feast], Roman Polanski's *Tess*, and many other films. Rassam was a talented drinker, a wild hedonist, who was in a liaison with Isabelle Huppert for several years and died of an overdose of tranquilizers in 1985.

On New Year's Eve before the wedding, we had a large party in Paris with Rassam, Carole, and many other guests. My friend Antonio Orlando disappeared into the cellar with Sofia Coppola, who was fourteen then. What a fuss there was! Sofia still half a child, and Antonio a cute little Neapolitan. The two of them reappeared, and I thought disaster was on its way, but Rassam turned up and punched Antonio, while Francis Ford Coppola came out of the other room, making for the pair of them. Rassam's punitive gesture averted the worst, as I had to explain to the shocked Antonio later that night. Rassam had saved him, because otherwise the old man would have gone on the attack. Sofia simply thought that Antonio was cute, which I could well understand.

Today Carole makes two or three films a year and appears onstage in the live theater too, for instance, in Jean Racine's *Bérénice* at the Théâtre des bouffes du nord, when Peter Brook was guest director. I wonder if she is making progress as a stage actress and can memorize those large quantities of text? She doesn't have a huge dramatic talent, but she likes acting and has plenty of work. Carole was in a relationship with Gérard Depardieu for a long time, and she has brought up two sons. She is a committed campaigner against the abuse of children and bad housing conditions. Today she is a beautiful woman who earns a fortune as a model for Chanel No. 5, so she has no financial worries. I like her very much.

Jean-Pierre Rassam would be worth a chapter of his own, and so would his sister. There have been various different kinds of encounters between us. The director Claude Berri is one of their family, Rassam's brother-in-law, married to his sister. His wife, Anne-Marie Berri, was a dear friend of mine, one of the few people with whom I have happily slept in the same bed. We were like brother and sister.

At the Venice Film Festival, Anne-Marie spontaneously gave me her wedding ring. She became aggressive when I said I couldn't take it. "You'll take it or I'll throw it in your face!" So I took the ring. It had belonged to Claude Berri's grandmother and was platinum, with a large solitaire diamond, valued at a hundred thousand marks. I got Antonio to take it back to her. Thereupon, she really did throw it in my face, and when I ran out of money, I thought I'd pawn it, but that seemed like a mean thing to do. In the end the valuable ring was stolen from me in the Philippines, when I was wearing it in bed, on a silver chain around my neck.

A blasphemous clan

When *The Ghost* had its première at the Berlinale in 1982, I introduced the film instead of Herbert Achternbusch, who couldn't be there. A few days later we were in trouble with my own film *Das Liebeskonzil* [The council of love], which is still banned in Europe and has even been the subject of legal proceedings at the European Court of Justice in Strasbourg. Years ago someone sent me the files, but I haven't kept them. If you spend your life going from hotel to hotel with a suitcase, or from friends to other friends, you don't drag a whole lot of files around with you. But I hear that there were even people who went on pilgrimage to the shrine of the Black Madonna at Altötting to pray for my soul to be saved. I could never understand all the fuss about *The Council of Love*, but the film can't be shown in the Tyrol, where 90 percent of the population are Catholic. Unfortunately, a judgment establishing a principle was passed in Strasbourg, stating that every film distributor must consider how much satire may be acceptable in each part of a country where certain forms of religion prevail. As a result, the film has disappeared from Austria because it is alleged to be blasphemous and likely to offend the religious sensitivities of the majority.

And yet it is harmless, witty, and kind at heart, being in essence a sequel to the trial for blasphemy of the author on whose work it is based. Oskar Panizza wrote his anti-Catholic satire in 1895 and had it published not at home in Bavaria but in Switzerland. After twenty-three copies had been sold in Munich, someone brought charges. Panizza did not deny that he had foreseen what would happen if he sold the work, or that he was proud of it. For this defiance of the authorities, he spent a year in prison in solitary confinement and was ruined by the costs of the trial.

Not until 1969 was his play *The Council of Love* performed again, in Paris, and then in Rome at the Teatro Belli in 1981. Peter Berling, who lives in Rome, went to the production, which amused the Roman audience mightily, and since my idea of filming *Querelle de Brest* and his plan for a ballet film about the Pan-American Highway had both fallen through, he suggested we make a film very quickly in collaboration with the Teatro Belli. The Duisburg film distributor and producer Hanns Eckelkamp provided some financial support; Dietrich Kuhlbrodt, the film critic who was also a district attorney and has been a friend of mine for forty years, since the days of alternative cinema, wrote the script for the framework action, and then we made *The Council of Love* as a low-budget film, shot by the cameraman Jörg Schmidt-Reitwein in ten days, working in day and night shifts on locations in Rome and Berlin. Catherine Brasier-Snopko helped me with the montage of the Italian and German sections.

The film follows the Italian stage production of *The Council of Love*, framed by scenes from the trial of Panizza. The German synchronization, in which I had made some alterations to the text, is better than the original. The stage production was modest, the wit not so sharp, and I improved it in the process of synchronization. Indeed, the synchronization may be the version that really has audiences falling down laughing.

Volker Spengler gives a great performance as God the Father, with the Holy Ghost, in the person of the dove, shitting on his head— I had trained the bird to do that. Also in the cast were Hans Peter Hallwachs as the Devil, Magdalena Montezuma as Mary Magdalene, Margit Carstensen as the prosecuting attorney, Heinrich Giskes as the attorney for the defense, Kurt Raab as the presiding judge, Antonio Salines, manager of the Teatro Belli, as the suicidal character of the real-life Panizza, and many other members of our ensemble. We made an abandoned cemetery in Berlin into Hell with smoke candles, and the Landwehr Canal stood in for the River Styx.

The play is set in the late Middle Ages, during the papacy of Alexander VI (Rodrigo Borgia), famous for his magnificence and his orgies—we had already staged a wild farce about his daughter Lucrezia Borgia in Bochum. In Panizza's play as we filmed it, God the Father is old and doddery, Christ is feebleminded, and his mother, Mary, is a clever intriguer. They take a look at the terrible state of affairs at the papal court—a passage, incidentally, that the Teatro Belli had tactfully cut. God needs a fitting punishment for mankind, but the human race must be capable of repentance and salvation, because God the Father is far too senile to create a new and better version of mankind. The Devil finds the suitable remedy— syphilis—and does a deal with God for a new portal to his dilapidated Hell in return. In addition, he can go on exerting his diabolical arts of seduction on earth with impunity.

When we screened *The Council of Love* at the Berlinale, Hanns Eckelkamp had posters put up showing a satyr with a huge erect penis. In the film, this statue had been enthroned on the Devil's piano—relegated to the background, but the Catholic Church was up in arms about it. There were protests, an enormous amount of fuss. Which prompted Eckelkamp to cancel his own provocative advertising strategy. I was indignant. Eckelkamp's fear of the Inquisition was scandalous. Peter Berling and I telexed protests. "Dear Eckelkamp, you have created a paper dragon with your own invocations of something 'spectacular' and 'commercial,' and now you run away from it screaming. I am not going along with this undignified and schizophrenic spectacle. . . . The censored Panizza extracts will be handed out to the public at the festival, and Panizza's memorable quotations will be displayed at the Atlas distribution stand, or the curtain will not go up. I wish you a little more courage and freedom—yes, and faith too—in the future. Ever yours, Werner Schroeter. PS: I am awaiting payment for the final installment of the fee due to me in Berlin as stipulated in the contract."

Réveille-moi à midi

We were just celebrating the première of *Don Carlos* in Frankfurt am Main when the news of Rainer Werner Fassbinder's death hit us. It was a great shock. True, I had been furious, disappointed, and jealous when he snapped up the chance of filming *Querelle de Brest*, which was so close to my heart, and indeed I had felt more painfully injured than I liked to admit publicly. But with his death, I lost someone whom, in spite of everything, I loved like a brother.

Recently I had found the real Fassbinder, the one who meant something to me, in his wonderful film *In a Year of Thirteen Moons*. The love depicted in it was given with such total, unconditional prodigality. The character of the transsexual Elvira, played by Volker Spengler, who has become a woman out of love for a man, meets with nothing but mockery and rejection. It went far beyond the usual sort of melodrama: it was a film born of pain, a memorial to Fassbinder's dead lover Armin, who took his own life after Fassbinder left him. Fassbinder's mother found him dead days later, in the apartment that I knew only too well. I kept imagining the graphic image that my mind presented to me of the body eaten by worms. Fassbinder had been about to play Iago in a production directed by Peter Palitzsch at the Frankfurt Theater—a curious idea—but instead he created this dense, intense film about love and the inability to love. Together with *The Marriage of Maria Braun*, *The Merchant of Four Seasons*, and *Katzelmacher*, *In a Year of Thirteen Moons* has always represented the peak of Fassbinder's work to me.

A strange kind of peace came over me at his funeral and was noticed by his film family and people on the Munich scene, who sounded disconcerted when they broached the subject to me. We were of the same generation; we felt that an era was ending, one in which we had left our mark on the German cinema by dwelling on the subjects of revolution and a new departure. All that year, conversations centered on our loss. I made my own sense of it by thinking that Fassbinder had made a pact not exactly with the devil but with his own soul, had dispensed with love for other, real people in order to win the favor of the public instead. I felt that the real tragedy was his unprecedented passion for work.

A good many people blamed me for my composed, fatalistic reaction to Fassbinder's death, which came far too soon. I was aware that there was a quantum of arrogance in it, but I couldn't help being an expert on states of mental danger. It had nothing to do with the decadent longing for death that some liked to impute to me. Don't we love life for the very reason that we must die?

For the rest, my ironic attitude was necessary to overcome the fear of all mankind's fragility. I was surrounded by those who were endangered. Many were addicted to drugs, and when an epidemic of AIDS began spreading, we heard new and terrifying reports of sickness every day. People whom I knew well were dying like flies. The worst news of all reached me a few weeks after Fassbinder's death. In the summer of 1982 we learned, with shattering certainty, that Magdalena Montezuma, not yet forty years old, was suffering from terminal cancer.

Feelings of grief, fury, and despair were no use at all. In spring that year, we had been working together at the Frankfurt Theater on Schiller's *Don Carlos*, in tandem with a production of Pirandello's

Tonight We Improvise. As well as directing, I had designed the set, and besides acting in the play, Magdalena had designed the costumes. We weren't to know that it would be our last work for the theater together. Magdalena was now recognized as a fine actress in her own right, very distinctive, and still developing her range of roles. But her cancer meant the end of such plans. In the course of 1983, when I was working in Argentina for months on end, I had to come to terms with the realization that she did not have much longer to live. We would work together creating something for as long as possible: that was our declaration of love for one another.

In that sad summer of 1983 we took the Frankfurt production of *Don Carlos* on tour to the Avignon Festival. But in fact we pulled a switch: the production of Friedrich Schiller's great drama was announced, but along with Eva Schuckardt, Carola Regnier, Hans Peter Hallwachs, Rainer Will, and members of the Frankfurt ensemble, we performed Luigi Pirandello's play *Tonight We Improvise* instead. In this work, a theatrical company is studying the tragic tale of a marriage in which an unhappy wife wants to leave her jealous husband, who prevents her from becoming an actress by violence. The audience watches the actors as the play develops and is constantly interrupted by their own conflicts, so that the marital drama and the real lives of the actors intermingle like stones in a mosaic.

I felt that Pirandello's plays were a wonderful expression of the fact that the theater is never just a world of illusion but becomes reality at the very moment when the actors construct it. There is no flight from reality in the theater. That year, there was a strong protest movement against the extension of Frankfurt airport, and an even stronger one against the stationing of American Pershing rockets on German soil. I was less interested in the depressing scenario of possible nuclear war than in the demonstrations, the social movements, and how the awakening ego of the individual was manifested in them. We didn't want to provide subsidized theater for the fat cats of the Frankfurt banks, nor did we want to stage dramas with an obvious message. We dreamed of opening up to new groups of spectators, of a new form of theater as a moral institution, exactly what Schiller himself had suggested. Hence our titular *Don Carlos.*

Pirandello's theme of jealousy in *Tonight We Improvise* also touched on the tricky points of our relationships in love, friendship, and work, not least in connection with Magdalena. Onstage, the question was whether to live out these relationships or suppress them. The company in the play is struggling against a tyrannical director who stirs up rivalry between them. We wanted to take this outmoded model and set other forms of relationship against it; social change seemed to me more important than politics. My view was that jealousy is the negative form of passion, and without it human relationships do not exist. I was pleading for the jealous to be understood, but within limits. Otherwise, jealousy, as the play shows, leads to death by suffocation. Speaking in public and giving interviews, I backed the wise proposition that love must give the loved person scope instead of forcing him or her to be subservient. Clinging together is an unattractive relic of the heterosexual norms of relationship. But freedom as I lived it was a strain, for other people too. With my innate individualism, and the friction that arose when I came up against bourgeois forms of life, I allowed myself the freedom that I wished, with all my heart, for everyone to have. I was spontaneous, nomadic, unreliable, a demanding and challenging lover. On the other hand, I needed people who would listen to me, help me, drive me around, and sit up half the night with me until I had finally solved the terrible problem of dropping off to sleep.

I shared in Magdalena's suffering only from a distance for a long time, as well as I could in my uneasiness and with my fear of sickness. Our plan to shoot a film occupied my mind a great deal, and at the same time I was preparing for my visit to Argentina. In parallel, I was working to complete a film on the history and culture of the Philippines as I saw them, my commentary on the rise of a dictatorship. I went to Manila four times in order to make this documentary film essay, which was entitled *Der lachende Stern* [The laughing star]. In this film, I reverted for the last time to my old methods of working: writing the script, directing, acting as my own cameraman, and doing the cutting with the help of Christel Orthmann. Peter Kern, the Viennese actor and director, was my producer. We had worked together on many theatrical productions—for instance, Shakespeare's *Comedy of Errors* in Berlin, also staged in 1983. Once again, Channel Two television was involved in *The Laughing Star*, in the form of that patient editor Christoph Holch.

The Laughing Star was supposed to have been propaganda *for* the regime of the Philippine dictator Ferdinand Marcos, but in fact I ended up with a portrait made up of bits and pieces, the story of a country under American influence, and in the middle of it, not least, was the comic obscenity of the president's wife, Imelda Marcos.

At this time the Philippines was suffering increasingly under the corrupt Marcos dictatorship. Looking for a suitable method of whitewashing the situation, Imelda, always over the top, came up with the idea of holding a great film festival, intended to rival even Cannes. And it actually took place in 1983, in a frightful Festival Palace built almost overnight, at the cost of the lives of many workers buried under its concrete because the dictatorship thought nothing of safety measures.

In 1979 I had already been invited by Imelda Marcos's office to make a film in the country. Since Francis Ford Coppola's *Apocalypse Now*, the Philippines had been a good location for international productions. Imelda, the former beauty queen with her vast collection of shoes, her curious puff-sleeved gowns, and her jet-set airs and graces, wanted to shine as "Minister for Human Settlement" with expensive cultural projects. I accepted the dubious invitation, intending to explore the country, which I did not know. But Asia had always interested me, and I wanted to see behind what the mirror of the regime showed. In the end I had a kaleidoscopic picture of a country torn apart. I asked actors to narrate the traditional myths, and amateurs, including impoverished rice farmers, immigrants to the cities, and former extras from *Apocalypse Now*, to improvise scenes from their own lives. I filmed actors in the savage Christian Passion plays at the height of their delirium and blatantly horny porn stars from the gay bars of Manila—both of those, incidentally, were enormously popular tourist attractions even before Coppola and his team had visited the archipelago. Hollywood brought up the rear, so to speak, of the American army, which had taken on the role of the former Spanish colonial system since the end of World

War II, and the corrupt regime profited by that dependency. I was able to observe Imelda Marcos at close quarters when she spoke at the opening of the festival, offering a pack of lies about humanity, development, and human resources and belting out the song "Feelings" to the best of her ability. *The Laughing Star* of the title refers to a game in which a Philippine boy put matchsticks together in the form of a cross and then set it moving by means of drops of water. After many attempts, the star took on the shape of a structure with jagged points similar to the star on the Philippine national flag. And I wanted to realize my next film project, in Buenos Aires, in the same personal manner as my critical approach to Manila.

The Rose King

The Rose King was the first of my films in which Elfi Mikesch, behind the camera, designed an incomparably magical world of images without batting an eyelash. It was her first 35 mm film, and a great challenge in that respect as well. The film is dense and colorful, and it is very, very important to me, more as a matter of the heart than anything else. Making it was a real necessity to me.

Three people from my own life play the main parts. At the center is Magdalena Montezuma, accompanied by Antonio Orlando and Mostefa Djadjam. Those three were my best friends, and my life was entangled with them in the most complicated way. The story told in the film arose, not from a surreal dream, but from a real existential one, uniting those three people in what they meant to me in life and in art.

When Magdalena, for so long my companion and colleague, had known for a year that she would soon die of cancer, I dreamed of that cruel fairy tale. Maybe the dream came to me so that I could answer loss and death with re-creation, with a work of art, and thus somehow or other exorcize it. It was a primeval dream born of the situation in which the three of us were linked. Magdalena died less than four weeks after the film was shot, but she insisted that she wanted to be in it, and she contributed to the subject and the dialog. *The Rose King* is dedicated to Magdalena.

The impulse behind *The Rose King* is the idea that day is a form of life, night is a form of life, and in this case their synthesis is death. The film critic Karsten Witte described it well: "a Rose King is a legend. He has no kingdom except in the land of dreams. The Rose King is an artificial figure who personifies the deadly dangers of art. He lives in art and succumbs to it, in earthly and masculine terms, by no means as a saint. The halo of sanctity is worn by Magdalena Montezuma. She is the Rose King's mother and guesses at the disaster inherent in beauty."

Magdalena plays the owner of a rose plantation on the Atlantic coast, Mostefa takes the part of her son, who has mastered the mysteries of rose breeding and shares with his mother the anxiety of imminent bankruptcy, but he turns away from her and to the handsome Italian laborer played by Antonio. He takes him prisoner, wants him all to himself, and in the apotheosis of the film maltreats the poor fellow like a beautiful plant from which he thinks he can breed something even more beautiful by the technique of grafting. It is a dark dream about an artist who falls in love with the handsome young laborer but renders him helpless. If we leave out *White Journey*, then *The Rose King* is my only film on the subject of a myth of sexual passion.

Magdalena was already terribly thin and transparent, but she worked to the last on the shooting, affirming life to the end. I can see nothing morbid in our film.

When I put the dream concept of *The Rose King* to the TV editorial team with which I had already made many experimental films, they all said no, there would be no money forthcoming for that film. But the clock was ticking; Magdalena was mortally sick. I could only turn directly to people I knew and ask them to donate money. Among those who did were Rudolf Augstein of *Der Spiegel*; Margarethe von Trotta; Juliane Lorenz, my good friend and reliable confidante; the Munich filmmaker and producer Katrin Seybold and her partner Thomas Harlan; and a number of other generous people who all understood the urgency of the matter and trusted Magdalena and me that the idea behind the film was a good one. We raised a sum that in modern terms would amount to about 130 thousand euros. The Portuguese producer Paulo Branco continued to finance the film and let me shoot it the way I wanted to. Hubert Bals of the Rotterdam Film Festival also contributed money from the Netherlands. So we had just enough to live well, eat well, and feel as well as possible in order to complete the film, paying no one any salary. In the end I was able to show a mixed and color-corrected copy.

The Rose King was shot in Sintra near Lisbon, a place with a strange microclimate of its own, dividing the area into two. One side of the valley is grown over with forest like a jungle; on the other side were the sea and the beach that Magdalena could see from her hotel room. Darkness and light alternated in this climate, and I was able to express my constant obsession with night to the full. As a result of Elfi Mikesch's work, you know in the film that it is day only when the inquisitive, voyeuristic children of Sintra put in an appearance. The whole effect was of a magical space, like a miracle reminding us that in death one really does disappear into such mysteries.

The old houses in Sintra and the old barn that we found in Montijo, not far from Lisbon, made time travel possible. They reflected the stories of the people who lived in them. There are still very many old houses in Portugal, but unfortunately, the legendary painted tiles have now been stripped from the walls and sold individually to tourists.

We left everything just as it was, even in rooms full of cobwebs— sad to say, a gigantic mother spider lost her life during the filming. We shot the film in a much eerier house than our location in *Willow Springs*, in a place that may not have been opened up for a hundred and fifty years. You felt at one with history and the genius loci there—signs that made us aware of Magdalena's imminent death.

We reacted to her strength and her pain, ignoring any other plans and what the script specified by way of daytime and nighttime. The film was our existential life-form, and whenever I saw *The Rose King* again, I always felt sure that accounted for its timeless effect. We were all upset by Magdalena's efforts to rise above her sickness and her pain. Antonio Orlando went back on heroin, which he had given up a little while earlier. I should add that he managed to kick the habit again after we had finished making *The Rose King*. I suffered torments because I saw every female tourist as a possible rival to me in the affections of my beloved Mostefa Djadjam. We all reacted in our own ways, but we flung ourselves wholeheartedly into the film. Our extreme reactions became its wealth; no one was pretending, and without ostentatious lamentations on our part, our feelings flowed into the film.

Because this was a sinister fairy tale, beautiful and strange animals appeared in it. For instance, a Portuguese poisonous toad that we called Paula crossed my path. She looked to me like an old witch under a spell, so I inveigled her into the film. She survived the shooting safe and sound and got a good salary in the form of worms to eat. Then there was Mafalda, the brilliantly talented white rat—I gave him that name as an insult. The kids in Montijo brought us Mafalda; he was a real rat king of high birth, no ordinary laboratory rat. He was very affectionate and kindly did as he was asked. He shared a bed with either Elfi or me, usually sleeping in my hair. I'm sure that Mafalda dreamed. His professional career came to a glorious conclusion when Elfi smuggled him back into Germany under her sweater, and he lived happily in Hamburg—for a short time, at least, for Mafalda became addicted to nibbling Ata toilet cleaner and died of liver cancer despite all the veterinarians' efforts to save his life.

Cats are divine beings and are part of what beauty brings into our lives. In *The Rose King* the desperate woman played by Magdalena crucifies a cat. She transfers the crucified Jesus to the animal world, doing a terrible thing with reference to a cruel religious idea. It is remarkable that, after the accusations of blasphemy leveled against Herbert Achternbusch's *The Ghost*, no one felt indignant enough about *The Rose King* to take us to court. I can say only two things on that subject: I was and still am a convinced Christian, but no lover of churches. I like to quote the theosophist Uta Ranke-Heinemann, who said, of Martin Scorsese's interesting film about Christ, that Scorsese did not finally get Christ down from the cross either. In that sense, I would have no objection to my *Rose King* being taken as criticism of the church. There is also a scene in which the young man who is held captive asks a statue of the Madonna to help him, or otherwise, he says, he will kill her. I don't want to interpret the scene symbolically. Whenever people try pinning me down to symbolism, I have objected. I am provoking, in the sense of the Latin verb *provocare*, which means only "to call forth." The idea of my films is not to express a heightened form of drama. I want to *call forth* something that makes me feel joy, grief, sorrow. I was happy for everyone to take his own idea of a film home from the cinema.

The Rose King could not be used in the AIDS campaign protesting against the stigmatizing of homosexuals. It was not meant to be topical or advertise anything.

Magdalena died on 15 July 1984 in Berlin. Our film, her last, was not finished until 1986. The material stayed with Juliane Lorenz until we could begin the montage. It wasn't a matter of money but of feeling that we *had* to do it. We were all trying to do our very best for the film, and that is why it is still so precious, at least to us . . .

I and alcohol—alcohol and I

"Io regna la droga,"said my friend Antonio Orlando, meaning "I rule the drugs; I am in charge of the drugs." We all of us, at least all sensitive, creative people who look for more in life than bourgeois stability, come into contact very early with the "miracles" that drugs can perform. In our society, alcohol has been the drug of choice since time immemorial. I must say that I have tolerated it very well. To me, it has always been a wonderful inspiration. I have never been drunk, even after imbibing large quantities. I haven't drunk in the evening just to get drunk either, only in the day while I am at work or when I am shooting at night. It has always been a pleasure to me, up to the point when one realizes that the second part of the phrase— the "alcohol and I" part—no longer refers to a euphoric sensation but to a physical need, a dependency. Then it becomes an agent, just enough to get you going but no help to your imagination and aesthetic sense. That is the point where many people are unlucky enough to find that they can't do without their drug of choice. I noticed that at the end of the eighties and tried to get by with inspirations of a different kind. But nothing really replaces its euphoric effect. You have to find something else in yourself.

I was lucky and succeeded. But what do I mean by lucky? When I was sick, drinking a lot was no fun. And then there was the struggle to find an existence in which life, having shaken off its dependency, sets free a different kind of creative and euphoric energy. I sometime thought I was physically dependent, an alcoholic in the sense that without alcohol I couldn't think or concentrate, or felt uncertain. In my case, fortunately, that wasn't so, because if I abstained from alcohol for quite a long time, I felt no ill effects—none at all.

Now, in the year 2009, if I drink alcohol, it is as a useful stimulant, taken on medical advice because it gives me a little energy, helps to build me up, and in the small quantities that I drink these days it really does give me a light, pleasant feeling. It's like a new beginning; once again I am drinking in the old way, just to feel more lightness of heart.

I began with cognac. My mother must have brought home tons of Hennessy. A good French cognac on special offer cost fourteen marks at the time! That was affordable. In extreme cases I might be drinking a bottle of cognac a day. I aimed to emulate the dramatist Heiner Müller, whom I revered and who was drinking a bottle of whisky a day—and was never drunk either. Never! It didn't impair the witty brilliance of his intellect. An absolute phenomenon.

Then I began drinking more and more, and after a while it simply felt like too much. Your stomach tells you when that comes, and you notice that you don't want to eat if you are drinking so much cognac and other spirits. So I went over to drinking mainly dry white wine or dry champagne. Today I drink white wine spritzers; I don't like anything else. And sometimes a little cognac in my coffee or a little rum in my tea or a drop of cassis to color the white wine. I prefer noncarbonated white wine spritzers, because my throat, since being treated for cancer, can't take the fizzy effect anymore. With white peaches—that's good.

I write about this subject because I have known some unfortunate cases in this connection. Many of the people with whom I was involved in strong loving, nostalgic relationships were inclined to numb their feelings with drugs and alcohol. For instance, and tragically, there was my beloved Antonio Orlando, my Neapolitan friend and creative colleague. He took heroin; he both sniffed and injected it. I tried to be as paternal and moral as possible and to preach as little as possible too. But the effect of the heroin was rather paradoxical in Antonio. He didn't get into the situation where the curtain went up and he could think, and then the curtain came down again. Instead, the drug stimulated him, he was wide awake, except when he had taken too much, which he never did while working. He could discipline himself. However, I watched this with great sorrow over the course of time. I managed to get him to stop for a while, but that didn't last long, and then he drank heavily. Under the influence of alcohol his behavior was very unpleasant, brutal and aggressive.

It went so far that I even tried buying heroin for him, so that at least it would be good quality and not mixed with rat poison and Penaten powder. This was the time when people were found sitting in the underground trains in Berlin and looking as if they were asleep, but they were dead because the dealers had cut the heroin with rat poison.

I went all over the place with Antonio, to New York, Palermo, London, and Paris, everywhere. When I spoke to him about drugs, he always came out with the old claim: he said he was in charge of the drug; the drug wasn't in charge of him. That is a fatal mistake; every heavy drinker also says the same, and always at the moment when he knows it's too late. Only someone who is already so dependent that he *can't* see clearly anymore, and is also prevented from seeing by his own inner urges, will make that stupid claim. And at that point the drug has already won.

There are always ups and downs, which is really very sad. However, Antonio's work was always wonderful. Then he came down with hepatitis B in Prague, where we were shooting the film *Day of the Idiots*. He was put in quarantine, a very brutal regime. He had had hepatitis once before, no doubt catching it from used syringes. That battle left its mark on our relationship, and it got worse and worse. This kind of sick dependency always involves telling lies. I have nothing against lying; maybe the truth is the greatest lie of all if someone presumes to claim that he knows, as Hugo von Hofmannsthal so cleverly has Clytemnestra saying in his *Electra*. But then an addict will not keep any promises and steals money. The drive is stronger than any ethical duty, stronger than human reason. And I loved him very much.

So there was my friend Antonio, who loved young girls because he was not first and foremost homosexual, and as well as that relationship I had my great passion for Mostefa Djadjam and Håkan Dalström. I had never made possessive claims on anyone, and I wasn't addicted either. I was so glad that I had those three friends, partly because going from one to another made evasion possible, and thus life was considerably easier. If I had had only Antonio to care about, it couldn't have gone well.

All who are strongly dependent on drugs or alcohol drag other people down with them in their addiction. There are many good accounts of this phenomenon. Those others are dragged down into hell, a terrible fate. I have caught myself emptying the glasses of heavy drinkers who were friends of mine when they had gone to the bathroom—I drank more, so that they wouldn't drink so much. That's a typical example. But it did no good; the alcoholic ordered the next drink as long as there was money available.

I struggled with my paternalistic behavior toward Antonio. I restrained myself and talked to him about it. I didn't want to do that. It's pointless and disgusting; no young man will accept what an older man preaching to him says. Apart from which, it is not a good way to behave.

But there was some kind of magic between Antonio and me. He was born on 7 April 1955 at 5:30 in the morning; I was born on 7 April 1945 at 5:30 in the morning. I was born in Georgenthal near Gotha; he was born in Naples. His mother was very worried about him. She would phone me, begging, "*Salva mio figlio*—save my son!" But I couldn't make any promises that I couldn't be sure of keeping, because it all became too much for me. I was working the whole time and leading a busy life that was a great strain on my strength.

At first, Antonio would say, "You try some heroin too." That is a typical gesture. You think you will understand the other person better, so you try it. Luckily, the effect on me was hair-raising. I felt hot and disturbed, unwell, and my mood was gloomy, disastrously gloomy. I spent hours puking with my head over the lavatory pan.

I lay on my bed, and when I moved, I felt terrible again. Just as well it had such a powerful effect on me. I can't imagine anyone overcoming that phase and then getting addicted. The attraction seems to be something that just eludes me; either that or I react particularly badly. It was quite different with Antonio. He became very active, clearheaded, and witty.

His death at far too young an age in 1989 shook me badly. Ida Di Benedetto told me when we were sitting in the plane on our way to a small festival. "Antonio is dead." She hadn't dared to tell me that for several days. It was a shattering setback for me, a cruel blow.

He had been in an accident. He was in a car with a friend, Antonio was driving, coming down from the mountainous country around Quartieri to the Via Roma, also called the Via Toledo, a busier road, and he ran into a bus. There are almost no fatal road accidents in Naples. The Neapolitans drive fast and in their own virtuoso style, and hardly any of them die in towns in an accident like this one. I assume that either he was suffering withdrawal symptoms from heroin, or he had injected too much of it, because he usually drove very well. Ultimately, it was that outside influence and the drugs that killed him, and I could do nothing to save him.

The people around me who took such drugs were always the most gifted and sensitive that I knew. They were not those who had gone downhill and grumbled despairingly to themselves but the most delicate and sensitive souls, and those are also the easiest to destroy.

I couldn't save and protect them, but I have always been attracted by sensitive people like Magdalena Montezuma and Antonio Orlando, people who look up at the stars or have taken Kant seriously when he speaks of "the moral law within me, the starry sky above me." That covers a wide spectrum of yearning, sensitivity and tenderness, which, as I see it, proves the existence of God.

No one will ever *want* to stop creative people experimenting. But if they come to the point I have described above, when "I and alcohol" becomes "alcohol and I," and the same is true of drugs, then at that crucial parting of the ways one must issue a warning, even if it sounds authoritarian. That is the only possible point from which an addict can return. I have seen so many people die of those addictions, as many as die of AIDS. An addict has to sense that point and then withdraw, find therapy, and try to turn his needs in a new direction. It is difficult, but at that point it is still possible—after that, it is very hard indeed. I know of very few cases where there has been a late recovery.

Grief, Longing, Rebellion

I met Marie Louise Alemann in 1980 at the Palace in Paris, a wonderful disco-theater where I had been directing a show for Ingrid Caven. We were going to celebrate the end of the show with a party. Marie Louise, an elegant blonde, came up the sweeping staircase from the foyer with a tall black man and a very handsome young Arab. I saw the three of them, in particular the Arab between the other two, flung myself at his feet on the stairs and cried, "Je vous aime!" All I got in return was laughter; they went on up the stairs, while I ran to the toilet, beside myself, yelling, "*Tuez-moi!*—Kill me, kill me!" because I was so scared of the feeling that came over me. But of course I, too, was playing a game. Someone came up to me and slapped my face, and I was in possession of my senses again.

By now the three of them were sitting at a table. It turned out that Frau Alemann came from Buenos Aires. She was married to an Argentinian who owned a newspaper, the German-language paper in Argentina, and wrote for it herself. Marie Louise knew the two young men from her travels and was also familiar with my work, which made our conversation very much easier.

I fell hard for that wonderful young Algerian, Mostefa Djadjam, who was beautiful in a feminine way, and is still a handsome man today, as anyone can see in the French cinema and on French TV. My feelings for Mostefa became obsessive, although he is not homosexual. That summer, he accompanied me to the Festival mondial du théâtre in Nancy, where we made *Die Generalprobe* [The dress rehearsal] together, with Mostefa as my assistant director and conversational partner. When we were all sitting together, discussing love as *the* theme of the festival, and I said to him, "Je t'aime," I meant him directly and in particular.

We also worked together on my films *Day of the Idiots* and, finally, *This Night*, and when he made his documentary on my staging of *Tosca* at the Opéra Bastille, I was his subject. The most intense evidence of our friendship, however, is *The Rose King*. My friendship with Marie Louise Alemann grew from our first meeting. She had made experimental short films in Argentina and arranged events and exhibitions. Four years after my mother's death, she became something like a foster mother to me, and that was how she herself saw it. Marie Louise addressed me as "Adorado" in her letters, and we took an active interest in all of each other's ventures and passions. We made a great team, and she is one of my best friends to this day.

She had good connections at the Goethe Institute in Buenos Aires and at the university in that city, where she also held workshops and seminars about German cinema, and she was influential in getting me invitations to Argentina. It was exactly the kind of thing that I had known in Mexico City: the Goethe Institute didn't just want to provide knowledge about Goethe—with whom most of the students there, incidentally, were better acquainted than I was—but also wanted to promote exchanges with Argentinian culture. In 1983 I went to Buenos Aires for a seminar with students of the university there, arranged on Marie Louise's initiative. She and her friends thought that a filmmaker like me could shake things up a bit. In Argentina, the appalling military dictatorship under General Videla was moving into a final phase of terror and violence, and word of it got abroad, mainly through the *madres de la Plaza de Mayo*, the mothers of the "disappeared," who were demonstrating to get their children back, even if that meant their corpses. The ghastly news of the tortures inflicted by the military dictatorship, and the way the dead simply disappeared without trace, had filtered through to Central Europe.

In the three-month workshop, I made an attempt to counter the general distress with joint creativity. The seminar was entitled "Tango y realidad en Argentina" [Tango and reality in Argentina], and the reference was political. Although I could not have guessed it then, the title immediately put the secret services of the military government on my trail; they didn't trust me an inch, and rightly. They began threatening the students, because they knew they wouldn't quickly get rid of me by dint of threats.

I divided the students into groups, gave them recorders, and sent them out to interview artists, politicians, and people living in the low-income areas, anyone they trusted to speak openly about the situation and their hopes. The idea was to use this material for our work on films and the live theater. But before we got as far as that, anonymous phone calls began coming into the Goethe Institute: "If that pansy Schroeter doesn't leave the country, you can expect a bomb to go off in the institute."

At first we went on working; I wasn't about to be scared away, but it was risky, because hundreds of people went in and out of the Goethe Institute daily. I told the students about the threats that day, and—how else can I put it?—they put their lives on the line with incredible courage. Whenever we gathered to work, we counted to see if anyone was missing, always fearing that someone might have disappeared and had already been enclosed in a concrete block. In such a situation you see whether people are capable of defending themselves, and what freedom is worth to them. Despite the daily threats, not a single student backed out of the seminar. The amazing Ambassador Frauke Peters stood by us, and her staff told us about escape routes and emergency exits and used metal detectors to look for any hidden bombs. Not until a university professor and his wife received a threat that their baby would be killed if I stayed in the country any longer did I have to give in, after three months. The students' farewell to me, on the balcony of the assembly hall at the University of Buenos Aires, lasted more than three hours. The secret police and the military police stood by calmly, grinning. Every student embraced me, I embraced every student—ninety-nine of them—it took a long time, and many tears were shed because we knew something impossible and terrible was going on. It was the only time in my life that I lost my composure, and I couldn't help weeping when I said, "I am yielding to force; there can be no worse feeling, but still I am yielding to force."

Months later, the dictatorship was at an end, but to this day I have not come to terms with what happened. It will be a long time before I can do that; remember that here in Germany, after sixty-five years, we have not entirely come to terms with everything that went on in those dark days of genocide.

I was invited back the following year, when democracy had returned to the country, because we didn't want to let things rest after the debacle. I was in great distress because Magdalena had just died. The singer and actress Cipe Lincovsky, a star in Buenos Aires, wanted me to create a concept for a program entitled *Libertad*, a textual collage celebrating liberty, the love of beauty, and so forth. I knew Cipe Lincovsky only from what Marie Louise had told me; she didn't know my films. In Argentina, she was considered a star who could venture to make comments on those in power. But after my previous experiences, I thought we ought to go for political depth— *Antigone* rather than some song-and-dance show. I put Sophocles together with quotations from the Bible, Marx, and Pasolini, but it was difficult to get Cipe Lincovsky to understand what I was doing. Of course, there was also room for Lautréamont's *Songs of Maldoror* in my program, because "the horror that a human instills in fellow humans" was palpable in Argentina and affected everyone. There had been many informers under the military dictatorship, and even after the dictatorship had fallen, bomb threats still accompanied our performance in the Teatro Lola Membrives.

And to my astonishment, I found that Lautréamont, who had been born in Uruguay, was regarded in Argentina, paradoxically, as a bringer of bad luck whose name must not be spoken. Cipe Lincovsky almost fell off her chair when I came out with it. In the following year, 1985, I was back in Argentina, filming with the students whom I knew from the seminar. We were making *Por ejemplo Argentina* [*De l'Argentine*], a very personal documentary about the country in the 1980s. I realized how high the educational level is in Argentina, because all the students knew more about German literature than I did. So I studied and studied, read Goethe, who is not my favorite author, as well as Julio Cortázar and many other Latin American writers. I was very fortunate that in those years in Latin America I found a new sense of the inner necessity of self-defense. Luckily, no one was injured or, even worse, killed. My eyes had been opened by those brave young people and my Argentinian foster mother Marie Louise.

Marcelo

In preparing for the theatrical evening *Libertad* in Buenos Aires, I looked around for young actors and students. I needed a large number of young people, and I asked them to improvise something, so that I could decide between them. This went on for several days, during which I had some strange experiences. I saw a young woman stubbing out cigarettes in her bare hand; she was a victim of the dictatorship, utterly distraught and devastated. Terrible memories overlapped with ideas of what might yet happen in the "no more dictatorship" year of 1984.

One of the candidates who wanted to be in *Libertad* was a certain Marcelo Uriona, aged eighteen. I auditioned him several times, but he didn't convince me. Because I was trying to be friendly, if it seemed sensible I had personal conversations with rejected candidates, to tell them why I was turning them down.

So I was sitting with Marcelo and my assistant Carlos in a *bolice*, a bar, explaining why I didn't think he quite made the grade. I talked and talked, saying he still had to wait. Then, all at once, I said, "Why don't we go to bed? That'll be much better." He replied, "Why not?" So I went off into the night with him, and we became lovers.

We were together in Buenos Aires for a few weeks, and then I flew back to Europe and kept wondering if anything might come of our relationship, despite the twenty-year difference in our ages. In the end I invited him to come to Germany. He accepted. That was in 1985, when Juliane Lorenz and I were finishing the cutting and mixing of *The Rose King*.

At first Marcelo lived in Berlin, then in Bremen with me. We were both working at the theater. He was a beginner, but he had talent. In *Don Carlos*, for instance, he was very good. I had him follow

Benno Ifland, playing King Philip, around as a kind of phantom, so as to visualize the conflict between father and son. As a silent role it worked splendidly. He put King Philip's hand in his mouth in a scene merging nightmare and real life—Benno Ifland and Marcelo acted the scene magnificently.

Marcelo's first steps onstage went very well. His next role was a singing part, in 1986. In García Lorca's *Doña Rosita* at the Düsseldorf Theater, I added a boy singing Lorca's songs to the cast for Marcelo. He sang wonderfully well in his native language too. Marcelo had a great gift for languages, and in the course of two years, he mastered German so well that he could correct other speakers of the language. He was also very musical, a wonderful young tango singer. The tango evening *Grief, Longing, Rebellion*, an idea of his own that we staged for him in 1967, is still fondly remembered by his fans, including Ingrid Caven. The performance was by Marcelo, a small tango instrumental ensemble, with a bandoneon, and a fourteen-year-old ballet dancer, Sandra Kunz. It was a very good evening, full of poetry, with tangos and going beyond the tango. I also worked with him at the Cologne Theater, and we worked together for the last time on Schönberg's oratorio *Die Jakobsleiter* [Jacob's ladder].

In 1989 Marcelo learned that he was HIV-positive and entered on a phase of suffering that he bore with great courage. We went on working with one another as long as possible. In 1992 he was still with Hans Hollmann at the Basel Theater and was also in France with Raimund Hoghe, formerly assistant to Pina Bausch, who took his own excellent ballets on tour. Marcelo did not go back to his mother in Argentina but went on working to the end, until he could no longer walk, was bedridden, and to weak to travel anywhere. It is terrible when the heart goes on and on beating and there is almost nothing left of the body, for the heart is very strong in someone so young. Then he went to the Düsseldorf University Hospital, where I could visit him. Early in 1993, after two months in the AIDS ward, he died at the age of twenty-seven. He was a very strong character and accepted his sickness; Marcelo was capable of that kind of thing. And how could he defend himself? Of course, he had all the treatments that were available. Desperation is neither very productive nor very creative.

Naturally, there were also catastrophes of various kinds in our life together. Inconstancy, for instance, because I could not be faithful. Faithfulness is a lie if it is in conflict with one's desires. I wasn't faithful to him; that's more than anyone can ask. After all, it can happen, quite suddenly, that things just don't work out. Be that as it may, ours was a deep friendship that survived many hazards.

Malina

My film *Malina* came at an exciting time for me. It was my thirteenth year at the Düsseldorf Theater, where in the spring we staged a production of *King Lear* that caused uproar, and in the fall *Missa solemnis*—a celebrated staged performance of Beethoven's Mass that is still discussed today. In between those productions, the Munich cinema proprietor, film distributor, and producer Thomas Kuchenreuther came to see me and asked whether I would be interested in directing a film of Ingeborg Bachmann's novel. He thought I was the right person for the job. *Malina*, he said, was his favorite book; he had a passion for it. Kuchenreuther was working with his own money, something very unusual in Germany. He found Austrian co-producers and managed to get financial backing for the film, so that, with a budget of almost eight million marks, I was able to shoot my most expensive film so far.

Thomas Kuchenreuther came to Düsseldorf on purpose to meet me. It wasn't out of deliberate calculation that he thought of me; he just knew and liked my work in films and the theater. And in fact, there is a close connection between the female characters in my films, from *Malibran* and *Flocons d'or* to *Day of the Idiots*. They all express a yearning for the absolute and lose themselves in it, and the novel *Malina* presents just such an unconditional search for passion. Three years earlier, I had made a documentary about Ariane Mnouchkine and her troupe at the Théâtre du soleil, *À la recherche du soleil* [In search of the sun]; seven years earlier I had made *The Laughing Star*, my documentary essay about the Philippines, and in between came *The Rose King*. There was a great deal of time, and even more work in the theater, between my last films and *Malina*.

When Thomas Kuchenreuther and I were on our way to Vienna, a few weeks later, I told him that I had always loved the poetry of Ingeborg Bachmann, but I did not know *Malina* so well. I had read it carefully, but without dwelling on it. And in essence, that sums up my knowledge of Bachmann to this day. My love of her poetry began with a particular experience: a lecture that she once gave in Frankfurt and in which, among other things, she read some of her writings. One poem, I remember, was "Undine geht" [Undine leaves]. What a woman! First her glasses fell off, then she dropped her manuscript, but it was all like something from another world. I was fascinated by this strange, sensitive woman and also by the strange voice in which she read her poems. She was far away and yet self-aware— that's the best way I can put it. My favorite poem of hers is "Böhmen liegt am Meer" [Bohemia lies beside the sea], with a line that runs "Bin ich's nicht, ist es einer, der ist so gut wie ich" [If it is not I, then it is one as good as me], or something like that.

As the project took shape, I turned to my revered friend Elfriede Jelinek, whom I knew from a wide variety of occasions, and asked her whether she would like to write the script. She did so and published it later in a book about the film. My love of Bachmann had brought me to the novel, and I was inspired by what I remembered about it. Elfriede, who had read it more closely than I had, added something in her own turn. And so there were three stages to the work: Ingeborg Bachmann's novel *Malina*, Elfriede Jelinek's screenplay, and finally my revision, in which I first rejected parts of the earlier versions and then incorporated them after all. In those three stages, we created something with a reality of its own.

The first question was the casting of the main role, the nameless woman who is a writer and loses herself in relation to two men, her desires, and her art. We discussed various possibilities. Thomas Kuchenreuther naturally had ideas of his own. Ultimately, we weren't happy with any of the actresses we had discussed. I remember that Kuchenreuther was strongly in favor of Aurore Clément, whom I knew very well from my time in Paris.

Then I remembered Isabelle Huppert. I didn't know her personally and had seen her only once. That was in 1980, when I was directing Alexander von Zemlinsky's opera after a story by Oscar Wilde, *A Florentine Tragedy*, at the La Fenice opera house in Venice. At the same time, Isabelle had been playing the lead role in the film *The Lady of the Camellias*, with Mauro Bolognini, which was being shot in Venice, and there was a party at the hotel. I happened to be crossing the lobby when this small figure ran past me and impressed me very much. I had no idea who she was. I had never seen her on the screen or in the theater, and I told her so, incidentally, only after the award of the German Film Prize for best actress, which she won for her performance in *Malina*. I had seen her passing me; that was all. But I told Thomas Kuchenreuther that I thought she would be good as the lead in *Malina*. After that we met, and one thing led to another.

It seemed to Thomas Kuchenreuther and me that Mathieu Carrière could play the strange, smooth, cold figure of Malina himself in the spirit of Bachmann, and so he was cast. I could visualize Isabelle in a physical relationship with the second male character. We came up with the idea of the Turkish Hungarian actor Can Togay, who plays Ivan. I am particularly fond of the scene of the children's birthday party, in which he appears, along with the birthday cake. He was very upset, in fact furious, because for a split second his prick was visible. A strange and very sensitive man, but all the same excellent at representing the sensuous principle. The other, more abrasive principle was admirably personified by Mathieu Carrière, cold and emanating a kind of antipathy. For the other roles, some of them very small, we used the best actors I knew from my work in the theater: Elisabeth Krejcir, Fritz Schediwy, Peter Kern, Libgart Schwarz, Isolde Barth, Wiebke Frost, and many other good actors.

We made the film in a studio building belonging to Bavaria Film Production in Munich and shot exterior scenes and some interiors on location in Vienna. Alberte designed the rooms in the apartment where much of the film is set with high ceilings, glazed windows, and mirrors, the final effect being a confusing ambience.

When I began surrounding the apartment with more and more flames at the end of the film, so that it would burn while the characters inside it went on acting as if nothing were wrong, there was a great fuss with the studio company. They were anxious to keep the buildings created for the set intact, even though they belonged to our production. But they were worth almost a million deutsche marks in themselves, and the prudent folk at Bavaria Film wanted to preserve them and reuse them for something else later. They argued that the roof would explode, and there would be dust all over the place—but no, we did exactly as we had planned in our original concept. I remember the firefighters sweating in the studio, because it was high summer with a temperature of thirty-one degrees outside—in the studio it was probably something like forty-eight degrees. Only Isabelle Huppert made her way through the flames without showing a drop of sweat, and Mathieu Carrière always stayed cold-blooded anyway.

Once, however, one of the camerawoman Elfi Mikesch's sneakers caught fire. My hair stood on end—and it got so dry and brittle in the heat that I could have broken it off. Since I hate all technically manipulated special effects, of course everything in *Malina* was for real, directly in front of the camera, no tricks, no dissolves, no double exposures, nothing computer generated. The flames shown on film were real. That is how the element of fire ought to be shown to make a strong impression; it was very important indeed in the novel. Two years after the opening of *Malina*, Ingeborg Bachmann herself died in a fire.

In this second collaboration of ours, after *The Rose King*, Elfi worked brilliantly with me again, with some unusual framing effects and following her own principle: "I want just one thing: light and shade." Isabelle mastered her role in her own way, reflecting the woman's inner conflict in her motionless face, creating a profile of her own, a transcendent Bachmann character.

Giacomo Manzoni, who was having a great success at La Scala with his opera *Fausto*, wrote a score especially for *Malina*. I went through the script with him scene by scene, discussing the music and the timing, before the shooting began. After that, however, I used only part of his huge score, preferring to add other and contrasting music, for instance, Claire Waldoff's song "Wer schmeisst denn da Lehm?" [Who's throwing mud?]. I was very happy with Manzoni's excellent music and with Jenny Drivala's wonderful arias.

I had used film music composed especially for a film only once before, in *Day of the Idiots*, but that score had been written by Peer Raben after the film was made.

I have always taken a great interest in fragmentary expression in artistic work, whether in music or painting, in films or literature. How could one have tried presenting everything in a "complete" linear narrative form when that didn't correspond to the intentions of the novel?

I regard *Malina* as a successful filmed version of a book because it does not cling to the original, like many films based on literature these days—for instance, the films of *Buddenbrooks* and *Effi Briest*. Because Ingeborg Bachmann's novel is so disunited, fragmentary, and strange in itself, it was very suitable as the basis for a new creation, if we respected the fact that, between us all—Ingeborg Bachmann, Elfriede Jelinek, I, and the camera team, as well as Juliane Lorenz with the montage—we were indeed producing something new. The literary and film critics reviewed it positively, and when the film itself, Isabelle Huppert, and many who had worked on it won awards at the German Film Prize ceremony, it was hailed as the beginning of a new era in the filming of literature, an era of adapting books freely, not just chugging along in the wake of the original.

I remember one review, by Georg Seesslen. I can't interpret my films myself; I can only describe why and how they came into being. But I entirely agree with what Seesslen said: "Film acts as a metaphor for the contradiction between 'art,' which is only a model for a way of dealing with the world, and 'life,' which happens to be only a medium in which the impulses of lust, work, and death are expressed. Elfriede Jelinek thinks that disappearance is the real task of a woman in love, and the woman in *Malina* lives through that disappearance, showing its terror and its pain. Her masculine soul, even when molded by submerged and withered desires, protests against it and at the same time promotes it."

In my own words, I would say that *Malina* is a metaphor applicable to any difficult human being. Longing for sensuality and a fulfilled life with someone else also means finding yourself through and with that other person, and I take that idea personally. Seesslen also quoted Roland Barthes, a passage from *Fragments d'un discours amoureux* [Fragments of a lover's discourse], in relation to *Malina*: "The Other appears where I expect him, where I have already created him, and if he does not, then I see a hallucination of him." What can I say about that? Very clever. Expectation is always the worst kind of self-betrayal and is always bound to be tragically disappointed. That is why liberty means living without expectation. I try to do that, but I do not always succeed.

My theatrical family

Over the course of the years, when I was involved for quite a long time with the Düsseldorf Theater under the management of Volker Canaris between 1986 and 1996, the theater developed into my real home and sometimes my extended family. I was not really used to regular work rather than single engagements at a theater, but then the Düsseldorf Theater became my family and my home. Indeed, I have no home apart from wherever I happen to be, and in myself, my thoughts, and my friendships.

We were a really strong group in Düsseldorf, and once you were part of it, it was difficult to extricate yourself. I was passionately in love with this family of mine, so I came to love the place itself. After a long time, I had an apartment of my own again at last. That was what Marcelo wanted. Although I love plants, I had never been able to have any while I was living in hotels or with friends. Only with Marcelo did I furnish our place with plants; it looked like a jungle. I didn't really think of Düsseldorf as a city at the time but as the place where we lived at the theater. I didn't mind it in the least that I was making so few films between 1986 and 1996, because the family I had found gave me all I wanted. We had some amazing times in Düsseldorf, getting up to all sorts of things. I always kept the troupe moving. We would sit all night in the empty Gustav-Gründgens Square outside the theater. We simply took the tables from the bar there out into the square, drank, and talked to one another. That became legendary, because we did it even in winter. Evidently I was in robust health. We shivered with cold, but we were cheerful, talking, dancing, and laughing. We were notorious—no, famous for it. However that may be, new projects kept coming up as well.

I let myself be inspired by the group and my own ideas, or else—although not so often—the ideas came from the theater management. The first play that I directed there with the core members of the company, including Elisabeth Krejcir, was Federico García Lorca's *Doña Rosita; or, The Language of Flowers*. I was delighted, because I liked Lorca, and the play offered a chance to begin working on his texts. Enrique Beck's German translation, unfortunately, had slipped down to the level of romantic kitsch. I improved it by going back closer to the original; I knew Spanish well after the time I had spent in Mexico and Argentina.

It was my opinion, and still is, that the theater should stimulate imagination and thought—that is to say, the soul and reason. But you can't be sure how effective what you are doing is. At the most, you can tell when people come back another time, and maybe when the conversation at first-night parties is not about the elegant clothes that the guests are wearing or the fact that the sparkling wine is not well enough chilled but about the play that the audience has just seen. If it arouses questions in their minds, if they discuss it, and that discussion adds a new imaginative factor, you can see the effect that the theater has on spectators. That was what we were trying to do in Düsseldorf.

In 1987 I discovered Yukio Mishima's *The Tropical Tree* for us. It is an excessive, indeed an extremist play, and Mishima himself was such an extremist that in 1970 he committed hara-kiri in front of the soldiers of the emperor of Japan, with the students whom he had made into his private army. Mishima thought highly of Marguerite Yourcenar, and she, in return, was a fan of Mishima's. I knew what she had written about him, and that was one of the points from which our production set out. The fascinating thing about it was that Mishima's play is an adaptation of the Electra myth inspired by the Japanese Noh theater. Isamuo is the Japanese version of Orestes, the girl Ikuko corresponds to Electra, their parents Ritsuko and Keisaburo are Clytemnestra and Aegisthus. At first we were working with a translation by Ursula Schuh, the wife of the director and theater manager Oskar Fritz Schuh, but the original had been smoothed out far too much. For instance, when Ikuko, the Electra character, tells her brother, "You must do it, you must kill her; is it not enough that we crawled out of her gray and slimy cunt, out of that mother, that terrible mother who can blot out even the stars in the sky with her shit?" the translation by Frau Schuh was distinctly anodyne, something along the lines of "It is very bad that we were born as children of a woman capable of such evil." If you want to read the play as Mishima intended it to be read, you must go to the translation that I did with the assistance of Carola Regnier. It has the archaic force of the extraordinarily powerful dramatic work that it is.

Yet again I was working with the actors in the group. Elisabeth Krejcir, one of my regulars for over thirty years, and Peter Kern were the malign parents, Arpad Kraupa and Karina Fallenstein played the rebellious siblings. Our production won a prize at the World Theater Festival in Quebec, and so did our production of *Medea* a year later. I didn't go over to Canada for these occasions because I was already working on the next play. Unfortunately, there were often four productions a year, but as with everything I did, I regarded that as an organic process.

When I began on the rehearsals, of course I had a concept. I always knew what I wanted. But then I usually threw it out, just as I did when I was making films. To me the moment, the here and now, is the most important thing in life, and I always worked with the inspiration of the moment, with intuition. Onstage and in the cinema alike, you have to jettison plans that you have already made because you must let the actors surprise you at the moment when something new happens. If you aren't open to that idea, then live theater becomes boring and a film is just any old bureaucratic movie. That is unfair to the actors. I go along with Jean Cocteau's felicitous demand, "Étonnez-moi!" [Surprise me!]. At times, remarkable works of art can result from the surprise produced by the actors or, vice versa, from my own surprise.

A year before *The Tropical Tree*, standing in as an emergency doctor, so to speak, I took on a Düsseldorf production of Rainer Werner Fassbinder's *Katzelmacher* [Foreigners] that had fallen apart. With the fine actors I had available, I rescued it. It was enjoyable because we all communicated with each other so well. Such events in live theater are human and possible, and thus necessary, and with this particular production it was very clear that it had come into being without any quarrels or misunderstandings. I had told the theatrical manager Herr Canaris that I would tackle the production only if the previous director, Annette Rosenfeld (who, sad to say, is dead now), and her literary adviser agreed.

It quite often happens, as it did on this occasion, that a production is in a state of crisis after five weeks of rehearsal, as a result of anxiety or overzealousness. I call the feeling that you must make sure everything is absolutely perfect "fulfillment mania." It always reminds me of the children's book claiming that "there must be more to life." If one doesn't go about directing the play openly and patiently, the strain often shows. This little play by Fassbinder had been so overloaded that it lost its charm. We changed that, and then there was a tremendous fuss because one of the characters took a piss onstage, which was a really good effect. I still remember that one review was captioned "Dark Beer and Urine." Fassbinder depicted two harmless idiots, a couple of Bavarian neo-Nazis, to very good effect. When they get drunk, they pee in the corner, roll about in it, and say, "Oh, so warm and comfortable, like being in a U-boat." There was a tremendous fuss. The makeup artists were told to get the two actors well tanked up before the performance, one with herbal tea, the other with light beer, and then, when they were on the stage and that point in the play arrived, they couldn't help taking a leak. After the performance, the actors and I mopped it all up again. But that was against labor union rules, so a cleaning lady was hired to wipe up after them. That's what I mean about the fuss. In short, the production of *Katzelmacher*, complete with dark beer and urine, worked very well. It ran and ran and was a great success.

In general, the stage plays that I directed contrasted well with each other. In the same year as we staged Mishima's cruel play *The Tropical Tree*, we also put on Marcelo's tango evening, *Grief, Longing, Rebellion*; and the year after that, Maxim Gorky's *Children of the Sun*.

Shakespeare's *King Lear* in the spring of 1990 was produced especially for Volker Canaris. He was set on having Hermann Lause as Lear and me as director. Right, I said, we'll do it. Oh, my word!

Things went very far. Someone told me recently that in 2005 Jürgen Gosch's production of *Macbeth* was suggested by my *King Lear* in Düsseldorf, with all the violence to be found in Shakespeare's play.

The Düsseldorf *Lear* in 1990, with Hermann Lause in the title role, Eva Schuckardt, Christiane Lemm, and Elisabeth Krejcir as Goneril, Regan, and Cordelia, and Peter Kern as Gloucester, featured blood, sex, and violence and was so provocative that it created a shocking sensation at the première. For the first three-quarters of an hour there was total silence; you could have heard a pin drop. Then all hell broke loose, with the audience shouting, "Stop the show! Bastards!" and so forth. It was truly bizarre. Curiously enough, the moment in my production when King Lear begins to rape his daughters set off no audible reaction at the première. Hermann Lause crept under the skirt of Goneril, played by Eva Schuckardt, who had no underwear on, seemed to be nibbling her cunt, and came out again with pubic hair clinging to his mouth. But only when Lear made homosexual advances to the faithful Kent and grabbed his flies did they start shouting. Typical! The evening spent acting this wide-ranging, wise, and provocative play became a battle for survival so far as the actors were concerned. I encouraged them during the interval, and then, after the performance was over, Hermann Lause, in a state of total confusion, went to take his bow alone amid a storm of booing. I went over to him and led him off.

The scandal went as far as the Düsseldorf state congress. The Christian Democrats organized a witch-hunt against the actors, claiming they had been raped onstage and, furthermore, seemed to be enjoying it. There was a large press conference with members of congress, the actors, and me, recorded by West German Radio in its large studio. The actors dealt with it all very sensibly. At the time, Peter Kern said it was being insinuated that they were stupid, but in fact, Werner Schroeter was creating the production together with his actors, and everything had been agreed. The German press was foaming at the mouth, with the exception of a good review in the *Süddeutsche Zeitung*, which understood my view of the play. Finally, the Shakespeare Society in London commented, saying that they thought my production came very close to the reality of the play. *King Lear* became a cult production in Düsseldorf, and after the première audiences paid very close attention to it. Sad to say, however, it closed too soon, because Peter Kern or Hermann Lause, for some reason that I no longer remember, either didn't want to or couldn't go on appearing in it, and I didn't feel like recasting their roles.

Where words end, music begins

In the nineties, after the deaths of my friends, my father, and my brother, I looked around for a work that would address my feelings and my existential questions directly. I was thinking of Aeschylus's tragedy *The Persians* and Molière's comedy *The Misanthrope*, but I found that I was drawn more intensively to music than to either of them. I always enjoyed working with music, which had an incredibly therapeutic effect on my head and my heart. An old project came back to my mind, taking me back to my roots and enabling me to express loss and fear without any sentimentality.

It was the idea for a film that I had originally intended for Maria Callas. When I met her, she was profoundly unhappy. I wanted the two of us to explore the question of how love, longing, and pain left their mark on her expression of music, how her art emerged from her emotions. She once wrote to me on a postcard, "Dove finiscono le parole incomincia la mùsica, come ha detto il vostro grande poeta E. T. A. Hoffmann" [Where words end, music begins, as your great poet E. T. A. Hoffmann said]. Maybe Maria Callas was cautiously setting out on the way to herself at that time, but she died before I could put the idea for the film to her. So the project had been on the back burner for a long time.

In the following decades, Maria Callas remained for me both divine messenger and *prima donna assoluta*. Yet the more intensive my own theatrical work became, the less often I listened to her music. She and other great divas had been shining stars in my youth, and when I revived my project in 1995—now a project of a different nature, more in tune with modern times, with spontaneity and improvisation—I approached three great singers of the past: Martha Mödl, Anita Cerquetti, and Rita Gorr.

Poussières d'amour [Love's debris] was not planned from the first as a fully staged concert. On principle, I never touched conventional adaptations of concerts and operas. I hate filmed opera. So I felt it increasingly annoying to be described in Germany as "operatic." In the course of my forty years of work as a director, I had been overwhelmingly concerned with the spoken word onstage in live theater, and my operatic productions made up only a small part of my output. I thought of myself more as a musical director than an operatic director, with all the pomp and circumstance of that genre. My great love for music often had me working with singers on a reduction of effects. The soprano Montserrat Caballé once told me the secret of the way she worked—"I simply burn the stage"—but that attitude was the very reason I didn't think highly of her. I was more interested in a way of approaching the work that could sometimes be a release for the director: singers who had mastered their scores— that is to say, the music they were to sing—could often be more expressive than many straight actors because of the confidence that the musical score gave them.

The concept of something operatic, properly understood, is a great quality. The melodrama as Claudio Monteverdi and Jacopo Peri wrote it is a "complete" artistic invention, a total artwork comprising the stage set and costumes, orchestral music, song and dance. In it, the language used is cleansed of banality and raised to transparent, transfigural spheres. So if it was said of me that I was going to breathe new life into that total form of art, I valued the "operatic" attribute, but personally I took it as more of an insult than anything else, as if everything that I did was kitschy and highly colored.

Alexander Kluge, the writer and director, who loves poetry and music, which is a rarity among German filmmakers, was one of the few to understand what I was doing. His remark that opera is a "power plant of the feelings" went back to an idea of mine. It is a good expression for something precious in a country where the dissolution of feelings, as in the geological formation of karst, is regarded as progress toward greater profitability. My project for *Love's*

187

Debris was to center on the origin of the art of song but also on the question of how art can transcend death. In my youth, I had imagined suicide as a form of *Liebestod* and a self-confident step to take. That was just youthful pretension, of course, but beyond that, the power of art, playing around those frontiers, had always fascinated me. Even in adolescence, when I thought of myself as an artist in dying, I had never really been in danger of killing myself; the poetry of death always offered a glimmer of hope.

When you are directing films, stage plays, and operas, you let the here and now of the actors' presence capture you, and you wring form out of the transience of the moment. I had been magically attracted by that evanescence all my life, for the very reason that it represented permanent friction with the finality and transient nature of humanity. For forty years, I had made the great mistake of failing to distinguish between life and expression in my work, and so it was a matter of existential urgency to me to think that death can appear to be fooled, at least onstage. Jean Cocteau once said that filmmaking enabled you to watch death at work. I thought, on the other hand, that you can rehearse for it in films and onstage; you can direct and replay it. Art can stop time and play a melancholy game with the return of life. As long as you are siting in the cinema, the theater, the opera house, you are alive. Why else is the singing in operas so particularly beautiful when it is about death?

Playing the fool with our proximity to death or our distance from it was always a point on which my work touched, hence the line "Life is so precious . . . even right now!" when the dead eyes in *Eika Katappa* keep opening again and Christine Kaufmann's deranged claim "No one really dies! No one really dies!" in *Day of the Idiots*. Such a revolt against death, such a fine impulse in spite of the certainty that at heart nothing can change its power, is magically present in music, especially in the great operas. In them, paradoxically, death merges with a vitality and harmony that never really existed and never will but that all the same is comfortingly close.

In Giuseppe Verdi's operas, for instance, there are neither pitiful nor beautiful deaths, but there is a reality between beauty and pain on which it all depends. Maria Callas played Violetta's death scene in *La traviata* crying out, "I am alive, I feel new strength returning," before falling dead. That idea meant a lot to me, because it represents death as a kind of radiant light in a tunnel.

Love's Debris was to convey that consoling sense. I wanted to make a film about people who were professional singers pursuing a musical career and in it ask them about the vital origins of their work. The fact that they were all ready to respond to a phone call and to come and talk with full confidence in me showed how well we communicated. The film was based on that and on my plan to have no academically harsh tensions.

Martha Mödl, Anita Cerquetti, and Rita Gorr had already illuminated my youth with their art. With them, and younger singers such as Sergej Larin, Laurence Dale, Trudeliese Schmidt, Jenny Drivala, Gail Gilmore, Kristine and Katherine Ciesinski, with all of whom I had been friends in many long years of work, we found the subject that we would pursue in the short time of the eleven days it took to shoot the film.

I asked each artist to bring his or her partner, lover, or family for three days, work with me and the pianist Elizabeth Cooper, and be ready to talk in front of the camera. I asked them all about the meaning of love, passion, and death in their lives. It wasn't a case of formulating answers but of raising questions and discussing ideas. All the same, some of them were very sure what they wanted to say: the tenor Sergej Larin thought that God revealed himself in music; the soprano Kristine Ciesinski said, amused, that she sings with her ovaries—she says she has ten of them. Music as love's debris meant the fine dust that comes of life as it grinds us down, leading to entirely new structures. And in this way, casually, we succeeded in making a film about the culture of music and singing, language and communication.

The dramatic soprano Martha Mödl, later a mezzo-soprano, was one of the greatest German prima donnas of the postwar period, connected for many years with the German Opera on the Rhine in Düsseldorf and the operas of Wagner at the Bayreuth Festival, and she also had a great interest in new music. At the suggestion of the composer and conductor Eberhard Kloke, I had directed her in Bernd Alois Zimmermann's *Ecclesiastical Action* in 1992 at the Düsseldorf Theater, and in working with her I came to love the wisdom of her advancing age. She didn't want to know where her strength and her voice came from; she liked to say that in the old days, under the conductor Wilhelm Furtwängler, it was thought fair enough not to be entirely perfect. Martha sang with wonderfully unsentimental melancholy in *Love's Debris*, performing the Countess's aria of reminiscence in Tchaikovsky's *The Queen of Spades*, "Je crains de lui parler la nuit," her great role, which she was still performing onstage until shortly before her death in 2001.

We had mounted a major search for the Italian soprano Anita Cerquetti, the most ecstatic singer among my guests, and we did indeed find her in Italy. Until her retirement in 1960, Cerquetti had been one of the outstanding rivals of Maria Callas. She began her career at the age of nineteen but retired twelve years later after suffering a kind of stroke because of the permanent strain she was under. She could no longer sing, and yet singing had meant more to her than her private family life. That attitude, too, stands for the search for fulfillment and unity that we were presenting in *Love's Debris*.

Anita Cerquetti arrived with her whole family, the most important people in her life. But we couldn't refrain from including some amusing background disasters—for instance, when Anita's spoilt, grown-up daughter, who had never become independent, talked on and on, to her mother's annoyance. All the same, Anita loved her dearly. So the touching finale of the film was reserved for the great Anita Cerquetti, who seems to be singing once again, in playback, the aria *Casta diva* as she sang it in her prime.

I had also met the Belgian mezzo-soprano Rita Gorr in the 1950s, when she was a young Wagnerian singer, and I thought highly of her because of her dramatic volume of expression. Rita Gorr's repertoire of French song had something extraordinary about it, a sense of drama that I described as the inner and outer manifestations of the *tragédie française*. I asked her to sing an aria from *The Queen of Spades* in our film, one that Martha Mödl also sang, so as to show their two very distinctive voices.

Carole Bouquet and Isabelle Huppert, who were both interested in music and singing and always took an interest in my work as well, visited us during the shooting, and on the spur of the moment I invited them to join in. "Just come along, that's all," I told my friend

Isabelle. I knew that she loved singing. Carole Bouquet also proved a good friend by talking to Anita Cerquetti. Isabelle Huppert was very close to Martha Mödl in her musical sensitivity. Martha talked to her, without understanding a word of Isabelle's French, and I interpreted. "I can tell from the way Isabelle talks," said Martha, "that she is musical and has a real relationship with music."

What all the participants said about their personal lives depended on their family situations and the trusting, frank atmosphere. I let them surprise me. For instance, I knew Sergej Larin from our wonderful work together on *Luise Miller* in Amsterdam and *The Lady Macbeth of Mtsensk* in Frankfurt, as well as other operatic productions. I knew that he was married, lived in Bratislava, and usually traveled with his wife and family. But he turned up for our film with a shy young man, an Italian, who was his lover; no one had known about it. So his story was both a private and a public coming-out. I directed that part of the film in the same lyrical and poetic spirit, by showing a naked youth on horseback galloping through the great hall like an image from classical antiquity.

Elfi Mikesch was behind the 35 mm camera, as she had been in *Malina*. All the participants reacted in their own way to such situations, and together we created a poetic space that was enlivened now and then by our ironic glances. We found the right place for the scene of the musical banquet in the former Royaumont Abbey in Paris, a wonderfully compact thirteenth-century building that now accommodates a music college.

Yet again, this Franco-German film had only a small budget, and thrift encouraged our creativity. There were only eleven days available for us to shoot the film, and we had to make do with very brief rehearsals. Elfi Mikesch relied on spontaneous improvisation even more than in *The Rose King* and *Malina*, without ever impairing the aesthetic quality of the lighting and the framing. She captured the magic of the situation wonderfully well, and I often hardly felt that she was there, except when we exchanged glances. We had known each other ever since I began making films, and the fact that we could work together almost without words was the greatest compliment we paid one another. An atmosphere was established in which the camera followed the movement of the singers' breathing and their voices. The arias being rehearsed and then performed permeated their personal stories; music appeared as a part of life, just as I always wanted it to be. The artists felt liberated from any routine, something new could happen at any moment, and we would all go along with it. Singing a duet on the stairs of the abbey, my friends Kristine and Katherine Ciesinski were almost hit by a picture falling off the wall but went on singing with composure after the first moment of alarm, without any interruption.

Nothing was farther from our minds than any idea of making a dusty, old-fashioned film about opera. Reality had to find a way in. Elfi and I looked for pictures of interiors, architecture, and landscapes matching the inner quality of the singers' encounters, thus creating a second, contrapuntal plane. When Gail Gilmore sings a passage from Hector Berlioz's cantata *La mort de Cléopâtre* [The death of Cleopatra], in which the queen, about to commit suicide, sings of her fear that the gods will not commemorate her life with an honorable grave, the camera glides over panes of glass let into the ground. Looking through them, the viewer catches wonderful glimpses of a brook flowing beneath the glass, although in fact it is there only to cover the holes of the former monastic WC. This practical medieval arrangement really did have a poetic beauty that has been entirely eradicated from the modern surroundings of our chosen setting, particularly in the sordid suburbs of Paris.

We wanted that brutal reality to blow through our production like a biting wind, preserving the music from pathos, raising it above bland continuity, and opening viewers' eyes. Accordingly, Elfi and I sought out pictures of cold, unattractive buildings, squares, cemeteries, and highways expressing no humanity in Paris, even though we couldn't afford permits to film them. With a 16 mm camera under her arm, and without any exposure meter, Elfi smuggled herself into the elevator of the Eiffel Tower, and she actually did take a picture, although she was caught in the act of replaying it by an inspector. She pretended not to understand the language, but when he reacted with a simple *nyet* there was nothing to be done. In view of the many improvisations, we ended up with remarkably little material; it occupied about four hours, and my cutter Juliane Lorenz and I put them together into the finished film, working together for many weeks without any preordained plan.

When I see *Love's Debris* today, the film still seems magically present in my mind, although Sergej Larin, Trudeliese Schmidt, Martha Mödl, and Anita Cerquetti's husband left us many years ago. In the film they all, courageously, said they did not fear death. I was aware that the question concerned me very closely in my personal situation and my grief. I thought it neither too banal nor too intimate or obsessive, but intimate and obsessive at once, and therefore existentially important.

The Queen

When she was ninety years old, Marianne Hoppe once said to me that an artist who has left his childhood far behind him is no true artist and will never be one. She was absolutely right. That is why fairy tales are so important. We need to understand what they say about the soul and drawing on the soul. A child takes in everything, looks at everything, and on beginning to draw, maybe first on a slate or with a pencil, suddenly feels the urge to add color. The child hums while drawing, makes up little tunes, and then suddenly feels like making a hat, using whatever easily comes to hand. So in childhood we are absorbing everything, doing something creative with it, and soon we have a total work of art to play with. That freedom with the reality of ideas is what enables the child to master artistic design. For me, childhood itself is a total work of art in the sense that Marianne Hoppe meant.

When I was twelve years old, the Vienna Burgtheater brought a play by Eugene O'Neill on tour to Bielefeld, where we were living: *A Touch of the Poet*, with Paula Wessely, Attila Hörbiger, and Marianne Hoppe. It was terrible. I allow myself to say so, because it was so bad that even as a twelve-year-old I noticed. It was also one of my first experiences of the live theater. Such a tearjerker, as Wessely played it, and the booming, trombone-like voice of Attila Hörbiger! And then Deborah, the woman from the leading man Melody's past, came on. She was played by Marianne Hoppe in white with a white sunshade, moving from upstage right to downstage left. I sat there transfixed by what I saw. After that I tried to get her autograph. I think I even pinched her arm to see whether she was real and what would happen.

Then we had nothing to do with each other for a long time. Not until 1992 was I able to engage her as Martha Mödl's understudy in Bernd Alois Zimmermann's *Ecclesiastical Action*. We were to take that Düsseldorf Theater production on tour to Los Angeles, but Martha, who was afraid of flying, didn't want to go. So I sought out Marianne Hoppe in Berlin. She was living at the Academy of Arts on Hanseatenweg, where artists who were members could rent rooms for a short time—a very sensible idea, incidentally. I visited and offered her Martha Mödl's role.

It was a musical work by Bernd Alois Zimmermann, an enormous German composition. "I turned and saw all the injustice under the sun—Ecclesiastical Action." It consists of a dialog between the Grand Inquisitor and Christ, adapted from the Bible and *The Brothers Karamazov*. Zimmermann's philosophy of time fascinated me; his idea was that the passing of time does not really exist in our intellectuality, which basically is more real than time marked by the clock. Martha Mödl was playing the Grand Inquisitor in *Ecclesiastical Action*, and I needed someone musical enough to take the part in Los Angeles instead of her. "Well, my boy," said Marianne promptly, "what my young colleague can do, I can do too." She was eighty-three; Martha was eighty.

So we set to work. It went very well—and was quite different from the interpretation of the part by Martha Mödl, a gentle and incredibly kindly woman. Marianne Hoppe was also delightful, but she seemed to other people stern, and they were afraid of her. To me, however, she was always a dear friend.

Later, in our film about Marianne, Martin Wuttke said she had always played the grande dame and made him feel that he came from the industrial Ruhr valley. Be that as it may, she didn't have the same effect on me. We often met. I saw her in Heiner Müller's play *Quartet* and in Robert Wilson's production of *King Lear*. Then, in 1996/97, we made *Monsieur Verdoux*, after Charlie Chaplin's film, together at the Berlin Ensemble. She appeared with Martin Wuttke, Anna Thalbach, Zazie de Paris, and others. At the age of eighty-eight, Marianne was the oldest-ever bride of the wife-murderer Verdoux—only a small part, but she carried it off magnificently. Benjamin Henreich tore my production to shreds in *Die Zeit*, but he was fascinated by the way Marianne played her part. "Despair sends the soul to sleep"—I still remember that line. An increasingly close friendship developed between us at about the time of *Monsieur Verdoux*, and I often went out and about with her.

I visited her in her horrible senior citizens' care home in Berlin, where she was very unhappy, and I often took her to gay bars. At first she said, "This won't do; they'll be scared of me." But we found it amusing, and she enjoyed herself very much.

Ultimately, we decided to make a film about her while she could still participate, because at the age of ninety her memory was gradually failing her. With Monika Keppler, I wrote the screenplay and drew up a design for the production team and the TV stations that were also involved. Unfortunately, the production company went broke, and *The Queen* is hardly ever screened these days.

We took Marianne to Felsenhagen in the Prignitz district and the former country estate that she had loved so much as a child, before she left home to become an actress. In the studio, Judith Engel and Maren Eggert played scenes with her—it was all very concentrated, just as we had rehearsed it.

Marianne Hoppe didn't let the Nazis and Goebbels force her into anything. Whatever her propaganda function and the dubious power of Gustaf Gründgens meant in the enhancement of the appalling Nazi regime, it was my opinion that with her work and her life after the war, Marianne had atoned for it. When I presented our film *The Queen* together with her, she said, "Marianne Hoppe and Werner Schroeter, that engaged couple, welcome you! It's a terrible film, terrible!" But in fact she liked it very much.

Enough breath for my life

The Düsseldorf Theater, under Volker Canaris, made many things possible for me. And audiences were enthusiastic too. They always reacted strongly, and as I see it, that's the essential point in the theater. Being praised has never really interested me for its own sake. Just under six weeks after *King Lear*, in 1990, we put on Beethoven's *Missa solemnis*—"from the heart may it go further to the heart." As we produced this staged concert performance, it seemed so right for the theater that it was a joy. It began with the members of the orchestra going through the theater, and there was singing in the foyer. Biblical texts lured the audience into the auditorium. At a certain point I leaped up, crying, "Endless happiness!" in the middle of the pause between two of Beethoven's movements. The *Missa solemnis* was acclaimed as a triumph, but I was just as pleased with our controversial productions as those that went down well. These works left no one indifferent, and that is what matters, nothing else.

While I was at Düsseldorf I also directed works at other theaters and opera houses. The theater almost consumed me. I worked on several projects at the same time, directing more and more productions. That meant that I directed three or four major, demanding works within a year. For instance, in 1986, in between Georg Büchner's *Leonce und Lena* in Bremen and Lorca's *Doña Rosita* in Düsseldorf, I also directed the splendid Mexican première of Richard Strauss's opera *Salome* in Mexico City. I directed August Strindberg's *Intoxication*, Samuel Beckett's *Breath*, and Schiller's *Don Carlos* in Bremen, all with one of my favorite actresses, Traute Hoess. Monika Keppler, drama adviser in Bremen, worked with me on the text of *Don Carlos*, using Schiller's verse of 1805 as our basis, and when she moved to the management team of the Cologne Theater, I also directed works there at the same time as fulfilling my Düsseldorf commitments. And I directed operas in Italian houses and elsewhere: in 1987 Gaetano Donizetti's *Lucia di Lammermoor* in Livorno, with Jenny Drivala (who also played the part of an opera singer in *Malina*), as well as Luigi Cherubini's *Medea* in Freiburg, and then back to Mexico City to direct a fine production, together with Kristine Ciesinski. The following year I directed Tommaso Traetta's *Antigone* in Spoleto and Gaetano Donizetti's *Parisina d'Este* in Basel. In 1991 there was Giuseppe Verdi's *Luisa Miller* in Amsterdam, not forgetting Shostakovich's *Lady Macbeth of Mtsensk* at Frankfurt Opera, Jules Massenet's *Werther* in Bonn, and above all Puccini's *Tosca* at the Opéra nationale de Paris—a production that remained in the repertory until the summer of 2009.

But mainly I alternated between Düsseldorf and Cologne—to such an extent that at one point I was working in the mornings on a Cologne production of Eugène Labiche's *Le Prix Martin*, in a wonderful German translation by H. C. Artmann, again with Traute Hoess in the cast, and in the afternoons in Düsseldorf on Arnold Schönberg's oratorio *Jacob's Ladder*, in a double bill with Bernd Alois Zimmermann's *Ecclesiastical Action*. This was a production for the Düsseldorf Theater, with the Bochum Symphony Orchestra, soloists and all. Those taking part included Martha Mödl, Jens Berthold, Marcelo Uriona, Eva Schuckardt, many opera singers, and Eberhard Kloke as conductor. After that we were invited to take it to Los Angeles, where Marianne Hoppe stood in for Martha Mödl. It was a wonderful time! Both the rehearsal stages, in Düsseldorf and in Cologne for *Le Prix Martin*, were always very hot. But I relished the contrast between Schönberg and his tragic themes, on the one hand, and the frivolity of Eugène Labiche, on the other. I am sure that intriguing contrast was one of the reasons why both productions turned out so well.

There were many more productions too. In Cologne I also directed Jean Genet's *Haute surveillance* and Jakob Michael Reinhold Lenz's *Die Soldaten*, a play that I liked very much. My work in the theater went on uninterrupted—how could I have squeezed films into my timetable? For many years my work in the cinema simply lapsed, and life as a theatrical director also guaranteed me the kind of income that had never been possible while I was also making films.

Furthermore, the parallel programs of the two cities where I mainly worked were practical, and the conditions comfortable. The Cologne Theater had rented a small apartment for me, so that I went to Düsseldorf only for rehearsals or to visit Marcelo in hospital at the weekend. I couldn't complain. Once again, the situation was the result of an organic development, although naturally a driving force was at work, for if I felt I *had* to express something, then I sought out the place and the means to do it.

Yet it was also a terrible time, for in 1994 my brother was with me in Düsseldorf, and he was dying. He had arrived a few days before the première of *Ecclesiastical Action* and stayed for a long time. Weeks later, my cousin Gina took him back to Bavaria, and he died not long afterward. I had known Hans-Jürgen was sick since the spring, when I was told the day before my father's funeral. I saw my brother again and noticed how thin and frail he seemed. I told him he was looking good—handsome, not so massive. It was because he had cancer, only I didn't know that.

I simply went on working, for instance, on Jakob Michael Reinhold Lenz's comedy *Der neue Menoza* [The new Menoza], a cryptic comedy of errors set in Naumburg an der Saale and Spain. And in 1996 I directed *Divinas palabras* [Wonderful words] by Ramón María del Valle-Inclán, the great subversive Spanish author of the turn of the century—another play too seldom seen in Germany and one that I had had on my mind for some time. It is a picture of world pandemonium, not far from Hieronymus Bosch and quite close to the Spanish military dictator Franco. We staged this wonderful play, with the universal truths it expresses, as a crazed circus story. It can be seen as a confrontation with Franco, who had been dead for twenty years in 1996 when we put on *Divinas palabras*. Valle-Inclán's *Luces de Bohemia* [The glory of Bohemia] is another strange play for German audiences—all the more reason to produce it. Its lust for life, vitality, and sensuality, finding beauty even in wretchedness, are my own themes too. It draws its imaginative force from standing by itself, even in its brutal attitude to itself and others.

The Düsseldorf Theater even offered me the post of artistic director. They had already furnished an office for me, with all the appropriate copies of plays and other things necessary, but I hesitated. I asked the people who were really fond of me whether I should accept or not. They advised me not to, and they were right. I could never have dealt with such a job. Before making a final decision, I tested myself on what it would mean to be meddling with the work of other directors. I thought that one production in preparation for Düsseldorf was so much on the wrong track that I asked its director whether he had a little time to talk to me. I told him very moderately and quietly about my reservations and saw the horror with which he took it; he was rigid with shock. At that moment I realized that I didn't want to be artistic director. I had no liking for such conflicts or for wielding power. It wouldn't have given me any pleasure, and so it would have impaired my quality of life. Work *must* be a pleasure, or there's no point in it. I decided that telling others what to do and insisting on changes was not in my line.

In addition, I wouldn't have had enough breath left for my own life, my friendships, and the sense of community that was so important to me. Until now I had been in the same boat as everyone else, and that feeling would have suffered if I had become artistic director, quite apart from all the time it would have taken. I preferred to be together with other theater people, talking and getting ideas. I myself needed no set of rules from an artistic policy interposed between me and my work, because on the whole the theater went along with what I wanted, and I got almost everything I asked for.

A new management team took over at the Düsseldorf Theater in 1996, and I did not get along with it. It was no longer right for me to go on working there.

All that life devours

The last twenty-five years was really a very productive time for me. Even before the end of my era at the Düsseldorf Theater, I had been directing works for many other houses, and after I ended my personal association with the theater in Düsseldorf, the new manager kept a long list of my productions in the repertory—including some regarded as failures.

For instance, after I had directed a very successful production of *Tosca* for the Opéra Bastille in Paris, and *The New Menoza* in Düsseldorf, they were followed up by Aeschylus's *The Persians* for the

Cologne Theater. I failed with that one, although I have to add that I have never seen a successful production of *The Persians* onstage.

It was an unhappy situation, because I had originally planned to direct *Antigone*, in Hölderlin's translation, in Cologne with my dear friend the Austrian actress Almut Zilcher, but she was unable to make it. Günter Krämer, general manager at the Cologne Theater, still insisted on a work from classical antiquity, even though *Antigone* had fallen through, so I had stupidly agreed to his suggestion of *The Persians*. The problem was the speeches of the Chorus; nothing can be done with them in German. They usually sound terrible in the German language, and of a hundred directors trying to make something of them, maybe one will succeed. Einar Schleef is the only director I know who could work with them, and even in his production the conquerors and the conquered occupied the foreground. That is what I never liked about the choruses of classical plays in German. In productions directed by my friend and colleague Dimiter Gotscheff, the actors perform them in groups of two or three. I liked that, but with *The Persians* I had to get twenty actors involved.

This failure was followed in the same year by Molière's *The Misanthrope* at the Hamburg Theater, but I did not find the subject congenial enough. Misanthropy has never been a theme to interest me, but Frank Bambauer, general manager at Hamburg, insisted on the play, and so although it had a good cast, it was only a mediocre production. I had to immerse myself in something that did not really appeal to me. Today I would prefer to turn down commissions unless the proposition strikes a spark in me, and I really want to direct a play.

In that year of 1995 I thought, after *The Misanthrope*, this won't do, I can't have failure after failure. Then I had a lucky break: I got to direct Beethoven's *Fidelio* for the Darmstadt State Theater, whose general music director was Marc Albrecht, a production paired with Luigi Nono's *Intolleranza*. It was a coproduction with the Strasbourg Music Festival for New Music, and at last I had a success again. Then, because I hadn't given up, those were followed in the fall by my film *Love's Debris*, four years after I had made *Malina*.

The fact was that if I couldn't really relate to a play or an opera, that work held no interest for me. I never saw myself as a sausage factory constantly churning out sausages. It was just unfortunate that because of my urge to creativity, and because I had to keep on earning money, I kept having to begin all over again, and that made me accept many other commissions. Not that it was anything unusual in the kind of life I led. Living the high life meant that I had to earn plenty of money; life devours a lot of it, and I always had people around me who were earning less or nothing at all. So I paid, and that was a wonderful feeling so long as it worked.

Later, I did make an exception for a few commissions to direct works that I did not particularly care for. For example, Giacomo Puccini's *Madama Butterfly* was one of the operas that said nothing much to me, until I really came to know it better in 2002. Getting close to it, I suddenly saw what a brilliant opera it is. The production was a very good one, with Karine Babajanyan, a wonderful Armenian soprano who worked in Stuttgart later. But it was staged in Bielefeld, of all places, a city I did not like at all. I had been invited there too, as guest director, and I greatly enjoyed the wonderful collaboration with my assistant Birgit Kronshage, whom we were able to engage again in 2005 for the Bielefeld production of *Don Carlos*.

When a collaboration was as good as mine with Birgit Kronshage, I always tried to keep it going, and I was able to maintain that with a small group of colleagues, varying according to whether I was working on a theatrical, operatic, or cinematic project.

At the time, the organic development of my life and work, something that is very important to me, seemed to arise from a fateful combination of tragedies. The deaths of friends and family began with Marcelo's. He died in January 1993, then Arpad, then my father, then Jens, then my brother. All three of my friends were working at the Düsseldorf Theater, Marcelo ever since I had been there myself, Arpad arriving a little later, and the same was true of Jens, a wild, imposing, handsome man, who had played Prince Gonzaga in our *Emilia Galotti* and the villainous Edmund in *King Lear*.

Even before we met, Arpad Kraupa had learned that he was sick. I knew all along, at least after the middle of the eighties. Of those three friends of mine, Jens Berthold was the last to die, in the fall of 1994. Homophobia was rife then, as was only to be expected. It is still much stronger than anyone likes to admit but is more inclined to stay underground because it is no longer politically correct. At the time, however, it was clear to us that something of that reactionary nature would be washed up in the wake of AIDS. I wouldn't say that what I felt was shock exactly, but I was aware of the situation as a problem to be solved and a heavy burden to bear.

My own relationships with my friends never changed, and yet I was never infected. There are all manner of theories and hypotheses for that phenomenon. Many who are infected have had anonymous sex, a purely carnal desire for a fling with someone else, a man whose name they don't know and whose face they hardly see. The encounter takes place surreptitiously, in a dark room, a toilet, a pickup spot, and so forth. But I went to bed only with people I was fond of, whose minds, names, and presence were all close to my heart. I could call them by their names, and they meant a great deal to me. I never had protected sex either, although I wouldn't recommend that to anyone. One ought to wear protection.

It would be nonsense to ask me, "How have you managed to do so much in your life, Herr Schroeter? Starting from nothing, and with no education!" I can only say that I can't be taken as any criterion. You do what you have to do; you must follow your own path. If one sees connections in everything, then it is clear that, fundamentally, that time in Düsseldorf came to an end when my friends were all dead.

The last love, friendship

Isabelle Huppert and I have been great friends ever since *Malina*. Even after work on that film was over, we remained close and regarded our friendship as a great gift. Isabelle is very intuitive and has a calm center, a harmonious strength, that she has worked to find for herself, making it her own by dint of experience. Since we felt deeply for one another's lives, it was only natural for us to keep coming up with joint ideas.

In working on *Malina* I had already found that I could go further with Isabelle than anyone else, because she courageously and confidently embarked on our friendship. She was like a blank canvas on which I could paint. I asked her to shed tears more often than any other actress. Tears are a natural expression of her nature, a product of her body, emotional but not sentimental. She has great clarity of mind, but she can also depict the most complex ideas and feelings. I admired her stage presence when she delivered the two-hour monolog from Sarah Kane's *4.48 Psychosis* at the Théâtre de l'odéon in Paris. When Isabelle saw how far she could go, she was always glad, because she gained from it herself.

We could go through life through thick and thin, achieving something special and precious in our work. Our dream project was a film in which Isabelle was to play King Frederick the Great of Prussia in his youth, up to his coronation. But the mere idea of this great actress taking the role of a young king between the ages of fourteen and twenty-one seemed all wrong to people who thought in naturalistic terms, and they controlled the finances. My argument that naturalism has nothing to do with the cinema or the theater did no good. We could never scrape up the money for that wonderfully strange project.

Then, in January 2001, Paulo Branco surprisingly came to see me in Paris and asked whether, after our work together on *The Rose King*—a long time ago by then—I would like to make another film with him, a Portuguese, French, and German coproduction that we would be able to shoot in Portugal again. I was very glad of the offer, because it opened up another organic development in my life. At that time all my film projects were faltering, and I was also in a slack phase with operatic and theatrical productions.

Of course, Paulo Branco couldn't finance our idea about the youth of Frederick the Great, but we agreed that I would make a film for and with Isabelle. She was prepared to take time out for it at once, and within four weeks I wrote the screenplay for *Deux* [Two] with the young French scriptwriter Cédric Anger. It was really based on intense autobiographical experiences and dreams. Paulo Branco gave me a free hand to approach the film in as personal a way as I liked. In Germany, by way of contrast, I would have had to keep on explaining why a character did so much as to open or close a door.

I wanted to express a feeling that had been my theme, most recently, in *Love's Debris*. It was about the innermost experience of incorporating in oneself beings beyond the borders of sexual and social norms. That extravagant unity corresponds to perfect beauty if one can find adequate means of expressing it. But the old myths say, truthfully, that those who see themselves in the mirror as a duality, as identity in complete unity, will die. The myth of Narcissus and his romantic double, who meet in death, has fascinated me since my childhood. All my life I have been pursued by the idea that I really have an opposite number, only I have forgotten who he is. Someone sensitive will often follow a train of thought suggesting that he perceives the person who may be a part of himself, but either nothing still links them or too much does.

The images of this rift, a subject that I wanted to discuss with Isabelle, flowed out of me in a great torrent of memory, partly in anecdotes and key experiences of my youth, partly in literary quotations from the *Songs of Maldoror*. They assumed the form of an associative dream narrative outside time, one that we would develop further during the shooting with our spontaneous improvisations and the atmospheric wealth of the passing moment. I had to take the messages, always the same, that life prescribes and turn them into a riddle, a labyrinth in which, however, we would find our way at the end, in Juliane Lorenz's montage, as if following Ariadne's thread.

At the center of *Two* we meet a pair of identical twins, Maria and Magdalena, both lesbians, one living in Paris, the other in Sintra on the Atlantic coast of Portugal. Separated at birth, they know neither each other nor their fantastical mother, Anna. Each lives her own life, depicted in a kind of surreal overview of her friendships and love stories, her search for beauty, sex, poetry, and music. The remarkable lesbian double nature of the twins stood not for the simple opposition between good and evil but for something split into multiple parts that finds itself in itself, painfully misses its mark, and finally kills itself.

Most people who reacted to my film mentioned the scene with

Isabelle and Robinson Stévenin, in which she is a schoolgirl and he takes her home on his bicycle, telling her about a film with Diana Dors to which he wanted to invite her. This was my memory of Siegfried in Bielefeld, whom I loved so much, and who gave me that story before killing himself.

Isabelle would have had a much harder time incorporating the fine nuances in the various parts of the twins' lives as fascinatingly as she did if my friend Alberte hadn't created an atmosphere in the design of the production and costumes that acted as a historical pointer. When Isabelle is working on a part, she begins with the costume and shoes that she will wear. It is her way of approaching the character she is going to impersonate in front of the camera.

I managed to get Bulle Ogier for the part of the twins' mother, Anna, a woman who loses herself in transports of joy and disaster, as if hurtling through time. On an additional plane of association, Bulle also appeared in a video installation in the film, repeating the sentence "La violence commence à la naissance" [Violence begins at birth]. We are always inclined to forget that our own birth was painful for our mothers.

In Elfi Mikesch's pictures, Isabelle's face and body language shone with translucence as never before, and once again I rejoiced in the almost-wordless understanding between us. The light, the clouds, the gleaming breakers of the sea—everything in *Two* succeeded magically, three-dimensionally, without a wrong note. We filled dead objects with life and led the living into their dark interior.

When *Two* was shown in competition at the Cannes Film Festival of 2002, one critic wrote that he didn't understand it all, but he felt as if he had seen several centuries of European art history running past him. *Voilà*.

But I also drew inspiration from Indian myths; I made them a part of my personal universe, as a ritual between life and death. There is a custom in India of leading a corpse along on sticks, like a marionette, and literally walking it to its grave. We shot that scene on the beach at night, when Isabelle is burying the alter ego that she has killed and partially eaten, to the ecstatic sound of a tam-tam. And there is still a ritual in which the outcast eunuchs of India play music outside houses where children have just been born, telling the parents that if their child happens to be ugly, they are willing to take it away and raise it. That atavistic way of ensuring that they had progeny was a black symbol in my universe of images.

I took over another detail from the *Thousand and One Nights*, when a ghost appears to a young widow, telling her to eat the first thing she is given, and then she will get her husband back. When the dead man appears, he throws up in her face, she swallows the vomit, and he comes back to life. If I am not ready to accept everything that someone else gives me, I cannot create life: that was the meaning. I brought such ideas from a magical exterior into *Two*, merging them with the poetry of dark Romanticism. The idea of the actress as a puppet letting herself be led to the grave was not an image of horror to Isabelle but a key scene relating to her career, as she said at many presentations of the film.

But a few of the scenes were not easy for her. I included in the screenplay a reminiscence of my experiences with Michael O'Daniels, with whom I went around Los Angeles accompanied by a fox in the seventies. We really used three animals, trained as far as their talents would allow, but working with them was difficult, because ultimately the foxes could not be tamed, and they were always unpredictable. Isabelle did not conceal her fear of them, although a viewer wouldn't know it from the images in the film. It was an adventure for the fox, for the whole team, most of all for Isabelle, but there was a point to my idea. The fox is a wonderful creature, precisely because it will not be tamed. The trainers who supplied the foxes easily did tricks with lions and tigers, but the fox kept on looking dangerously and unwaveringly out of its eyes.

Arielle Dombasle, the wife of the millionaire and philosopher Bernard-Henri Lévy, took the part of the singing teacher of one of the twin sisters played by Isabelle. Her husband's right-wing philosophy has never been congenial to me, but it was entertaining to work with Arielle. She can sing reasonably well, has a trained voice, but performs an odd mixture of singing styles. I thought her splendid, a strange, strident, beautiful figure. Best of all was one day of shooting on the beach at Sintra when the sea had a heavy swell, and I wanted Arielle to let the waves knock her over, but she said, "Oh, Werner, never mind that nonsense!" Paolo Trotta, my wonderful Neapolitan assistant, was sitting near me and saw a huge wave rolling up as Arielle, gesturing grandly, belted out, "Ah, que j'aime les militaires, que j'aime les militaires!" [Oh, how I love the military men, the military men!]. He jumped up, but the wave caught Arielle off-balance, and there she was, lying in the water. Was she ever cross!

I enjoyed such moments of teasing, but I didn't merely laugh at her. I thought her delightful, totally acceptable. Arielle was a charming woman who, like all of us, enjoyed a crazy moment now and then. She has a sense of humor, or she wouldn't have given me an aquamarine in memory of my mother's favorite gemstone. She could get really cross with me, always saying, "You only want to torment me." But in the end she gave me that aquamarine—I always wear it around my neck these days—saying, "Here's my salary back." She would come to work elaborately "made over" and styled, looking as if she had taken out a lease on eternal youth. It didn't matter to me whether or not one could tell her real age; her stylized appearance was a plus for the story we wanted to tell. In any case a film like *Two* is the total opposite of everyday life, unless one sets out from the true everyday life of the soul that is always there underground, deep down and influential. In the manner of narrative that we chose, language, images, sounds, literary quotations, and music are all of equal value. Fragments from the *Songs of Maldoror*, those poems about the monstrosity of human beings roaming on this earth, were my leitmotiv in that film.

Rilke spoke of beauty as the beginning of all terror. Beauty can be unendurable in the most banal of lives, sad when those who think themselves ugly are together with the very beautiful. *Two*, however, circles around the gaining of beauty as classical tragedy knows it, whether the divine beauty of Greek mythology or, as in Shakespeare, the beauty of behaving in the right way.

Two was my return to Cannes, and I considered the film my masterpiece. It aroused great interest in France but couldn't find a distributor in Germany. I could have wished for more attention to be paid to the film in my own country, but nothing I could do myself was enough. I had slipped into a deep depression, partly my own fault, and had to deal with a mountain of debts that made me drink too much and suffer sleepless nights. It was both dramatic and banal that I had no real idea of my financial affairs, and really I always preferred to avoid thinking about them. And now I faced the fact that someone whom I had allowed to use my Düsseldorf apartment had cleaned out my bank accounts and gone off to who knew where. I was so confused and astonished that in interviews—for instance, in the journal *Cahiers du cinéma* and on the ARTE TV channel—I spoke frankly about my difficulties. I had to earn money, and soon after *Two*, since my films were never good earners, I began directing the production of Vincenzo Bellini's *Norma* at the Düsseldorf Opera House. Working on an opera brought in as much as two years' work or more on a film. And in my situation at the time, I had to take any chance that came along.

The way to something new

I've always liked to crack jokes about my catastrophes, my "great dramas." But my private misfortunes cast a dark shadow over my delight in that beautiful total artwork *Two*. All the same, I was glad that the film was properly screened at the 2002 Cannes Film Festival and was intelligently discussed—except in Germany, where the usual reaction was a total failure to understand it. Incidentally, seeing it again after an interval of some years, I realized that it did not date. For admirers of Isabelle Huppert who also have an eye for Alberte Barsacq's subtle décor and costumes and for Elfi Mikesch's wonderful camerawork, it is an unforgettable experience, but unfortunately, two of the production companies involved found themselves in financial difficulties, and as the situation is not yet clear, *Two* cannot be screened at the moment.

Personally, I was lucky enough to have good friends who helped me out as far as they could. I am grateful to them for their support. They stood by me in a very confused situation and made it possible for me to go on working, which is what matters to me more than anything. My friend Monika Keppler, who not only has been one of my most important artistic colleagues since I began directing productions in Bremen in the eighties but is also my close friend and partner in so much of my life, was on the point of founding a drama management agency in Berlin. She acted as my artistic manager and tried hard to cast light on the tangled thicket of my losses and liabilities; in addition, she suggested we share a place to live in Berlin. Leander Haussmann, to this day one of my best friends and to whom I owe many stimulating conversations, took in Monika and me as his guests until we had found an apartment. It was hard for me to get a clear view of my situation, because conflicts with my fellow men, negotiations, the signing of contracts, rental problems—in short, all the disagreeable incidental aspects of an artist's insecure life—were the kind of thing that I hated. In spite of everything, with the kindness of my friends I managed to set out on new projects for theaters and opera houses, in line with my inner necessities. Like a musician, I kept playing the same piece, except that every repetition was different in its own way.

Some examples of what I was doing in the years 2002–10: I often resisted pronouncing on political events of the day from the artist's viewpoint—and then did so all the same when an inner urge drove me to it. The war of the USA against Iraq, staged in 2003 like an example of the theater of the absurd in reaction to the attack of 11 September 2001, was an example of the kind of human insanity that art has reflected for thousands of years, independently of the concrete historical and political situation. In directing Bellini's *Norma* at the Rhine Opera in Düsseldorf, I was not so naive as to flash protest signs onstage proclaiming, "Make peace, not war," or "Down with President Bush." Instead, I saw my task as making a statement embedded in the art form, one that would make any open-minded member of the audience think.

That is really the most humane idea: feelings to convey expression, going hand in hand with thought. Opera is an ideal form of expression for that: a total work of art not in the ideological sense in which Richard Wagner used the term but as music theater with its intellectual content rooted in actual historical incidents and dilemmas and just as important as the element of sound. Music in itself is tedious; it means something only when it reaches out beyond itself. I saw Maria Callas as the messenger of the gods because she went beyond music into transcendent space. My opinion was that you must gain ascendancy over the art form in the theater, and the cinema too, so that a metaspace of the soul can come into being.

Vincenzo Bellini's opera *Norma* opens up such spaces. Its theme is a subject taken from the history of Gaul toward the end of the period of Roman culture in its prime, a story of occupation, oppression, and betrayal. At the end of the opera the priestess Norma sacrifices herself and the Roman proconsul Pollione, whom she loves. Although they are both innocent, they die on the pyre intended for others. This dilemma is a comment on the injustice of the world outside the opera, as it is and always will be. In the Düsseldorf production, for which I also designed the set, Norma, sung by the wonderful soprano Alexandra von der Weth, walked proudly, head held high, through an open cube beyond which the flames blazed. It was a metaphor for the passage through death but also a kind of image representing our limited perception of war, violence, and devastation by fire and the sword. To me, it was above all an image of the idea of mastering fear, something that was becoming ever more prominent in my thinking.

Opera as a medium for humanist thought has always been to the fore in my work. When I asked the singers in *Love's Debris* how yearning for the essence of life and how the questions "Who are you?" and "Who am I?" make the beautiful "debris" that we call art possible, as well as the perfect happiness of creativity, it was also clear to me that the same artistic passion must apply to society and politics. The operas that I love best express that humanist ideal. A fine example is Ludwig van Beethoven's *Fidelio*, which I directed in Darmstadt in 1995. It is set in a Spanish state prison in the seventeenth century. The protagonist, Leonore, disguised as the prison warder Fidelio, is intent on rescuing her husband, Florestan, a political prisoner there. She is told to dig a grave for a man condemned to death and, as she does so, looks frantically for her husband in the dark dungeon. In this scene she sings, "Nein, du sollst kein Opfer sein, ich komme dich zu retten, ich rette dich wer du auch seist" [No, you shall be no victim; I come to save you, to save you whoever you may be]. I insisted on having those lines of the libretto sung distinctly and not, as usual, thrown away by bad diction. I particularly value that moment in Beethoven's *Fidelio* when the heroine reaches out beyond the marriage bond to say that she will save the prisoner, *whoever he may be.*

In 2004 I returned to the methods of the grotesque theater that I had used in earlier works. For the Darmstadt State Theater, for instance, I directed Vladimir Nabokov's *Walzers Erfindung* [The waltz invention], a work that he wrote in exile in France in 1938. After the October Revolution, Nabokov lived as a refugee in the colony of Russian emigrants in Berlin for fifteen years, including the first years of Hitler's regime. *The Waltz Invention* is his revenge on the totalitarian mentality of the Germans, which he loathed like poison, and to that end he added satire, with elements of both Russian comedy and the commedia dell'arte. I liked the madhouse atmosphere of the play, which releases explosive laughter somewhere between the dramatic danger of Shakespeare and elements of low culture, which I enjoyed in Frank Castorf's approach to the theater. Nabokov's grotesquerie anticipated the invention of the nuclear bomb before anyone thought seriously of such a thing. With the help of an excellent ensemble, including my dear friend Elisabeth Krejcir in the leading role of the weary Minister of War, we tried to sharpen the malice, although unfortunately it didn't turn out as I wanted. The bomber Waltz threatens to blow up the world, and in the state where the play is set, that gives him power, at least until everything falls apart into nightmare. I had male actors playing women and female actors playing men, thus, as usual, baffling the German critics. My reply to that was that I myself didn't want to be the same person every day, and I was enjoying this excellent opportunity to play at being someone else.

Another work that I directed, in 2006, centered on my old theme: the attempt to create a new composition out of fragments, contrasts, music, and speech arranged in an open form. Producing a scenic and musical collage had fascinated me in my first films, because in that way I could translate antiquated forms into a new artistic reality. I had been working for more than two decades on experimental performances of that nature, for various theaters, often with

Monika Keppler as my creative dramaturgical adversary and with Eberhard Kloke as cocomposer. In 2006 the Düsseldorf Hall of Art invited me to direct a scenic and musical mosaic on the subject of Robert Schumann and Heinrich Heine, celebrating both artists on the 150th anniversary of their deaths. In cooperation with the conductor Roland Techet, we produced a tribute, entitled *The Beauty of Shadows*, taking a journey back in time to the nineteenth century and depicting a fictional meeting between the poet Heine and the musician and composer Schumann. Both artists had lived in Düsseldorf for a while, Schumann had set poems by Heine to music, and both had known the terrible experience of sickness and dying slowly in what Heine called the "tomb of the mattress."

The Beauty of Shadows linked Schumann's piano cycle *Kreisleriana* with songs by him, Arnold Schönberg, and Hans Werner Henze, sung by the young Austrian soprano Julia Kamenik. This was matched by Christoph Seibert's sound installation with staged dance episodes. The idea of Heine and Schumann as companions on their journey through life reminded me of Magdalena Montezuma and Christine Kaufmann in *The Death of Maria Malibran*, meeting one another as life and death. "What must remain incomplete," I wrote then about the poetry used in this game of fragments, "hovers over everything like a cloud of sound, a Utopia of the reconciliation of art, life, and love."

While I was in Düsseldorf, I suffered a horrible physical sensation that cannot be put into words. I felt that there was something wrong and that some inexorable power was taking possession of me. The realization that I had cancer, like my whole family before me, hit me like a physical blow. I fell into despair and panic, into a state of distress that my friends tried to share with me, although something was happening to me that was beyond my ability to express. I had often imagined the threshold of death as so ecstatic and rich in imagery that I longed for it, but now I felt, with full force, the fear of dying, which is not the same as the fear of death. Monika helped to find doctors, she and Alberte nursed me and looked after me, and Isabelle Huppert came to Düsseldorf to persuade me to have chemotherapy at the Hôpital Tenon in Paris. Calling on one of my favorite sayings, by Andreas Gryphius, "In Gefahr und grösster Not ist der Mittelweg der Tod" [In danger and the greatest need, Death is the middle way indeed], I agreed to have the painful treatment.

I was lucky in being able to stay with Alberte in Paris. She cared for me in my depressingly poor state of health for six months. Bulle Ogier, Isabelle, Nathalie Delon, Ingrid Caven, and many other friends tried to make the nauseating side effects of the disease and the therapy as bearable as possible. I lost strength, became unsteady on my feet, and could no longer master the pain. Step-by-step, I had to learn to overcome the fear we all feel of the end, and in my case I did, so far as I could be sure of myself. Since then I have had to go back to the hospital many times, and I have had operations at ever shorter intervals, observing all the rules of the art of surgery.

In the first year of my cancer, living in Paris was a help. Paris has always been a good place for me. In Germany, if I was not at the theater or with friends, I felt like a stranger. So many sad faces everywhere! When I smiled at people in the street in Germany, they looked away. When I filed my nails in the hospital and painted them to look pretty with colorless nail lacquer, the nurses whispered behind my back.

Maybe my poor health created a greater sense of distance; maybe, in my condition, my nerves became even more sensitive to the increasing calcification of my feelings. More and more often, I seemed to myself like a dinosaur from a time when no one knew any virtual worlds that could be entered by sitting alone in front of the computer or the TV set. Whenever I was asked about Germany, I missed no opportunity to express my alienation from it, and by then I really felt like the wandering prophet to whom Peter Berling had once compared me. Nobility of heart, the old virtue that my grandmother had possessed, was something that I lacked in my native land.

When I was in the hospital, I read crime novels by the dozen and had no option but to watch television, although I hate the kitsch of the mindless pap one sees there. On the nighttime programs, however, I did find some interesting new films by authors whose works ought to have found their way into the cinema. I was very surprised, for instance, by Matthias Glasner's film *Die freie Wille* [Free will], got hold of the phone number of his production company, and decided to call the director and the main actor, Jürgen Vogel. A very radical film, about the inner torments of a rapist. When I was working hard, I hardly noticed new films; they took my mind off my own work too much. But now I was getting to know films worth discussing whenever I met audiences enthusiastic about the cinema at my retrospectives or at festivals. I tried to cut my hospital stays as short as possible and get back as quickly as I could to my own projects and my friends.

This Night

I was in the middle of medical treatment in Paris when something extraordinarily cheering happened: Paulo Branco suggested that he and I might make another film together. Branco, who had had the courage to make *The Rose King* and *Two*, was thinking once again of a large-scale feature film—despite my poor health. This daring idea was first broached in a café in Paris, and our search for a suitable subject, work on the screenplay, and the details of casting were all discussed in French, but if the Berlin producer Frieder Schlaich had not been prepared to take part, as coproducer, in this Portuguese, French, and German production, the film *Nuit de chien [Diese Nacht—This Night]* would never have been made.

Making a huge effort, we got down to work on it in Paris, Porto, and Berlin in 2007 and 2008. Paulo Branco's team organized the shooting; the montage and postproduction were done by Schlaich's production company Filmgalerie 451. Sometimes I even slept in the cutting room, to reduce the time spent traveling, which put a great strain on me. As usual, the montage took many weeks, a trial to my own patience and that of all involved. Again, *This Night* was not created in the conventional way by sticking close to the script but was put together on the cutting table. No one expressed any concern about my poor health.

In my first rush of enthusiasm, I wanted to realize my old dream of filming James Baldwin's novel *Giovanni's Room* at long last. But for that we would have had to shoot the film in Paris, and there was no chance of financing such a project. Then Paulo Branco recommended that I read Juan Carlos Onetti's novel *Para esta noche*, which had appeared in France under the title *Nuit de chien*. I fell in love with it at once and was full of enthusiasm for its dark poetry.

The Argentinian novelist Onetti was born in Paraguay, and I already knew other books by him. In this novel, he described former freedom fighters who, in the face of their own failure to prevent the power grabs of the old regime, betrayed, hunted down, and terrorized one another. He portrayed a twilight of the gods, an inescapable cataclysm, yet one with glimmers of hope in its truthfulness despite everything. Onetti wrote his book during World War II, drawing on the accounts of exiles who had been tortured in Nazi prisons, and it also reflected the brutalities of the Spanish Civil War. As I read it, I was inevitably reminded of my visit to Argentina when the junta was wreaking havoc after losing the Falklands War, and the students in my seminar had been forced, under threat of violence, to give up our theatrical project. What I had seen in the agony of Buenos Aires in 1983, when the face of my assistant had been ravaged by torture, and the mothers of the "disappeared" courageously demonstrated in the Plaza de Mayo, strengthened my resolve to film this universal parable. Onetti's nightmare phantasmagoria was set in an imaginary city, but the story had general relevance and expressive power, over and beyond the actual historical events of the thirties and forties. In addition, Onetti was a poetic critic of the *condition humaine*, his black humor hard as bone and verging on cynicism. His account of disaster is free of guilt, as if the characters of the novel were helplessly caught up in their mutual destruction. There is no answer to the question of why war exists; yet we have to ask it again and again.

All these were good reasons for me to get together with the French scriptwriter Gilles Taurand to write a screenplay. Paulo Branco wanted a film that strictly followed the course of the novel's action, and so far as I was concerned he got it. All the same, I worked on the same principle as in *Malina*: I read the novel all the way through, but the screenplay was just a guideline. I knew intuitively that this was a story that must not exhaust itself plodding through everyday incidents.

In Titian's painting *The Flaying of Marsyas*, a violinist stops play-ing, and the Muse of music falls silent, as Marsyas is skinned alive by order of Apollo. Music and cruelty, beauty and violence, lie close together in this mythological scene. Apollo, the god of light and the music that is represented by his lyre, has the flute player Marsyas flayed because his wild music comes straight from nature, like the wind in the trees, instead of representing the measured accompa-niment of song and speech. Titian's picture is an allegory of the di-lemma that human beings cannot successfully live in a community. I placed that painting at the beginning of my film *This Night* instead of a prologue.

The action covers a single night that decides everything: Ossorio Vignal, played by Pascal Greggory, is a doctor and former freedom fighter who, after the defeat of the revolutionary troops with which he was fighting, returns to the city of Santa Maria to look for his lover, Clara Baldi, and with her leave the country on the last refu-gee ship waiting at the pier. But Clara has disappeared, Ossorio's search becomes an odyssey through the city, where those left be-hind are beginning to settle their scores. The chief of police makes arrests and has his prisoners tortured, getting false confessions and denunciations by means of violence. Onetti's novel cancels out the apportionment of blame; all who meet one another that night are possessed by their fear of death. I was convinced that fear, the con-vulsive fear of death, drives human beings to brutality, and so I also prefaced my film with Shakespeare's words on death, from *Julius Caesar*: "Of all the wonders that I yet have heard, / It seems to me most strange that men should fear, / Seeing that death, a necessary end / Will come when it will come."

Whenever I was in the northern Portuguese city of Porto, I was re-minded of C. G. Jung's remark that the Middle Ages were the last pe-riod when a magical view of the world prevailed, striking a balance between the soul and the reasoning mind. That towering old city, with its winding alleys, dark stone houses, and the colored tiles of its interiors, develops a black magic by night and a bright enchant-ment by day and seemed to me the ideal setting for the imaginary city of Santa Maria. Paulo Branco made it possible for me to shoot scenes in the medieval city center and in the cathedral, which is built on the highest ground of Porto. It watches over the city like a guardian angel, a place of refuge, but in *This Night* the interior represents a prison devoted to interrogations and torture, and we were able to shoot in the cathedral itself.

For weeks on end we worked exclusively at night, from six in the evening until seven in the morning. I relished the shifting of working hours to the night; it comes naturally to me, and I have often had problems when work is organized according to trade union rates and regulations. Working by night in Porto had all of us, the actors and the rest of the team, gradually falling into a trance that heightened the nightmarish atmosphere of the film. We moved along narrow alleys, between locked buildings, as if in a labyrinth that our cameraman Thomas Plenert, whom I had met in Berlin, immersed in a twilight suggesting the aura of a grand residence that had seen better days. Alberte was art director and created a wonderful scenographic concept emphasizing the nature of the film as a parable outside time. The refugees whom Ossorio meets in the city, for instance, wear costumes from different periods, and the taxis outside Porto rail station come from many cities all over the world.

All my films, including *This Night*, bear witness to my search for forms in which vitality communicates the joy in creativity and beauty that is such a gift to those in our career. In beauty, and in the recognition of beauty, there is hope *malgré tout*, in spite of everything. It expresses hope even when the subject of a film deals with the darkest nocturnal aspects of existence.

With this film I was returning to Portugal, a country that I had fallen in love with again quite recently when I was working on *Two*. The city of Porto, the erotic spirit of the landscapes, and the humor of the Portuguese, who are not vain, flowed subtly into our total work of art, and that life-affirming mood was ever present as a sublime contrast to the pessimism and nihilism of the story being told.

In creating ambivalent atmospheres, I have always found music of great importance in both my cinematographic and my theatrical work. I am well known for going everywhere with a small stereo system and playing a special selection of music from my own repertoire. Scarcely any of that music can be heard later on the sound-track of a film or in the incidental music for a theatrical production. It is there solely to lighten our feelings while we are working. The actors and I enjoy having something to concentrate on other than the text and its sense while we are shooting. Shakespeare says that music is the food of love. I have always found it a necessary meditative preparation and something to be heard during the intervals of a play to maintain the atmosphere. "Ruhe sanft, mein holdes Leben, schlafe, bis dein Glück erwacht" [Rest in peace, my dearest life, sleep till happiness awakes] runs the aria from Mozart's *Zaide*, which was one such work during shooting, and for *This Night* I also used the Rhapsody in G minor by Johannes Brahms, songs by Federico García Lorca, and some anonymous Czech music from the nineteenth century that I had found. Naturally, we also worked with military marches, some of them from the former propaganda machine of the Argentinian junta.

I was glad to be able, at last, to cast Pascal Greggory in the role of Ossorio Vignal. I had known him since 1978 as Patrice Chéreau's partner. At the time I thought him very attractive and tried to seduce him, but unsuccessfully. I followed his career in France, where he has become a great star. French actors tend to be clear and academic in their physical expression; in their tradition, the body acts as an adjunct to speech. My idea of it was different, and I wanted more sensuality in *This Night*, in the original French as well as other languages. Pascal Greggory, Bruno Todeschini, Sami Frey, and Jean-François Stévenin, all of them playing men who have come to grief in the gloomy dance of death, were happy to be able to explore another dimension in the game.

With the exception of Pascale Schiller, Lena Schwarz, and Oleg Zhukov, all the actors were French. My friends Nathalie Delon and Bulle Ogier took small but significant parts. Amira Casar, an actress who conveys a rigorous emotional charge of a kind seldom found these days, took the role of Irène, a whore who is forced to betray others and beaten up. When the film had its première in Venice in 2008, there was vehement criticism of such brutality to a woman. I countered that piece of political correctness with Goethe's line

"Öffne den umwolkten Blick" [Open up your clouded eyes], for transferred into an absolute, or if you prefer a mannerist artistic reality, the film opposes the reality of violence. I always liked the company of mannerists, and Pier Paolo Pasolini was one of the best. If the critics stamped one of my cheeks with the word "mannerist" and the other with the word "nihilist," it wouldn't bother me at all.

At the end of the film Ossorio takes under his protection the girl Victoria, whose father, Barcala, was head of the movement and killed himself. Originally, the producer Paulo Branco hoped to keep on the right side of his financiers by having this ill-assorted couple escape the inferno. And I did in fact shoot a happy ending, but the compromise was banal and kitschy. So the film ends with an adjutant and fellow traveler of the chief of police—the eternal zero, representing the horror of mediocrity—deciding on matters of life and death.

Whenever I was taxed with the pessimism of Onetti's view of the world in conversations with the public, I replied, "No, you're wrong; beauty wins the day." To quote Pyotr Tchaikovsky—it is a quotation that I love—I was concerned only with "the continuing contrast between pain and beauty," which reveals the only legitimate artistic search for truth. Without pain and the search for truth, there is no beauty. Those sayings stood like pillars; I could always develop a relationship from them and encourage others to look at their own experiences.

Figures of the Madonna and Christ suffering on the cross have often drawn attention in my films and theatrical productions, and some people have seen that as either folklore or blasphemy. It has been assumed that the cross that I wear around my neck is a piece of costume jewelry. To say these days that one is a Christian believer often meets with incredulity, but to me, as a convinced Christian, the cross has always meant a great deal. The torturer in *This Night* carries out his interrogations in the cathedral, and his table is not an altar but the desk of a perpetrator of evil deeds. That terrible alliance between the church and power, faith, and brutality was an important statement for me as both a Christian believer and an outspoken critic of the church. The history of the mistakes and crimes of the church is a catastrophe, and the film rejects it as betrayal. In full awareness of disaster, despite torture, viciousness, and intrigues, our longing for a possible community, a credible Utopia, is overwhelming. This hopeful hopelessness and hopeless hope is my own conviction. I am a hopeful man.

AFTERWORD

CLAUDIA LENSSEN

In the summer and fall of 2009, we recorded some fifty hours of conversations. I was dealing with a charismatic personality who cultivated his own presentation via understatement, humor, and nonchalance. Schroeter loved delivering monologs, but he always established an intimate atmosphere and addressed the listener directly. His speech was fascinating, with a style and sound all his own, interspersed with literary quotations and colloquial expressions. In meeting with him, I always felt as if I was attending an original performance that defied textual form. Schroeter scored points with the sudden sound of his own eccentric laugh. He thought in several languages and was inclined to put important adjectives after their nouns in the French manner. His exclamations of "Terrific!" "Great!" "Wonderful!" exaggerated everything. Occasionally, he would pause and let out a melodious "Hmmm," allowing his pleasure over what he had just said to linger. His world was populated by strange comic-strip figures and soft toys, in line with the child that he still partly was. Once he even hired a Donald Duck impersonator to appear in the doomsday revue *Die göttliche Flamme* [The divine flame] in Oberhausen in 2002. Another habit he had was to doodle on notepads, paper napkins, letters, tickets, and theater programs; the doodles were always cheerful little matchstick men with strikingly long noses.

We met in cafés and restaurants, usually outdoors so he could smoke his inevitable cigarette. He didn't seem to mind if the surroundings were private or not. His books, letters, gramophone records, photographs, everything that could have been a bridge to the past had been put in storage, mislaid, or given away—or so he said. A restless man, who always carried a black fabric bag, he did not want to be encumbered with anything.

I first met Werner Schroeter in 1999 at the Academy of Arts in Berlin. There he cut the figure of a *grand seigneur*, clad in leather, his long hair combed straight back and tied at the nape of his neck, his voice rich with the timber of good living.

He had come to the academy to participate in a conversation about emotions on-screen and the fear of excessive emotion in the contemporary cinema. Martina Gedeck was saying how she dealt with that dilemma; Werner Schroeter joined in with casual arrogance and, before you know it, had persuaded the actress to take part in an episode of his documentary film on Marianne Hoppe, *The Queen*.

Ten years later his cancer had severely affected his appearance. Slender, stooped, still wearing black, plus a large, elegant hat, he looked like a memento mori on two legs. He knew that pictures of him were being circulated in the media with voyeuristic glee, but he took it with composure, noting the slight differences between them. He never forgot unflattering photographs. He often dwelled on his appearance, describing himself without sentimentality as a dead man walking, but he did not take kindly to such grisly images when they came from journalists.

He walked with care, his head tipped over to his bad side. After radiotherapy and chemotherapy, his voice cracked now and then during our conversations. He had to drink still water, without ice or a slice of lemon, because swallowing was difficult. He would often stand up abruptly and go to a nearby bar to express a special wish. Cafés were his natural habitat, even when he was sick, although he lost his temper more and more often if the waiters were not attentive enough. He would also jump up restlessly for no obvious reason and simply walk out.

On a chain around his neck Schroeter wore an aquamarine the color of his blue eyes, with a gold crucifix glittering beside it, and a brooch in the form of a lizard set with gemstones on his lapel. His hands were adorned with aquamarine rings, and it really caught the eye when he reached out into the air and seemed to catch an imaginary bird in his fingers, holding it close with a grand, operatic gesture.

Our work on the material we had collected was only one of his many activities. Sometimes Schroeter disappeared for weeks. He would stay temporarily with various friends. Sometimes he confused official invitations with a vacation, would travel to the event by rail, and then expect to convalesce at festivals or seminars celebrating his work, though convalescence was of course out of the question.

It was impossible to talk with him before the afternoon. Schroeter used to say that he had been a chronic night owl all his life, but in the summer of 2009, despite his controlled demeanor, it was impossible not to notice how his condition was tormenting him. In an offhand manner, but with glances betraying the horror of it, he would talk about the pain raging in his wasted body; sleeping and eating were all but impossible.

He spoke openly about his cancer, and spontaneously, when he received information that shocked him. At the end, though, he declined company, support, and help. His films always portrayed death as a communicative event, a finale leading to aftereffects, but in my personal proximity to him it became increasingly clear that he knew he must face dying on his own. Being there to silently share his fears was all that a friend could do; expressions of sympathy provoked downright derision.

Writing these memoirs grew ever more connected to his sickness. I would collect him from the doctor's office to take him for radiotherapy. I was expected to bring the forbidden cigarettes and a small cognac to the hospital for him. Then he would talk spontaneously about his symptoms. He had been living with cancer for four years, but he was still trying to confront it as "something new" in terms of the book—he would come up with an idea for a chapter heading, a chapter that was never written. He admired the way his friend Christoph Schlingensief made his own cancer a story for the media: after all, the disease is rampant, an epidemic affecting the entire modern world and of enormous public interest. But for himself, he absolutely rejected that approach.

Over the months he came to value the fact that I could pick him up wherever he happened to be in Berlin. We spent a good deal of time in my car, where he told me much about himself that I then tried to set down later in my notes. Schroeter gradually accepted me into his world, was glad for the small experiences we shared, the situation of the moment, rather than the progress of his memoirs. I drove him to his favorite CD stores, and in return he pointed out the best and cheapest recordings of, say, the opera singer Magda Olivero or James MacMillan's *Seven Last Words from the Cross*, about which he spoke with natural expertise, but writing such opinions down in a book seemed to him too abstract and cost too much strength.

His memoirs are the story of his life as he ran it past his inner eye in his final months. We had to hurry to get down a record of it at least in broad outline, and as far as possible in his own inimitable words. To reflect on what had been said, and go deeper into the material, I sometimes brought transcripts to our meetings. But his restlessness, the pain he was in, the malaise of his daily life at this time distracted him from concentrated work on the text. He often came to our meetings without a draft of the work we had just done, preferring to make brilliant suggestions on how to approach the next chapter. The harder it was for him to stay on top of the cancer, the more irritable he grew if he thought one incident or another was already on record in our work. He increasingly and impatiently referred me to newspaper archives or the files he had given to the German Kinemathek Film and Television Museum. He would recapitulate from memory whole passages from earlier interviews, needing the complete texts I had written only as a crutch so that he wouldn't have to "say everything twice."

Schroeter was aware of the striking lack of commentary on his work, but he wasn't so ambitious as to put forward any theoretical propositions of his own. Earlier stagings, overlapping comparisons between his media of film, theater, and opera seemed to him hardly worth attention, apart from his brief verdicts on the works concerned or praise for individual contributors to them. His pride in his vast artistic achievement through the course of his life was expressed in his pleasure in drawing up inventories, endless lists of what plays and operas he had directed when, and at which theater or opera house. He took every comment from the public as a reason to talk about the concrete circumstances of a work's background and the adventure of directing it, but in principle he felt suspicious of anything "academic" that might impair the power of association. A profound script or screenplay, he believed, must always come straight from life, from ideas and emotions; they gave rise to the situation to which an artist like him reacted.

I came to know Schroeter as an extremely cultivated and well-read man who knew his own place in cultural tradition, always drawing on a wealth of references in the form of quotations, fragments, and the associations they evoked.

Schroeter began work on his memoirs by taking great pleasure in going back to his early memories. He became so sick, however, that the longer the chronicle of events went on, the harder he found the work. It was possible for him to touch only briefly on the abundance and variety of the plays and operas that he had directed in the last twenty years of his life.

He liked nothing better than escaping to the warmth of the Atlantic coast of Portugal. Early in the summer of 2009 he dreamed of making a film in Lisbon and working on his memoirs with me there. But he lacked money, health, and mobility. Sometimes work on the book faltered as he composed handwritten appeals for money, fees still due to him, and we would go to a copy shop or a generous restaurateur to have them sent off by fax. Sometimes he hardly had enough cash to pay for the use of the fax machine. Sometimes he went to the supermarket so that he could cook someone a meal—with good ingredients, of course.

Schroeter fought for his life in style. As long as he could be out and about and could communicate, he managed, in spite of his plight, to enjoy his own vitality in momentary experiences such as visiting with friends, enjoying books. Even in pain, he maintained his charm. Almost immediately after yet another operation, he would get back into his dandified but ever-simpler black clothing and go off, with the inevitable fabric bag, wandering around cafés, meeting friends, attending theatrical rehearsals, conversing with producers, and appearing at public events in his honor. His fatalism, his humor, and his deep sense of religion combined into something that may have acted as a magical form of self-hypnosis—something very personal that merits our admiration. Perhaps his mania for drawing up lists of his works was his own version of Ariadne's thread, leading to the center of his inner labyrinth. Looking back on his life gave him strength to bear his illness, and this book is an expression of that retrospective search.

Werner Schroeter did not hide the fact that he was a devout Christian. He considered the crucifix that he wore on his chest to be not jewelry but a visual confession of faith, a tiny, intimate clue among all the many signs of Christian iconography in his films and the stage plays he directed. The broken, ecstatic, transcendent body of Christ was one of the key images in his aesthetic, philosophical, ambivalently erotic universe. When I was with him in the year we created this book, it was clear, from the power of conviction in his spontaneous outbursts, how seriously he moved in that universe and how important prayer was to him. Once, when I asked him on the day of yet one more terrifying diagnosis, whether he could bring himself to go through another operation, he suddenly exclaimed, "I can decide that only with the help of my God!" I had to stop the car at once by the side of the road; he jumped out of it and disappeared.

There was so much more that I would have liked to ask him, but in late fall 2009 we lost touch. He was barely able to get through the rehearsals of *Quai West*. During the Berlinale 2010, he received, in a touchingly straightforward manner, the Teddy Award (the German gay and lesbian film prize) for his life's work, and a little later he and Elfi Mikesch received the F. W. Murnau Prize of the city of Bielefeld. A little later still, he viewed the exhibition in his honor at the Gay Museum of Berlin. He made one more trip to Paris, where cineasts had offered to let him plan the program for an evening in his honor. The film clips of his appearance, which I saw later, show him in a terrible physical state, but with his mind as sharp as ever. At that farewell occasion he set the seal, once more, on his love for and friendship with Carole Bouquet. The program, however, was a heart-rending appeal to the emotions. He confronted the audience with the American documentary film *Winter Soldier*, as a flashback to the cinematic experiences that had molded his own attitudes. In the film, young veterans of the Vietnam War confess their cruelties to the Vietnamese population at a public investigation and, by revealing the barbaric murders they had committed, call for the end of the war. As a provocative contrast, hard to take but typical of him, he set it against his film *Love's Debris*. The message he bestowed on the disturbed audience was that only beauty can combat barbarism.

I never saw him again. On 12 April 2010, five days after his sixty-fifth birthday, he died in a hospital in Kassel. These memoirs were left in a fragmentary state. Questions that might have added yet another dimension to his story remained unanswered. What part did the small distinction between fact and fiction play in his life? What was the relationship between dream and reality? What was left undone in an irregular life like his?

Schroeter left me fragments for the close of the book. Fragments were his most important artistic instrument; he would contrast them with each other to make "something new" in the minds of the public. In that, the open-ended finale of his memoir also matches his enigmatic dialectical approach to the pain and beauty of the world. It must be left to readers to draw their own conclusions.

Schroeter said: "It may sound bizarre, but what has always fascinated me about the theater is its ephemeral nature. When the curtain has fallen at the end of the performance, and the lights onstage go out, all that is left, as Lessing put it, is 'a trembling vibrato in the auditorium.' To me, that has always been the best image of life, recognizing that it is fleeting, and one day the end will come."

December 2010

APPENDIXES

THE PRIMA DONNA'S BROKEN HEART

WERNER SCHROETER

O cuore dono fatale
Retaggio di dolore,
Il mio destino è questo:
O morte, o amore!

[O heart, sad gift,
the legacy of pain;
my fate is death,
is death or love!]

From Amilcare Ponchielli's La Gioconda

Much as all-expressive human power can derive only from injury and suffering, profound passion, and the close knowledge of oneself and the world inevitably bound up with it, so while the voice of Maria Callas was naturally a low mezzo-soprano, she herself, as if plucking stars from ashes to fling them at the sky, raised it to that higher pitch that gave me nosebleeds in my excitement when I was seventeen years old.

In our time, Maria Callas was unique, isolated like a woman of the Romantic era accidentally stranded in the wrong century. She has often been judged by the so-called aesthetic qualities of her voice, which is fundamentally nonsense, because the bourgeois aesthetics of our time are only another definition of smooth conformity.

The qualities of Maria Callas's vocal instrument can be judged only by an archaic criterion of aesthetics holding that truth gives rise to beauty, not the other way around.

She herself once told me, "The only time I myself have been moved to tears onstage was at the open-air production of Beethoven's *Fidelio* in the arena of Epidaurus in 1944, a performance put on for the German soldiers of the occupying forces. While I was singing, '*Komm Hoffnung* . . . come, Hope, let not the last star go out, the star of the weary, shed light on their goal however far away; that goal is love, is love, and they will reach it,' just as I was singing that passage the evening star appeared in the sky of Greece, which, until that moment, had been overcast."

Maria Callas herself was the only criterion by which to judge those larger-than-life heroines whom she brought to life onstage and in the recording studio, and in the long run probably more or less the criterion by which to judge her own performance, although many thought that she was driven by extraordinary ambition.

However, that ambition was not, as people liked to assume, to find herself a capitalist on the grand scale one day, settling down in a small castle, but to live out the few basic human factors of musical and dramatic expression to the utmost—conveying those few entirely valid feelings for life, love, joy, hatred, jealousy, and the fear of death, seen in their totality and without psychological analysis.

To that end, Maria Callas chose a now unusual musical form in the shape of early nineteenth-century Italian bel canto opera (for instance, Bellini's *Norma*, Donizetti's *Lucia di Lammermoor*), so of course she did not move in the social milieu of other great so-called stars such as Janis Joplin or Elvis Presley but by that very choice was forced into an artistic and social sphere that in our time, unfortunately, seems less vital to society.

At the time of Giuseppe Verdi, for example, the general population took as great an interest in opera as they do in the louder kind of pop concerts today, and an opera could set off a social revolution, as it did in Belgium, in the case of Auber's *La muette de Portici* [The mute girl of Portici], while the choruses calling for liberty in Verdi's early operas led to the downfall of the Austrian occupying power in Italy. But those days are long gone.

As a performer of as much intensity as Jimi Hendrix, Maria Callas had to present herself to a society in which the moribund upper class made her fine recitals into smug social events. That did not trouble Maria Callas herself. She came from a petit bourgeois family of pharmacists in Brooklyn, New York, and saw her rise to the top of her profession as a social necessity.

As if moving from darkness into light, and contending at first with diffidence, clumsiness, and hysteria, she had developed her style into the total artwork to which she remained true all her life, even after she had to give up her real singing career in 1965. Not that it was a short career, far from it. At the age of fifteen, she was already singing the main role of Santuzza in Mascagni's *Cavalleria rusticana* [Rustic chivalry] at the Athens opera house. That was in the tradition of such great prima donnas of the nineteenth century as Maria Malibran and Giuditta Pasta, many of whom began by singing the most difficult of roles between the ages of thirteen and eighteen, and who, like Maria Callas, had sung themselves out relatively soon. At least Maria Callas's ability to work, with the gifts so typical of her, lasted for twenty-seven years.

The American singer Beverly Sills once said, "Better to sing for ten years in as unique and intense a manner as Maria Callas than to sing like me for nearly thirty years"—although she herself certainly did not suffer from excessive modesty and was one of the most famous singers of our time.

It has always amazed me that a woman to whom life onstage acted like a drug was able to survive, both psychologically and physically, the final break with her true calling in 1965. Apparently, and to all outward appearances, Maria Callas was still particularly beautiful and healthy for a woman of her age in 1976. I seemed to myself some fifteen times less fit and more in need of help, far more run-down and unfortunate.

But with the same discipline that she brought to bear on mobilizing her own enormous powers and her sensitivity to sing us all back into the dream of a true Romantic world, she hid her own unhappiness from herself, and most of all from the outside world, with the natural pride peculiar to her.

To me, the strange end of Maria Callas, supposedly a heart attack, at a time when she might have been expected to undertake a different kind of work on the stage as an actress, and when her private life seemed to be on an even keel, is evidence that she shared the fate of all who, by squandering their own powers and personalities too generously, are bound to perish in an environment that does not suit them, since they can never receive anything comparably beautiful in return. The sensitivity of Marilyn Monroe, the brash forcefulness of Janis Joplin, and the death of James Dean when little more than a teenager are features of a degenerate consumer society where there is no real hope of honest friendship based on mutual understanding.

If Maria Callas had been born in the nineteenth century, her public would have carried her coffin to the grave with their own hands, in friendship and as a necessary tribute of gratitude. Instead, her funeral will have been as cold as the last years of her life probably were, leading to a woman of fifty-three, still vital and very beautiful, dying of a heart attack. In the more warmhearted days of the poet Novalis, such a death would surely have been described as dying of a broken heart.

I have never understood how she could bear, even in the last years of her life, to live in the sterile and violent atmosphere of what is known as high society, so that she was never able to abandon the position that her fame had brought her, leaving her set in it as if in concrete.

For instance, at a reception at the Greek Embassy in Paris, where she had spoken as naively as a young girl about a woman's need to devote herself entirely to a man, and she was clearly making much of a French lover whom she seemed to like very much, an American oil-baron type told me later, "It must be wonderful to have your cock blown with *La traviata* on the voice cords." I could have strangled him. It must have been very strange to live with the consciousness and awareness that the people to whom she had given the greatest of gifts responded with a kind of curious contempt.

Those who knew the character and work of Callas as her musical colleagues for many years see her very differently. Here is Piero Tosi, describing the première of the production of *La traviata* at La Scala, Milan, on 28 May 1955, directed by Luchino Visconti, with Carlo Maria Giulini conducting: "The curtain has gone up on the last act. We notice that when Maria Callas rises from her bed she looks like a corpse, like some kind of mannequin from a waxworks show, no longer a human being but a living corpse. And she sings in a thread of a voice, very sick, very weak, very moving—it is only with a great effort that she reaches her dressing table, where she reads old Germont's letter and then sings the 'Addio del passato.' We see the lights of the carnival crowd passing by outside the window, and their shadows falling on the opposite wall. Only shadows: to Violetta the world is now a shadow and nothing else. She summons her maid and begins a terrible struggle to get dressed. Then comes the moment when she tries to put on gloves but cannot; her fingers are already stiff and rigid as death approaches. Only now does Violetta realize that there is no escape, and in that realization Maria Callas, with overwhelming intensity, utters her cry of 'Dear God! So young to die!' She is stunning.

"That broken, suffering, destroyed skeleton of a woman is fighting in vain for her life. For the moment of death itself, Visconti demands all Callas's genius as an actress. When she has finally accepted her fate, and has given Alfredo a locket with her picture in it, Violetta speaks the famous closing lines. Radiant, she tells Alfredo that her pain has gone away, and new strength and life have come into her. And with the words, 'O joy! O joy!' she dies, her large eyes wide open and staring sightlessly at the audience. Even after the fall of the curtain, her dead eyes still stare into a void. The whole audience thus shares Alfredo's pain, having felt the moment of death themselves."

In the same performance, after Giulini had ended the prelude to the first act and the orchestra moved into the festive *allegro* that is the signal for the curtain to rise, he says he felt something that he describes as follows: "My heart missed a beat; I was overpowered by the beauty that I saw before me. It was the most sensitive and extraordinary performance that I had ever seen. The illusion of art, or perhaps of theatrical artificiality, disappeared. I had the same feeling every time I conducted this production, on over twenty occasions. To me, reality was on the stage. All that was behind me, the audience, the auditorium, the theater itself, seemed artificial. Only what lived and breathed onstage was truth, was life itself."

It would be absurd to claim that the wish for beauty and truth is a mere illusion in a romantically capitalist society. No doubt the desire for an exaggerated, larger-than-life kind of wish fulfillment, one that we find everywhere in traditional art, but that we may also associate with modern trivial media like the cinema and television, denotes a common human need. Our ultimate destiny in death, only too strong and the one objective fact of our existence, annuls any prospect of concrete happiness in advance. So the expressive factors in art, driven to extremes, whether in architecture, music, or any other form, represent nothing but a need to stop time, that is, to ignore the finitude of human needs, giving them credibility in an exceptional case, and with that their pride.

Of all the women singers I know, it was Maria Callas who, in the strength of her expression, could make time stand still long enough for all fear to disappear, even the fear of death itself, and for a condition similar to what might be called happiness to be attained.

As a blind man develops a better sense of hearing and touch than someone sighted, Maria Callas was evidence of the fact that without following stupid regulations in a narrow system—she was too near-sighted ever to see the conductor's baton from the stage—one can draw on one's own resources to turn all weaknesses into creativity.

When she sang the words from the opera *La Gioconda* quoted at the beginning of this piece, she transformed a platitude of the inevitable dialectic of our existence into something bright. The unconditional nature of her feelings does not by any means entail stupidity, for unconditionality already means two possibilities: death or love.

With childlike naivety, Maria Callas defended a form of music that German musico-neurologists had dismissed as just boring and undemanding. In the process, of course, they had entirely overlooked the genius of such musicians as Bellini, Rossini, and Cherubini, the composer of *Medea*.

Maria Callas was not an intellectual. She said, to the considerable and cynical amusement of many other women singers, things that, in view of her unsurpassably beautiful interpretation of Richard Wagner's Isolde, may sound incredible but are not. "In Bellini, every note must have its due. Every note costs me all my strength and gives me a chance to express myself as precisely as imaginable. But Wagner sings itself; you have a whole huge orchestra behind you providing the harmonies; you simply cannot go wrong. You only have to open your mouth and the right sound comes out. It's purely a question of physical strength."

The close of an obituary of her in a Ruhrland newspaper struck me as very fine. "Maria Callas died at the age of fifty-three. But we may suspect that every year of her career onstage counted three times over." To which I would add that I hope every year of her whole life counted for as much.

CANCELING OUT UNBEARABLE REALITY

A CONVERSATION BETWEEN MONIKA KEPPLER
AND CLAUDIA LENSSEN

CLAUDIA LENSSEN. Frau Keppler, *Days of Twilight, Nights of Frenzy*, the title of Werner Schroeter's autobiography, derives from a witty remark of Ingrid Caven's. What would you say on the subject?

MONIKA KEPPLER. The day belongs to those who cope well with everyday life, the night to those who want to distance themselves from the promptings of everyday life as determined by society, to live in their imaginations, in fantasy and in art. Werner Schroeter liked the idea of raising his unsuitability for the world of everyday to a life-form in itself, stylized as an attitude of protest.

C.L. Werner Schroeter kept mentioning certain poets, philosophers, and famous directors. His quotations from Hölderlin, Lautréamont, and Bloch appear in many of his program notes as indirect manifestos. Was that insistent form of repetition in his comments his way of mounting an offensive on the state of the world?

M.K. There are indeed recurrent quotations in his writing, whether literary, philosophical, iconographic, metaphorical, or musical. But that doesn't really distinguish him so very much from other artists. He was always concerned with the conflict of the individual and his intellectual and emotional options in the face of reality—social and political reality, I mean.

C.L. Does that run counter to his emotional side and his obsessive concern with death?

M.K. No, it's about a better world, and that includes the idea of escaping this world for a place free from the adversities of life, for a world of nostalgia. His dreaming was lucid dreaming.

C.L. Not the end, but a beginning?

M.K. Or finding fulfillment, in a much wider sense, in self-liberation.

C.L. At the beginning of his career he emphasized his anarchism. How did his ideas change?

M.K. If he described himself as an anarchist, it was never in any concrete political sense. He was an individualist in his anarchism. He wrote, in one set of program notes: "Isn't every work of art, every artistic creation, yet another attempt to cancel out the unbearable nature of reality? An attempt to take reality off its hinges, by an act of yearning. Artists and anarchists are united in refusing to submit to what is intolerable in the world as it exists. They have the courage to break the norms of ordinary life." That was written in 1985, when he was directing the opera *La Wally* in Bremen. One night at the beginning of our work together, in the context of one of the first productions on which I acted as drama adviser, August Strindberg's *Intoxication*, we came upon a saying by Ernst Bloch: "It must never be forgotten that happiness, unlike intoxication, shows that a human being is not beside himself but is coming to terms with himself and what is his, to our here and now."

C.L. Did he interpret Bloch with a social community in mind?

M.K. How can we deal with the intolerable nature of life without suffering from it all the time? As he says in the autobiography, "yearning [is] a word easy to say . . ." Later, he changed it to "Love, a word easy to say / and yet so hard for me. / The stream is shallow as the day / but I dream of the sea." The image of the sea, with all its waters gathered together, included everything.

C.L. The place where he could always keep that search going was the theater, the opera house, the location where he was shooting a film. How interested was he in finding the happiness that means someone's "coming to terms with himself and what is his" outside art as well?

M.K. His longing for harmony, friendship, and love was so immense that any small conflict, the kind of thing we all have to deal with every day, could irritate and distress him. But he also had a good sense of humor, and if something went against the grain with him and a conflict became obvious, he liked to quote Marquis Posa in *Don Carlos*: "The sun will bring it to light."

C.L. His idea of the role of a director was as primus inter pares. But that's a naive dream, since there are always hierarchies and conflicts within a group. Did he manage to make them productive?

M.K. Of course, there were sometimes conflicts, but not often. He could deal with anything in his artistic work and was the most patient of men. He seduced other people. He did not like aggression but resolved it and made it creative by means of associated imagery and music. He was well liked for that. In his work he was open, free, and generous. In fact, he was always generous, but particularly so in his work, and he paid attention to everyone. However, there were conflicts in his generally sunlit life.

C.L. Would you say there was an aura of failure around him?

M.K. He sometimes felt desperate in daily life. That may have been what made him sick, but he never did fail. He had so many people around him, close friends who were always there for him, as he was there for them. Not all of them, unfortunately, are mentioned in the autobiography because it remained a fragment.

C.L. In his last years, did he ever feel the need for a place to which he could withdraw, a place molded by him and the things around him?

M.K. He did have a place like that, with all the "things" that he owned and were left to him. However, it was something else that he longed for.

C.L. What was it that drove him?

M.K. If there was no harmony, he ran away.

C.L. How did he cope with the fact that conflicts followed him, and the same pattern was constantly repeated?

M.K. He could see that there were always explosions at the same points. The main problem in his life was money. He had no idea how to manage his finances.

C.L. What did he think about that? Did he blame other people, saying his parents should have taught him better, that sort of thing?

M.K. No, never. He didn't blame anyone; he was just baffled and didn't know what to do. He was earning relatively well for a while because he worked so hard, but if you simply don't think of such things as taxes for years on end, the system is going to break down sometime. It wasn't a question of understanding; many things simply weren't real to him.

C.L. Back to the autobiography. Werner Schroeter didn't get around to describing his operatic productions and his work with singers in any detail. Is there anything of that nature in his literary estate? Did he leave any studies, working diaries, or analyses of operatic material?

M.K. He collected everything like a hoarder and kept it somewhere. I'm sure I shall find something more, but fundamentally he was an artist who never made notes for himself while he was working. The logic whereby one thing must lead to another in writing was alien to his method of work. He was more of an associative thinker. But there were many conversations with drama advisers, colleagues,

242

and people like the conductor Eberhard Kloke, and they put a good deal down in writing, making it available for posterity. And a number of other inspiring conversations are still on record in our heads. In addition, Alexander Kluge made some fascinating recordings and transmissions with Werner Schroeter for television, and there are equally fascinating written publications and interviews with Dietrich Kuhlbrodt, Wolfgang Storch, Frieder Schlaich, and many others.

C.L. Was any dialog with such people recorded in his work on program notes?

M.K. Program notes don't primarily deal much with the concept of dramatic cooperation. They come at the end of work on a production and at most consist of the opinions of the director and his drama adviser and their interpretation of the work concerned and give information on the data and ideas that are illuminating for an understanding of the work of the playwright or composer and his views. Discussion begins long before the start of rehearsals and is crystallized in a first version of the text at that point, while dialog continues right up to the dress rehearsal. And after it as well. At most, he would give me a few pages of handwritten notes, directions, and quotations, and it was up to me to make a coherent version or formulate a text from those. He read widely, listened to a great deal of music, and absorbed all that he read and heard. He drew on that fund of knowledge to combine everything in terms of images.

C.L. He was a collector and also a vagabond—how could those two things be reconciled?

M.K. That was the result of his rejection of any kind of bourgeois life. What he liked best was when someone phoned, and he could say, "I must pack quickly. I have to go to Paris tomorrow." He liked to travel and absorb the world.

C.L. You own the rights to Werner Schroeter's films.

M.K. When I began looking after his business affairs at the start of the century, we drew up an agreement whereby he ceded his rights in the films to me. Initially, the agreement was meant to be put away in a drawer, just for safety's sake. Those are the rights to the films that he produced or coproduced himself, mainly the early films, and the contextual archive that, at his own wish, went to the German Kinemathek in Berlin. The filmed material, if it wasn't there already, went to the Munich Museum of Film. Stefan Drössler, director of the museum, is committed to reprocessing and restoring the films, and Werner Schroeter was able to see the restoration of his early films himself. Anne Even, who worked on many of Werner's films as an editor for ZDF and the ARTE channel, helped and is still helping with that. And the filmmaker Katrin Seybold, a close friend of Werner's, has made the filmed material in her possession available, so something is being put together. Some of the major later films are not available at the moment because the producers are insolvent. The recording, reprocessing, and preparation of such a large body of work, at present scattered all over the world, entails a great deal of expense, so it cannot be adequately documented in a short time—and as a result the appendix to the book is only a fragment itself.

C.L. During his illness, Werner Schroeter had a special charisma. Where did he find the strength to deal so confidently with the disease?

M.K. He wanted to live. He wanted to realize his dreams and realize himself. He accepted his illness but did not want to let it get the better of him. He thought very hard about what there still was for him to do, and it amounted to a great deal . . .

C.L. What was his last project?

M.K. "Josefine and Me," a wonderful story by Hans Magnus Enzensberger. Ingrid Caven wanted Werner to film it, and she was going to play Josefine. We met Hans Magnus Enzensberger, he agreed to the project and wrote a treatment, and Wim Wenders was prepared to support us. But in the end nothing came of it.

Berlin, December 2010

LIFE'S WORK

FILMOGRAPHY

This filmography lists first all extant completed films by Werner Schroeter, then preliminary studies for his films, fragments, and films never completed or lost. The data are coordinated with those in the Munich Museum of Film and collections of film and video copies. Since most of the films up to 1978 have no opening credits, many of the facts are based on information from Werner Schroeter himself or others involved in them. The première dates of the early films that were not shown in cinemas or on TV cannot be established. The figures given for length correspond in 8 mm films to a speed in performance of eighteen frames per second and in 18 mm and 35 mm films to a speed in performance of twenty-five frames per second.

A   actors
C   camera
Ct   cut
D   director
Dc   décor and costumes
F   type of film used
L   length
M   music (mentioned only when it was specially composed)
P   production
Pr   première
S   screenplay
ZDF Zweites deutsches Fernsehen (Channel Two)

1967

Verona / Two Cats

    D, S, C, Ct, P: Werner Schroeter. F: 8 mm, silent, black and white. L: 10 minutes.

1968

Portrait of Maria Callas

    D, S, C, Ct, P: Werner Schroeter. F: 8 mm, separate soundtrack, color. L: 15 minutes.

Mona Lisa

    D, S, C, Ct, P: Werner Schroeter. F: 8 mm, separate soundtrack, color. L: 35 minutes.

Maria Callas Sings, 1957, Elvira's recitative and aria from Giuseppe Verdi, *Ernani, 1844*

    D, S, C, Ct, A, P: Werner Schroeter. F: 8 mm, separate soundtrack, black and white. L: 10 minutes.

La morte d'Isotta

    D, S, C, Ct, P: Werner Schroeter, from texts by Lautréamont's *Les chants de Maldoror*. A: Rita Bauer, Joachim Bauer, Knut Koch, Truùla Bartek, Werner Schroeter. F: 8 mm, separate soundtrack, color. L: 37 minutes.

Himmel Hoch

    D, S, C, Ct, P: Werner Schroeter. A: Steven Adamczewski, Rita Bauer, Joachim Bauer. F: 8 mm, separate soundtrack, black and white. L: 12 minutes.

Paula—"je reviens"

    D, S, C, Ct, P: Werner Schroeter. A: Heidi Lorenzo, Rita Bauer, Suzanne Sheed, Knut Koch, Werner Schroeter. F: 8 mm, separate soundtrack, color. L: 35 minutes.

Aggressions

    D, S, C, Ct, P: Werner Schroeter. A: Heidi Lorenzo. F: 16 mm, separate soundtrack, black and white. L: 23 minutes.

1969

Neurasia

D, S, C, Ct, P: Werner Schroeter. A: Carla Aulaulu, Magdalena Montezuma, Rita Bauer, Steven Adamczewski. F: 16 mm, magnetic soundtrack, black and white. L: 37 minutes.

Argila

D, S, C, Ct, P: Werner Schroeter. A: Gisela Trowe, Magdalena Montezuma, Carla Aulaulu, Sigurd Salto. F: 16 mm, double projection, separate soundtrack, color + black and white. L: 33 minutes.

Eika Katappa

D, S, Ct: Werner Schroeter. C: Werner Schroeter, Robert van Ackeren. A: Gisela Trowe, Carla Aulaulu, Magdalena Monte-zuma, Knut Koch, Alix von Buchen, Rosy-Rosy, René Schönberg. F: 16 mm, magnetic soundtrack, color. L: 143 minutes. Pr: 10 October 1969, International Film Week, Mannheim.

1970

The Bomber Pilot

D, S, C, Ct: Werner Schroeter. A: Carla Aulaulu, Mascha Rabben, Magdalena Montezuma, Suzanne Sheed, Werner Schroeter, Daniel Schmid. P: Werner Schroeter, for ZDF. F: 16 mm, magnetic soundtrack, color. L: 65 minutes. Pr: 3 November 1970, ZDF.

1971

Salome

D, S: Werner Schroeter, after the play by Oscar Wilde. C: Robert van Ackeren. Ct: Ila von Hasperg. Dc: Elfi Mikesch (cos-tumes). A: Mascha Elm-Rabben, Magdalena Montezuma, Ellen Umlauf, Thomas von Keyserling, René Schönberg, Joachim Paede. P: Ifage, for ZDF. F: 16 mm, magnetic soundtrack, color. L: 81 minutes. Pr: 11 May 1971, ZDF.

Macbeth

D, S, Ct: Werner Schroeter, from themes by William Shakespeare and Giuseppe Verdi. C: Horst Thürling. Dc: Magdalena

Montezuma (costumes). A: Annette Tirier, Stefan von Haugk, Michael Bolze, Sigurd Salto, Magdalena Montezuma, Suzanne Sheed. P: Hessian Radio. F: MAZ, color. L: 60 minutes. Pr: 18 December 1971, HR III.

1972

The Death of Maria Malibran

D, S, C: Werner Schroeter. Ct: Werner Schroeter, Ila von Hasperg. A: Magdalena Montezuma, Christine Kaufmann, Candy Darling, Manuela Riva, Ingrid Caven, Annette Tirier, Einar Hanfstaengl. P: Werner Schroeter, for ZDF. F: 16 mm, optical sound, color. L: 104 minutes. Pr: 2 March 1972, ZDF.

1973

Willow Springs

D, S, C: Werner Schroeter. Ct: Werner Schroeter, Ila von Hasperg. A: Magdalena Montezuma, Christine Kaufmann, Ila von Hasperg, Michael O'Daniels. P: Werner Schroeter, for ZDF. F: 16 mm, magnetic sound, color. L: 78 minutes. Pr: 3 April 1973, ZDF.

1974

The Black Angel

D, S, C, Ct: Werner Schroeter. A: Magdalena Montezuma, Ellen Umlauf. P: Werner Schroeter, for ZDF. F: 16 mm, magnetic sound, color. L: 71 minutes. Pr: 7 May 1974.

1975

Johanna's Dream

D, S, C, Ct, P: Werner Schroeter. A: Magdalena Montezuma, Christine Kaufmann, Candy Darling. F: 16 mm, magnetic sound, color. L: 22 minutes.

1976

Flocons d'or [Flakes of gold]

D, S, C: Werner Schroeter. Ct: Cécile Decugis. A: Magdalena Montezuma, Ellen Umlauf, Christine Kaufmann, Andréa

Ferréol, Bulle Ogier, Ingrid Caven, Isolde Barth, Udo Kier, Ila von Hasperg, Rainer Will. P: Werner Schroeter, for ZDF / Les films du Losange I.N.A. F: 16 mm, magnetic sound, color. L: 160 minutes. Pr: 20 May 1976, ZDF.

1978

The Kingdom of Naples / Neapolitan Siblings

D: Werner Schroeter. S: Werner Schroeter. C: Thomas Mauch. Ct: Ursula West, Werner Schroeter. M: Roberto Pregadio. Dc: Alberte Barsacq, Franco Calabrese. A: Antonio Orlando, Cristina Donadio, Dino Mele, Renata Zamengo, Liana Trouche, Laura Sodano, Raúl Gimenez, Margareth Clémenti, Ida Di Benedetto. P: Dieter Geissler Filmproduktion / Peter Berling Cinematografica / ZDF. F: 16 mm blowup, optical sound, color. L: 130 minutes. Pr: 8 June 1978, ZDF.

1980

Palermo or Wolfsburg

D: Werner Schroeter. S: Giuseppe Fava, Werner Schroeter. C: Thomas Mauch. Ct: Ursula West, Werner Schroeter. Dc: Alberte Barsacq, Roberto Lagana, Magdalena Montezuma, Edwin Wengobowski. A: Nicola Zarbo, Ida Di Benedetto, Magdalena Montezuma, Antonio Orlando, Brigitte Tilg, Harry Baer, Ula Stockl, Tamara Kafka, Isolde Barthm Rainer Will, Claude-Oliver Rudolph, Otto Sander. P: Thomas Mauch Filmproduktion / Arco Film / ZDF. F: 35 mm, optical sound, color. L: 170 minutes. Pr: 1980, International Film Festival, Berlin.

La répétition générale [The dress rehearsal]

D, S: Werner Schroeter. C: Franz Weich. Ct: Catherine Brasier. A: Mostefa Djadjam, Catherine Brasier, Colette Godard, Lew Bogdan, André Engel, Pat Olesko, Kazuo Ohno, Pina Bausch, Reinhild Hoffmann, Ortrud Beginnen. P: Laura Film, for ZDF. F: 16 mm, magnetic sound, color. L: 88 minutes. Pr: 7 September 1980, Mostra del Cinema di Venezia.

White Journey

D, S, C, Ct: Werner Schroeter. Dc: Harald Vogl. A: Jim Auwae, Tilly Soffing, Margareth Clémenti, Maria Schneider, Harald

Vogl, Ursula Rodel, Trudeliese Schmidt, Marion Varella, Werner Schroeter. P: Eric Franck / Werner Schroeter. F: 16 mm, magnetic sound, color. L: 51 minutes. Pr: 10 December 1980, Paris.

1981

Day of the Idiots

D: Werner Schroeter. S: Dana Horáková, Werner Schroeter.
C: Ivan Slapeta. Ct: Catherine Brasier. M: Peer Raben.
Dc: Alberte Barsacq (costumes), Zbybek Hloch (set).
A: Carole Bouquet, Ingrid Caven, Christine Kaufmann, Ida Di Benedetto, Carola Regnier, Mostefa Djadjam, Magdalena Montezuma, Tamara Kafka, Ellen Umlauf. P: Oko-Film Karek Dirka / Bayerische Rundfunk. F: 35 mm, optical sound, color. L: 104 minutes. Pr: 31 October 1981, Hof International Film Festival.

1982

The Council of Love [Il concilio d'amore]

D: Werner Schroeter. S: Dietrich Kuhlbrodt, Roberto Lerici, Horst Alexander, after the play by Oskar Panizza. C: Jörg Schmidt-Reitwein. Ct: Catherine Brasier. Dc: Klaus Meyenberg, Bruno Garofalo (costumes), Magdalena Montezuma (costumes). A: Antonio Salines, Magdalena Montezuma, Kurt Raab, Agnès Nobécourt, Renzo Rinaldi, Margit Carstensen, Roberto Tesconi, Kristina van Eyck, Heinrich Giskes, Gabriela Gómez-Ortega. P: Saskia-Film GmbH / Trio Film GmbH / Antea Cinematografica Sr.l. F: 35 mm, optical sound, color. L: 90 minutes. Pr: 1982, International Film Festival, Berlin.

1983

The Laughing Star

D, C: Werner Schroeter. S: Werner Schroeter, Peter Kern.
Ct: Christl Orthmann, Werner Schroeter. P: Luxor-Film Beteiligungs GmbH / ZDF. F: 16 mm, optical sound, color. L: 108 minutes. Pr: 2 December 1985, Hof International Film Festival.

1985

De l'Argentine [For instance, Argentina]

D, S: Werner Schroeter. C: Werner Schroeter, Carlos Bernardo Waisman. Ct: Catherine Brasier, Claudio Martinez. A: Mothers of the Plaza de Mayo, Libertad Leblanc, Oriana Fallaci. P: Out On / FR 3 / Ministère de la culture. F: 16 mm, optical sound, color. L: 91 minutes. Pr: 2 December 1985, Cinémathèque française.

1986

The Rose King

D: Werner Schroeter. S: Werner Schroeter, Magdalena Montezuma, Rainer Will. C: Elfi Mikesch. Ct: Juliane Lorenz. Dc: Caritas de Witt. A: Magdalena Montezuma, Mostefa Djadjam, Antonio Orlando, Karina Fallenstein. P: Werner Schroeter Filmproduktion / Futura Film Munich / Metro Films Lisbon / Juliane Lorenz Filmproduktion. F: 35 mm, optical sound, color. L: 101 minutes. Pr: 1 February 1986, Rotterdam Film Festival.

1987

In Search of the Sun [À la recherche du soleil]

D, S: Werner Schroeter. C: Wolfgang Pilgrim. Ct: Juliane Lorenz. A: Ariane Mnouchkine, Hélène Cixous, Ensemble du Théâtre du soleil. P: Regina Ziegler Filmproduktion, for ZDF. F: 16 mm, magnetic sound, color. L: 94 minutes. Pr: 10 October 1987, 3sat.

1991

Malina

D: Werner Schroeter. S: Elfriede Jelinek, after the novel by Ingeborg Bachmann. C: Elfi Mikesch. Ct: Juliane Lorenz. M: Giacomo Manzoni. Dc: Alberte Barsacq. A: Isabelle Huppert, Mathieu Carrière, Can Togay, Fritz Schwediwy, Isolde Barth, Libgart Schwarz, Elisabeth Krejcir, Peter Kern, Jenny Drivala, Wiebke Frost. P: Kuchenreuther Film GmbH / Neue

Studio Film GmbH / ZDF / ORF. F: 35 mm, optical sound, color. L: 121 minutes. Pr: 17 November 1991, Munich.

1996

Poussières d'amour [Love's debris]

D: Werner Schroeter. S: Werner Schroeter, Claire Alby. C: Elfi Mikesch. Ct: Juliane Lorenz. M: Elizabeth Cooper. Dc: Alberte Barsacq. A: Anita Cerquetti, Martha Mödl, Isabelle Huppert, Trudeliese Schmidt, Rita Gorr, Kristine Ciesinski, Katherine Ciesinski, Laurence Dale, Jenny Drivala, Gail Gilmore, Sergej Larin, Carole Bouquet, Werner Schroeter. P: MC 4 / Imalyre / Schlemmer Film / La Sept / ARTE / WDR. F: 35 mm, optical sound, color. L: 125 minutes. Pr: 24 October 1996, Hof International Film Festival.

2000

The Queen—Marianne Hoppe

D: Werner Schroeter. S: Werner Schroeter, Monika Keppler. C: Thomas Plenert, Alexandra Kordes. Ct: Florian Köhler. M: Peer Raben. Dc: Alberte Barsacq, Isabel Branco. A: Marianne Hoppe, Evelyne Künneke, Lola Müthel, Einar Schleef, Elisabeth Minetti, Martin Wuttke, Robert Wilson, Maren Eggert, Judith Engel, Ursina Lardi, Martina Gedeck, Barbara Nüsse, Gerti Blache, Benedikt Hoppe. P: Mira Filmproduktion / SFB / ARTE / NDR. F: 16 mm blowup, optical sound, color. L: 101 minutes. Pr: February 2000, International Film Festival, Berlin.

2002

Deux [Two]

D: Werner Schroeter. S: Werner Schroeter, Cédric Anger. C: Elfi Mikesch. Ct: Juliane Lorenz. Dc: Alberte Barsacq. A: Isabelle Huppert, Bulle Ogier, Manuel Blanc, Arielle Dombasle, Annika Kuhl, Philippe Reuter, Jean-François Stévenin, Tim Fischer, Zazie de Paris, Elizabeth Cooper, Alexia Voulgaridou. P: Gemini Films / Mandrogoa Filmes / Road Movies / France 2

Cinéma. F: 35 mm, Dolby stereo sound, color. L: 117 minutes.
Pr: 19 May 2002, Cannes International Film Festival.

2008

Nuit de chien / This Night

D: Werner Schroeter. S: Werner Schroeter, Gilles Taurand, after
the novel *Para esta noche* by Juan Carlos Onetti. C: Thomas
Plenert. Ct: Julia Grégory. M: Eberhard Kloke. Dc: Alberte
Barsacq, Isabel Branco. A: Pascal Greggory, Bruno Tode-
schini, Jean-François Stévenin, Marc Barbé, Amira Casar,
Sami Frey, Elsa Zylberstein, Nathalie Delon, Eric Caravaca,
Bulle Ogier, Lena Schwarz, Pascale Schiller, Oleg Zhukov.
P: Alfama Films / Clap Filmes / Filmgalerie 451. F: 35 mm,
Dolby stereo sound, color. L: 118 minutes. Pr: 2 September
2008, Mostra del Cinema di Venezia.

TEST FILMS, FRAGMENTS, INCOMPLETE PROJECTS

1968

Callas Walking Lucia

D, S, C, Ct, P: Werner Schroeter. F: 8 mm, silent, black and white.
L: 3 minutes. Preliminary study for the Callas film. Original
in the Munich Museum of Film.

Callas Text with Double Exposure

D, S, C, Ct, P: Werner Schroeter. F: 8 mm, silent, black and white.
L: 5 minutes. Preliminary study for the Callas film. Original
in the Munich Museum of Film.

Rehearsals with Actors

D, S, C, P: Werner Schroeter. A: Magdalena Montezuma, Carla
Aulaulu, Steven Adamczewski, Werner Schroeter. F: 8 mm, silent, black and white + color. L: 30 minutes. Nine uncut rolls,
preliminary studies for longer films. Original in the Munich
Museum of Film.

Grotesque–Burlesque–Picturesque

D, S, C: Werner Schroeter, Rosa von Praunheim. F: 8 mm. L: 33
minutes. The Munich Museum of Film contains only the
soundtrack of this film, intended for use as a radio play.

Faces

> D, S, C, Ct, P: Werner Schroeter. A: Heidi Lorenzo. F: 8 mm, silent, black and white. L: 20 minutes. Preliminary study for *Aggressions*. Original in the Munich Museum of Film.

Virginia's Death

> D, S, C, Ct, P: Werner Schroeter. A: Magdalena Montezuma, Heidi Lorenzo. F: 8 mm, silent, black and white. L: 9 minutes. "An unpublished fragment that obviously has not been seen by anyone" (Walter Schobert). The film has not been preserved. The Munich Museum of Film has a soundtrack entitled *Flowers or the Grave* that may be the track of this film.

1969

Nicaragua

> D, S, Ct: Werner Schroeter. C: Robert van Ackeren. A: Carla Aulaulu, Magdalena Montezuma, Gavin Campbell. P: Peter Berling. F: 35 mm, CinemaScope, black and white. L: 18 minutes. According to Werner Schroeter, the film was cut but never shown. The material has not been preserved.

1970

Anglia

> D, S, Ct: Werner Schroeter. C: Jörg Schmidt-Reitwein. A: Magdalena Montezuma, Carla Aulaulu, Mascha Elm-Rabben, Kathrin Schaake, Ulli Lommel, Stefan Hurdalek, Hannes Gromball. P: Atlantis Film. F: 16 mm, color. According to Werner Schroeter, the film was never completed, and the material has not been preserved.

1971

Radio Exhibition 1971—Hitparade

> D, S: Werner Schroeter. P: ZDF. F: MAZ, color. The material filmed by Werner Schroeter was not used and has not been preserved.

LIVE PERFORMANCE (PLAYS, MUSICAL THEATER, OPERA, DANCE THEATER)

Under the heading of A for actors and other interpreters, the protagonists and those who worked with Werner Schroeter for many years are listed alphabetically. All the facts are taken from programs where they were available.

A   actors
C   costumes
D   director
DM   director of music (mentioned only for all operatic
      productions and for plays for which a director of music
      created his or her own compositions)
FGP   first German-language production
OP   other participants
Opr   original première
Pr   première
S   soloists
SD   set design

1972

Gotthold Ephraim Lessing, *Emilia Galotti*

    D: Werner Schroeter. SD, C: Bernd Holzapfel. A: Hans Peter Hallwachs, Christine Kaufmann, Magdalena Montezuma, Gisela Trowe, etc. Pr: 28 May 1972, German Theater, Hamburg.

1973

Oscar Wilde, *Salome*

    D: Werner Schroeter. SD, C: Werner Schroeter, Magdalena Montezuma, Jan Moewes. DM: Peer Raben. A: Ingrid Caven, Christine Kaufmann, Magdalena Montezuma, Friedrich-Karl Praetorius, Rainer Will, Fred Williams. Pr: 16 March 1973, Bochum Theater.

1974

Victor Hugo, *Lucrezia Borgia*

D: Werner Schroeter. SD, C: Werner Schroeter, Magdalena Montezuma, Katharina Schüssler. DM: Peer Raben. A: Magdalena Montezuma, Tamara Kafka, Siemen Rühaak, Fritz Schediwy, Rainer Will, etc. Pr: 6 November 1974, Bochum Theater.

1977

August Strindberg, *Miss Julie*

D: Werner Schroeter. SD, C: Werner Schroeter, Alberte Barsacq, Jan Moewes. A: Ingrid Caven, Tamara Kafka, Wolfgang Schumacher, etc. Pr: 21 September 1977, Bochum Theater.

Gotthold Ephraim Lessing, *Miss Sara Sampson*

D: Werner Schroeter. SD: Werner Schroeter, Alberte Barsacq. C: Alberte Barsacq. A: Elisabeth Krejcir, Wolfgang Schumacher, Heiner Stadelmann, etc. Pr: 30 November 1977, Kassel State Theater.

1978

Heinrich von Kleist, *Das Käthchen von Heilbronn*

D: Werner Schroeter. SD: Werner Schroeter, Hans Peter Schubert. C: Alberte Barsacq. A: Tamara Kafka, Knut Koch, Elisabeth Krejcir, Gottfried Lachmann, Magdalena Montezuma, Tana Schanzara, Wolfgang Schumacher, etc. Pr: 7 December 1978, Bochum Theater.

1979

Richard Wagner, *Lohengrin*

DM: James Lockhart. D: Werner Schroeter. SD: Werner Schroeter, Walter Perdacher. C: Alberte Barsacq. S: Barbara Honn, Arley Reece, Rose Wagemann, etc. Pr: 30 September 1979, Kassel State Theater.

1980

Corrado Alvaro, *Lunga notte di Medea*

DM: Rosa Balistreri. D: Werner Schroeter. SD: Cesare Berlingeri. C: Alberte Barsacq. S: Piera Degli Esposti, Yorya Lambropoulos, Laura Mereu, etc. Pr: 19 January 1980, Teatro Niccolini, Florence.

Ingrid Caven chante
> D: Werner Schroeter. DM: Peer Raben, with words by Hans Magnus Enzensberger, Rainer Werner Fassbinder. A, S: Ingrid Caven. March 1980, La Palace, Paris.

Alexander von Zemlinsky, *A Florentine Tragedy*
> DM: Friedrich Pleyer. D: Werner Schroeter. SD: Paolo Potoghesi. A, S: Hans-Jürgen Demitz, etc. Pr: 4–5 October 1980, Teatro La Fenice, Venice, Biennale Venezia.

1982

Luigi Pirandello, *Tonight We Improvise*, production announced as *Don Carlos*
> D: Werner Schroeter. SD, C: Werner Schroeter, Magdalena Montezuma. A: Hans Peter Hallwachs, Albert Kitzl, Magdalena Montezuma, Sonja Mustoff, Carola Regnier, Eva Schuckardt, Rainer Will, etc. Pr: 16 May 1982, Frankfurt Theater, coproduction with the Munich Festival Theater and the Avignon Festival.

1983

Tango y realidad en Argentina 1983
> Workshop and staged production at the invitation of the Goethe-Institut, Buenos Aires. D, SD, C: Werner Schroeter.

William Shakespeare, *The Comedy of Errors*
> D: Werner Schroeter. SD: Werner Schroeter. C: Alberte Barsacq. A: Karina Fallenstein, Peter Kern, Claude-Oliver Rudolph, Eva Schuckardt, Wolfgang Schuhmacher, etc. Pr: 2 September 1983, Freie Volksbühne, Berlin.

1984

Libertad: A Scenic Collage
> D: Werner Schroeter. SD, C: Alberte Barsacq. Teatro Lola Membrives, Buenos Aires.

1985

Horst Laube, from themes by Carlo Goldoni, *Finale in Smyrna*
   D: Werner Schroeter. SD, C: Alberte Barsacq. A: Michael Alt-
   mann, Christa Berndl, Jürgen Holtz, Monika John, Peter
   Kern, Heinz Kraehkamp, Eva Schuckardt, Lena Stolze, Rainer
   Will, etc. Opr: Bavarian State Theater, Munich. Pr: 24 Febru-
   ary 1985.

Alfredo Catalani, *La Wally*
   DM: Pinchas Steinberg. D: Werner Schroeter. SD, C: Alberte
   Barsacq. S: Kristine Ciesinski, Nelly Boschkowa, Jeanne
   Brügemann, Mihai Zamfir, etc. Pr: 24 November 1985, Bremen
   Theater.

1986

Georg Büchner, *Leonce und Lena*
   D: Werner Schroeter. SD, C: Alberte Barsacq. A: Benno Ifland,
   Hertha Martin, Birgit Walter, Isolde Barth, etc. Pr: 12 April
   1986, Bremen Theater.

Richard Strauss, *Salome*
   D: Werner Schroeter. DM: Francisco Savin. S: Kristine Ciesinski,
   etc. Pr: 25 July 1986, Teatro de bellas artes, Mexico City.

Federica García Lorca, *Doña Rosita*
   D: Werner Schroeter. SD, C: Alberte Barsacq. A: Karina Fallen-
   stein, Peter Kern, Elisabeth Krejcir, Christiane Lemm,
   Christine Schönfeld, Hanna Seiffert, Marcelo Uriona, etc.
   Pr: 15 November 1986, Düsseldorf Theater.

1987

August Strindberg, *Intoxication*
   D: Werner Schroeter. SD, C: Alberte Barsacq. A: Ludwig Boettger,
   Traute Hoess, Hertha Martin, Martin Reinke, Birgit Walter,
   etc. Pr: 16 January 1987, Bremen Theater.

Rainer Werner Fassbinder, *Katzelmacher* [Foreigners]
   D: Werner Schroeter, Annette Rosenfeld. SD: Manfred Dittrich.
   C: Dorothea Katzer. A: Gerhild Didusch, Arpad Kraupa, Mar-
   garete Oesterreich, Bernd Stegemann, Franziska Weber, etc.
   Pr: 2 May 1987, Düsseldorf Theater.

Yukio Mishima, *The Tropical Tree*

> D: Werner Schroeter. SD, C: Alberte Barsacq. A: Karina Fall-
> enstein, Peter Kern, Arpad Kraupa, Elisabeth Krejcir, Petra
> Redinger. FGP: translation by Ursula Schuh. Pr: 20 June 1987,
> Düsseldorf Theater.

Gaetano Donizetti, *Lucia di Lammermoor*

> DM: Anton Guadagno. D: Werner Schroeter. SD: Werner
> Schroeter, Florian Etti. C: Alberte Barsacq. S: Jenny Drivala,
> etc. Pr: 7 July 1987, Teatro di Villa Mimbella, Livorno.

Luigi Cherubini, *Medea*

> DM: Eberhard Kloke. D: Werner Schroeter. SD, C: Alberte
> Barsacq. S: Kristine Ciesinski, Neal Schwantes, etc. Pr: 19 Sep-
> tember 1987, Freiburg Theater.

Grief, Longing, Rebellion: An Evening with Tangos

> D: Werner Schroeter. SD, C: Florian Etti. A, S: Marcelo Uriona,
> etc. Pr: 4 October 1987, Düsseldorf Theater.

1988

Friedrich Schiller, *Don Carlos*

> D: Werner Schroeter. MD: Monika Keppler. SD, C: Alberte
> Barsacq. A: Frank Albrecht, Ludwig Boettger, Traute Hoess,
> Benno Ifland, Hertha Martin, Marcelo Uriona, Birgit Walter,
> etc. Pr: 16 January 1988, Bremen Theater.

Maxim Gorky, *Children of the Sun*

> D: Werner Schroeter. SD, C: Alberte Barsacq. A: Karina Fallen-
> stein, Peter Kern, Elisabeth Krejcir, Christiane Lemm, etc.
> Pr: 21 May 1988, Düsseldorf Theater.

Tommaso Traetta, *Antigone*

> DM: Alkis Baltas. D: Werner Schroeter. SD, C: Alberte Barsacq.
> S: Jenny Drivala, etc. Pr: 24 June 1988, Festival dei due mondi,
> Spoleto.

Gerlind Reinshagen, *Die Feuerblume* [The flame-flower] (Opr)
Arnold Schönberg, *Pierrot Lunaire*

> D: Werner Schroeter, Günter Krämer. DM: Antony Beaumont.
> SD, C: Ulrich Schulz; A, S: Ludwig Boettger, Therese Dürren-
> berger, Eva Gilhofer, Traute Hoess, Benno Ifland, Herbert
> Knaup, Birgit Walter, etc. Pr: 1 October 1988, Bremen Theater.

Gaetano Donizetti, *Parisina d'est*

  DM: Baldo Podic. D: Werner Schroeter. SD, C: Alberte Barsacq.
  S: Paolo Gavinelli, Dalmacio Gonzales, Jolanda Omilian, etc.
  Pr: 6 November 1988, Basel Theater.

1989

Hans Henny Jahnn, *Medea*

  D: Werner Schroeter. SD: Florian Etti. C: Beatrice von Bomhard.
  A: Gerhild Didusch, Bernt Hahn, Elisabeth Krejcir, Peter
  Lohmeyer, Barbara Nüsse, Marcelo Uriona, etc. Pr: 23 January
  1989, Düsseldorf Theater.

Richard Wagner / Klaus Huber, *Spes contra spem* (Opr)

  DM: Eberhard Kloke. D: Werner Schroeter. SD, C: Alberte Barsacq. S: Kristine Ciesinski, June Card. A: Elisabeth Krejcir,
  Bernt Hahn, etc. Pr: 22 February 1989, Düsseldorf Theater,
  coproduction Bochum Symphony Orchestra / Düsseldorf
  Theater.

Samuel Beckett, *Breath*

  SD, C: Ulrich Schulz. A, S: Eva Gilhofer and ensemble. Pr:
  16 April 1989, Bremen Theater.

Eugene O'Neill, *Long Day's Journey into Night*

  D: Werner Schroeter. SD, C: Alberte Barsacq. A: Stephan Biss-
  meier, Inka Friedrich, Elisabeth Krejcir, Norbert Schwientek,
  Michael Wittenborn. Pr: 10 December 1989, Basel Theater.

1990

William Shakespeare, *King Lear*

  SD: Florian Etti. C: Lioba Winterhalder. A: Jens Berthold,
  Bernt Hahn, Peter Kern, Elisabeth Krejcir, Hermann Lause,
  Christiane Lemm, Eva Schuckardt, etc. Pr: 25 March 1990,
  Düsseldorf Theater.

Ludwig van Beethoven, *Missa solemnis*

  DM: Eberhard Kloke. D, SD: Werner Schroeter. C: Werner
  Schroeter, Andrea Markhoff. S: Melinda Liebermann, Ruth-
  Marie Nicolay, Alexander Stevenson, Daniel L. Williams.
  A: Petra Kuhles, Ellen Umlauf, Arpad Kraupa, Walter Spiske,
  Bernd Stegemann, etc. Pr: 3 June 1990, Düsseldorf Theater,

coproduction Bochum Symphony Orchestra / Düsseldorf
Theater.

1991

Gotthold Ephraim Lessing, *Emilia Galotti*
  D: Werner Schroeter. SD, C: Alberte Barsacq. A: Ernst Alisch,
  Jens Berthold, Gerhilt Didusch, Herbert Frisch, Elisabeth
  Krejcir, etc. Pr: 12 January 1991, Düsseldorf Theater.
Samuel Beckett, *Breath*
  D, SD, C: Werner Schroeter. A, S: Margarete Österreich, Marcelo
  Uriona, ensemble. Pr: 4 February 1991, Düsseldorf Theater.
Alfred de Musset, *Marianne—les caprices de Marianne*
  D: Werner Schroeter. SD, C: Alberte Barsacq. A: Heikko
  Deutschmann, Gerd Kunath, Jan Josef Liefers, Carola Reg-
  nier, Oscar Ortega Sánchez, etc. Pr: 6 April 1991, Thalia
  Theater, Hamburg.
August Strindberg, *The Dance of Death I and II*
  D: Werner Schroeter. SD, C: Alberte Barsacq. A: Ernst Alisch, Jele
  Brückner, Bernt Hahn, Eva Schuckardt, etc. Pr: 13 October
  1991, Düsseldorf Theater.
Giuseppe Verdi, *Luisa Miller*
  DM: Carlo Rizzi, Julian Reynolds. D: Werner Schroeter. SD,
  C: Alberte Barsacq. S: Kallen Esperian, Sergej Larin, Neil
  Shicoff, etc. Pr: 2 December 1991, Nederlandse Opera,
  Amsterdam.

1992

Jakob Michael Reinhold Lenz, *The Soldiers*
  D: Werner Schroeter. SD: Werner Schroeter, Ulrich Schulz. C:
  Carlo Diappi. A: Karine Fallenstein, Bernd Grawert, Herbert
  Knaup, Hansjoachim Krietsch, Marcelo Uriona, Birgit Wal-
  ter, Rainer Will, Almut Zilcher, etc. Pr: 5 June 1992, Cologne
  Theater.
Arnold Schönberg / Bernd Alois Zimmermann, *Jacob's Ladder /
Ecclesiastical Action*
  DM: Eberhard Kloke. D: Werner Schroeter. SD, C: Alberte Bar-
  sacq. S, A: Martha Mödl, Jens Berthold, etc. Pr: 18 September

1992, Düsseldorf Theater, coproduction Bochum Symphony Orchestra / Düsseldorf Theater.

    S, A: Marianne Hoppe, Markus Boysen, etc. Pr: 11 February 1993, Long Beach Opera, Los Angeles.

Eugène Labiche, *The Martin Prize*

    D: Werner Schroeter. SD: Werner Schroeter, Ulrich Schulz. C: Carola Brandes. A: Traute Hoess, Herbert Knaup, Almut Zilcher, etc. Pr: 24 October 1992, Cologne Theater.

Jean Genet, *Under Surveillance*

    D: Werner Schroeter. SD, C: Werner Schroeter, Ulrich Schulz. A: Bernd Grawert, Ernest Allan Hausmann, Nicki von Tempelhoff, Rainer Will. Pr: 22 December 1992, Cologne Theater.

1993

Giuseppe Verdi, *Luisa Miller*

    DM: Carlo Rizzi. D: Werner Schroeter. SD, C: Alberte Barsacq. S: Kallen Esperian, Neil Shicoff, etc. Pr: 1 February 1993, Grand théâtre de Geneve (guest production of the Nederlandse Opera, Amsterdam 1991).

Dmitri D. Shostakovich, *Lady Macbeth of Mtsensk*

    DM: Eberhard Kloke. D: Werner Schroeter. SD, C: Alberte Barsacq. S: Valeri Alekseev, June Card, Kristine Ciesinski, Ryszard Karczykowski, Sergej Larin, etc. Pr: 7 March 1993, Frankfurt Opera.

Samuel Beckett, *Breath*

    D, SD, C: Werner Schroeter. A: ensemble. Pr: 20 May 1993, Basel Theater.

Jules Massenet, *Werther*

    DM: Michel Sasson. D: Werner Schroeter. SD, C: Alberte Barsacq. S: Francisco Araiza, Thomas Mohr, Lani Poulson, etc. Pr: 11 July 1993, City of Bonn Opera.

Eugene O'Neill, *Mourning Becomes Electra*

    D: Werner Schroeter. SD, C: Alberte Barsacq. A: Ernst Alisch, Markus Boysen, Jele Brückner, Ernest Allan Hausmann, Elisabeth Krejcir, Eva Schuckardt, etc. Pr: 25 September 1993, Düsseldorf Theater.

Tony Kushner, *Angels in America*

> D: Werner Schroeter. SD, C: Alberte Barsacq. A: Stephan Biss-meier, Monica Bleibtreu, Markus Boysen, Matthias Fuchs, Ernest Allan Hausmann, Barbara Nüsse, Zazie de Paris, etc. Pr: 19 November 1993. FGP: German Theater, Hamburg.

1994

Albert Camus, *Caligula*

> D: Werner Schroeter. SD, C: Ulrich Schulz. A: Samuel Finzi, Jan Schütte, Almut Zilcher, etc. Pr: 4 March 1994, Cologne Theater.

Giacomo Puccini, *Tosca*

> DM: Spiros Argiris. D: Werner Schroeter. SD, C: Alberte Barsacq. S: Sergej Larin, Sergei Leiferkus, Carol Vaness, etc. Pr: 13 May 1994, Opéra nationale de Paris, Bastille.

Jakob Michael Reinhold Lenz, *The New Menoza; or, The Story of Prince Tandi of Cumba*

> D: Werner Schroeter. SD, C: Alberte Barsacq. A: Ernst Alisch, Tonio Arango, Dietlinde Hillebrecht, Benno Ifland, Elisabeth Krejcir, Christiane Lemm, Dieter Prochnow, Michaela Steiger, etc. Pr: 15 October 1994, Düsseldorf Theater.

1995

Aeschylus, *The Persians*

> D: Werner Schroeter. SD, C: Alberte Barsacq. A: Heinrich Baumgartner, Therese Dürrenberger, Traute Hoess, Jan Schütte, etc. Pr: 5 March 1995, Cologne Theater.

Jean-Baptiste Molière, *The Misanthrope*

> D: Werner Schroeter. SD: Katja Hass. C: Reinhard van der Than-nen. A: Stephan Bissmeier, Markus Boysen, Martin Horn, Inka Friedrich, Elke Lang, Martin Lindow, etc. Pr: 30 April 1995, German Theater, Hamburg.

Ludwig van Beethoven, *Fidelio*

> DM: Marc Albrecht. D: Werner Schroeter. SD, C: Alberte Barsacq. Chorus master: André Weiss. S: Jayne Casselman, Wolfgang Neumann, etc. Pr: 18 June 1995, Darmstadt State Theater.

Luigi Nono, *Intolleranza 1960*
  DM: Marc Albrecht. D: Werner Schroeter. SD, C: Alberte Barsacq. Chorus master: André Weiss. S: Wolfgang Neumann,
  etc. Pr: 16 September 1995.

1996

Ramón del Valle-Inclán, *Words of God*
  D: Werner Schroeter. SD, C: Alberte Barsacq. A: Ernst Alisch,
  Wolfgang Maria Bauer, Jele Brückner, Ernest Allan Haus-
  mann, Elisabeth Krejcir, Christine Schönfeld, Michaela
  Steiger, etc. Pr: 24 April 1996, Düsseldorf State Theater, main
  auditorium.
What Remains Is Disaster, Horror, or Lust: Revue Heiner Müller
  D, SD, C: Werner Schroeter. DM: Elizabeth Cooper. A: Jörg
  Michael Koerbl, Zazie de Paris, Volker Spengler, ensemble.
  S: Carol Wyatt. Pr: 30 December 1996, Berliner Ensemble.

1997

Charles Spencer Chaplin, *Monsieur Verdoux* (theatrical production
from the screenplay of the same name)
  D: Werner Schroeter. SD, C: Alberte Barsacq. A: Marianne
  Hoppe, Eva Mattes, Angelika Waller, Anna Thalbach, Jörg-
  Michael Koerbl, Zazie de Paris, Uwe Steinbruch, Martin
  Wuttke, etc. Pr: 19 January 1997, Berliner Ensemble.

1998

Lars Norèn, *Sangue*
  D: Werner Schroeter. SD, C: Alberte Barsacq. A: Marina Malfatti,
  Guido Morbello, Paolo Graziosi, etc. Pr: 24 February 1998,
  Teatro Carcano Milano.
Richard Wagner, *Tristan und Isolde*
  DM: Zóltán Peschkó. D: Werner Schroeter. SD, C: Hans Joachim
  Schlieker. S: Bodo Brinkmann, Renée Morloc, Wilhelm
  Richter, Raimo Sirkiä, Johann Tilli, Linda Watson, etc. Pr:
  6 June 1998, German Opera on the Rhine, Theater of the City
  of Duisberg.

Slobodan Snajder, *The Bride of the Wind*

> D: Werner Schroeter. SD, C: Alberte Barsacq. A: Maren Eggert, Wolfram Koch, Andreas Pietschmann, etc. Opr: Bochum Theater. Pr: 13 November 1998.

1999

Tennessee Williams, *The Glass Menagerie*

> D: Werner Schroeter. SD, C: Alberte Barsacq. A: Marina Malfatti, Valeria Milillo, Luca Lazzaeschi, Luigi Saravo. Pr: 16 January 1999, Teatro Eliseo Rome.

Georges Bizet, *Carmen*

> DM: Marc Albrecht. D: Werner Schroeter. SD, C: Hans-Joachim Schlieker. S: Fredrika Brillembourg, Hans Christoph Begemann, Doris Brüggemann, Thomas Fleischmann, Jon Ketilsson, Mary Anne Kruger, Fernando del Valle, Anton Keremidtchiev, Michaela Schuster, etc. Pr: 12 June 1999, Darmstadt State Theater.

Jean B. Racine, *Phaedra*

> D: Werner Schroeter. SD: Alex Harp. C: Caritas de Wit. A: Margit Carstensen, Ralf Dittrich, Samuel Finzi, Eva-Maria Hofmann, Annika Kuhl, Andreas Pietschmann, etc. Pr: 4 December 1999, Bochum Theater.

2000

Giuseppe Verdi, *A Masked Ball*

> DM: Peter Sommer. D: Werner Schroeter. SD, C: Alberte Barsacq. S: Ki-Chun Park, Alexia Voulgaridou, Elisabeth Whitehouse, etc. Guest performance in San Sebastián 2004. S: Francisco Casanova, Anna Maria Sanchez, Marina Prudenskaya, etc. Pr: 13 April 2000, coproduction Mannheim National Theater / San Sebastián Festival.

Giuseppi Verdi, *La traviata*

> DM: Marc Piollet. D: Werner Schroeter. SD, C: Alberte Barsacq. S: Yikun Chung, Nora Sourouzian, Alexia Voulgaridou, Tito You, etc. Pr: 13 September 2000, Kassel State Theater.

Tennessee Williams, *Orpheus Descending*

    D: Werner Schroeter. SD, C: Barbara Rückert. A: Tatjana Clasing, Ernest Allan Hausmann, Andreas Maier, Zazie de Paris, etc. Pr: 15 December 2000, Oberhausen Theater.

2001

Giuseppe Verdi, *Otello*

    DM: Roberto Paternostro. D, SD: Werner Schroeter. C: Alberte Barsacq. S: Fernando Cobo, Richard Decker, Alfred Kim, George Stevens, Tito You, etc. Pr: 22 September 2001, Kassel State Theater.

2002

The Divine Flame; or, The Longest Second

    A theatrical evening by Werner Schroeter and Monika Keppler. D: Werner Schroeter. SD, C: Barbara Rückert. DM: Michael Barfuss. A, S: Jennifer Julia Caron, Raffaele Irace, Andreas Maier, Daniel Wiemer, Zazi de Paris, Oleg Zhukov, etc. Pr: 31 May 2002, Oberhausen Theater.

Wolfgang Amadeus Mozart, *The Abduction from the Seraglio*

    From a concept by George Tabori. DM and overall management: Christoph Hagel. D: Werner Schroeter. C: Barbara Naujok. A, S Matthieu Carrière, Sylvia Koke, etc. Premières: 27 July 2002, Kaiser Wilhelm Memorial Church, Berlin; 17 August 2002, New Synagogue, Berlin; and 27 August 2002, Islamic Alevite Prayer House, Berlin.

Georg Kreisler, *Adam Schaf Is Afraid; or, The Song of the End*

    D, SD: Werner Schroeter. DM: Thomas Dörschel. C: Caritas de Wit. A, S: Tim Fischer, Steffi Kühnert, etc. Opr: Berliner Ensemble. Pr: 4 December 2002.

Giacomo Puccini, *Madama Butterfly*

    DM: Peter Kuhn. D, SD, C: Werner Schroeter. S: Karine Babajanyan, Nina Feldmann, Sergio Panajia, etc. Pr: 4 December 2002, Bielefeld Theater.

2003

Vincenzo Bellini, *Norma*

DM: John Fiore. D: Werner Schroeter. SD: Barbara Rückert.
C: Alberte Barsacq. S: Jeanne Pilaud, Gabriel Sadé, Chrisoph-
oros Stamboglis, Alexandra von der Weth, etc. Pr: 16 May
2003, German Opera on the Rhine, Düsseldorf Opera House.

Alban Berg, *Lulu*

DM: Roman Kofman. D: Werner Schroeter. SD, C: Alberte Bar-
sacq. S: Fabrice Dallis, Anat Efraty, Carmen Fugiss, Karsten
Gaul, Hanna Schwarz, Pavio Hunka, Adalbert Waller, etc.
Pr: 1 October 2003, Bonn Theater.

2004

Roland Dubillard, *Madame fait ce q'elle veut*

D: Werner Schroeter. A: Maria Machado. Pr: 2 March 2004,
Théâtre du rond point, Paris.

Vladimir Nabokov, *The Waltz Invention*

D, SD: Werner Schroeter. C: Susanne Thaler. A: Achim Barren-
stein, Elisabeth Krejcir, Till Sterzenbach, Christian Wirmer,
Uwe Zerwer, etc. Pr: 8 May 2004. FGP: Darmstadt State
Theater.

Heinrich von Kleist, *Amphitryon*

D, SD: Werner Schroeter. C: Barbara Rückert. A: Manuela Al-
phons, Juan Carlos Lopez, Andreas Maier, Wolfgang Rützer,
Daniel Wiemer, etc. Pr: 1 October 2004, Bonn Theater.

2005

Giuseppe Verdi, *Don Carlos*

DM: Peter Kuhn. D: Werner Schroeter. Musical direction: Birgit
Kronshage. SD: Werner Schroeter, Alexander Schult. C: Wer-
ner Schroeter, Eliseu Roque Weide. S: Michael Bachtadze,
Jacek Janiszewski, Vladimir Chmelo, Alexander Marco-
Buhrmeister, Irina Makarova, Ki-Chun Park, Irina Popova,
Alexander Vassiliev, etc. Pr: 19 February 2005, Bielefeld The-
ater, Rudolf Oetker Auditorium.

"I Can Sleep When I'm Dead": A Tribute to Rainer Werner Fassbinder on His Sixtieth Birthday

>D, SD, C: Werner Schroeter. Musical direction Harry Baer.
>A: Harry Baer, Rudolf Waldemar Brem, Margit Carstensen, Ingrid Caven, Hans Hirschmüller, Irm Hermann, Günther Kaufmann, Doris Mattes, Katrin Schaake, Elga Sorbas, etc. Pr: 4 June 2005, Bonn Theater.

Jan Müller-Wieland, *The Madmen; or, Fishing by Night*

>DM: Wolfgang Lischke. D, SD, C: Werner Schroeter. S: Julia Kamenik, Holger Falk, etc. Pr: 28 September 2005, coproduction Bonn Theater / Bonn Beethoven Festival / Art and Exhibition Hall of the Federal Republic of Germany.

2006

The Beauty of Shadows: Heinrich Heine and Robert Schumann; A Tribute by Werner Schroeter and Roland Techet

>DM: Roland Techet. D: Werner Schroeter. Musical direction: Monika Keppler, Thilo Rheinhardt. A: students of Professor Karl Kneidl's class in set design, conducted by Ruth Gross; and students of Professor Laurids Ortner's class in architecture, conducted by Christian P. Heuchel. A, S: Alexis Bug, Julia Kamenik, Alexandra Kunz, Lisa Marie Landgraf, Roland Techet, Oleg Zhukov, etc. Pr: 12 March 2006, Düsseldorf Hall of Art.

2007

Thomas Adès, *Powder Her Face*

>DM: Thomas Wise. D: Werner Schroeter. Musical direction: Jan David Schmitz. SD: Werner Schroeter, Ansgar Baradoy. C: Werner Schroeter, Gabriele Natascha Richter. S: Jennifer Chamandy, Nikolaus Meer, Eva Resch, Mark Rosenthal, etc. Pr: 15 March 2007, Bonn Theater, in cooperation with the Art and Exhibition Hall of the Federal Republic of Germany and Bonne chance! Experimental Music Theater.

2009

Wolfgang Amadeus Mozart, *Don Giovanni*

DM: Sébastien Rouland. D: Werner Schroeter. SD, C: Alberte Barsacq. S: Elaine Alvarez, Jean Broekhuizen, Konstantin Gorny, Tuomas Pursio, Tiberius Simu, etc. Pr: 31 January 2009, Leipzig Opera.

Friedrich Hölderlin and Hugo von Hofmannsthal, after Sophocles, *All Is Dead—Forms of Loneliness: Antigone/Electra*

Concept: Werner Schroeter, Monika Keppler. D: Werner Schroeter. SD: amphitheater by Bert Neumann. OP: Jochen Hochfeld. C: Alberte Barsacq. DM: Sir Henry. A: Dörte Lyssewski, Anne Ratte-Polle, Pascale Schiller, Almut Zilcher. Pr: 17 June 2009, Agora, Volksbühne on Rosa Luxembourg Square, Berlin.

A Tribute to Lautréamont and Christmas

A production with texts from *The Songs of Maldoror* on the occasion of the exhibition *Autrefois et toujours: Photographic Works by Werner Schroeter, 1973–2009*. Curator: Christian Holzfuss, Fine Arts Berlin. D: Werner Schroeter. SD, C: Werner Schroeter, Jochen Hochfeld. A: Anton Andreew, Pascale Schiller, Werner Schroeter, Almut Zilcher. Pr: 26 December 2009, House on the Lützowplatz, Berlin.

2010

Bernard-Marie Koltès, *Quai West*

D: Werner Schroeter. Musical direction: Monika Keppler. SD: Werner Schroeter, Jochen Hochfeld. C: Alberte Barsacq. A: Sebastian König, Toks Körner, Peter Kremer, Maria Kwiakowsky, Christoph Letkowski, Uwe Preuss, Silvia Rieger, Pascale Schiller. Pr: 10 March 2010, Volksbühne on Rosa Luxembourg Square, Berlin.

CHRONOLOGY

1945   7 April, Werner Schroeter born, son of Hans Otto Schröter and Lena Schröter, née Buchmann, in Georgenthal (Thuringia), brother of Hans-Jürgen Schröter.

1952   The family moves to Bielefeld.

1958   Death of Werner Schroeter's maternal grandmother.

1959–66   The family moves to Heidelberg-Dossenheim. Schroeter goes to school in Heidelberg, also spending several months at a school in Naples, and finally takes his graduation examination at the high school at the Anglo-American Institute, Heidelberg.

Meets Erika Kluge in Heidelberg, whom he renames Magdalena Montezuma. She works on all his productions with him under that name until her death in 1984.

Makes his first double 8 mm films.

Matriculates at the University of Mannheim to study psychology. Begins studying at the Munich University of Television and Film. In all, these two periods of "study" last only a few months.

1967   Visits the EXPRMNTL Film Festival in Knokke-le-Zoute, Belgium, where he meets Rosa von Praunheim.

1969   Wins the Josef von Sternberg Prize at the Mannheim International Film Festival for *Eika Katappa*. The film is bought for TV. Many of his subsequent films and stage productions will be shown on Zweites deutsches Fernsehen (ZDF), Channel Two of German public service television, in the *Little TV Theater* slot.

1970   Takes part in the Quinzaine des réalisateurs at the Cannes International Film Festival, with *Eika Katappa*. Meets Henri Langlois, director of the Cinémathèque française in Paris, who will do a good deal for the distribution and recognition of Schroeter's films in France.

1971   After the TV transmission of the film *Salome*, shot in Lebanon, receives offers from Jean-Pierre Ponnelle, Peter Zadek, and Ivan Nagel to direct theatrical productions.

First long visit to the United States, researching in New York for the film *The Death of Maria Malibran*.

1972   Shoots *Willow Springs* in Willow Springs, in the Mojave Desert, California.

Directs his first theatrical production, *Emilia Galotti*, at the German Theater, Hamburg.

First retrospectives at the Cinémathèque française in Paris, the Metropolitan Museum, and the Museum of Modern Art, New York.

1973–77   Meets Maria Callas, whose art has influenced him since his youth and has inspired him to make several films.

Retrospectives in London and Vienna.

Lectures at the University of California, Berkeley, and the University of California, Los Angeles; holds a workshop at the San Francisco Art School.

Several long visits to South America.

Makes the films *The Black Angel, Johanna's Dream*, and *Flakes of Gold*. Directs stage productions of *Salome, Lucrezia Borgia*, and *Miss Julie* at the Bochum Theater.

1975	In Paris, meets the costume designer Alberte Barsacq, who will accompany him on many of his stage productions and films as an inspiring designer of sets and costumes and a personal partner.
1976	Death of his mother.
1978	International success with the feature film *Il Regno di Napoli* [The Kingdom of Naples], which in German is misleadingly entitled *Neapolitanische Geschwister* [Neapolitan siblings], from a book by Franz Werfel.
1979	Directs an opera for the first time: *Lohengrin*, at the Kassel State Theater.
	Shoots *Palermo or Wolfsburg* in Sicily, Wolfsburg, and Berlin.
1980	Wins the Golden Bear award at the Berlin International Film Festival (the Berlinale) for *Palermo or Wolfsburg*.
	Shoots *White Journey* and *The Dress Rehearsal*.
	Andre Müller interviews him in *Die Zeit* about the film *Palermo or Wolfsburg*; the interview creates a scandal. Asked about Franz Josef Strauss as a candidate for chancellor of the Federal Republic of Germany, Schroeter says he hopes Strauss bursts "because he's so fat. Someone ought to feed him a little bomb in the form of a Bavarian white sausage." Strauss takes this as public incitement to murder, and the city fathers of Augsburg, with the backing of the heirs of the composer Richard Strauss, prevent Schroeter from directing a production of the opera *Salome*.
1981–83	Directs theatrical productions in Frankfurt, Berlin, and Buenos Aires. Lengthy visits to Brazil and Argentina, where he shoots films. Makes the films *Day of the Idiots*, *The Council of Love*, and *The Laughing Star*.

1984	At a casting session for *Libertad* in Buenos Aires, meets Marcelo Uriona, who comes to Germany in 1985 and lives and works with Schroeter until his early death.
	Shoots *The Rose King* in Portugal, with Magdalena Montezuma.
	Begins working with Elfi Mikesch as his camerawoman; she had already worked with him on several projects as photographer and designer.
	On 15 July, a few weeks after the end of shooting *The Rose King*, Magdalena Montezuma dies in Berlin.
1985–89	Directs operas and plays in Bremen, Düsseldorf, Spoleto, Freiburg, etc.
	Works on shooting *In Search of the Sun* and *De l'Argentine*.
	After staying in friends' apartments for a long time, Schroeter (with Marcelo Uriona) rents an apartment of his own in Bremen, then moves to one in Düsseldorf two years later and lives there until 2002.
1990	Shoots *Malina*, working with Isabelle Huppert for the first time.
1990–95	Directs operas and plays in Basel, Cologne, Frankfurt, Düsseldorf, Hamburg, Darmstadt, Kassel, Rome, Milan, Amsterdam, and Paris.
1993	Death of Marcelo Uriona.
1994	Schroeter's father dies in February; his brother dies in November.
1995	Shoots *Love's Debris*.
1996–2001	Directs operas and plays in Düsseldorf, Berlin, Milan, Bochum, Rome, Darmstadt, Mannheim, Kassel, and Oberhausen.
2002	Shoots *Deux* [Two], with Isabelle Huppert.

2003–7	Directs operas and plays in Oberhausen, Berlin, Biele-feld, Düsseldorf, Bonn, Darmstadt, Paris, and San Sebastián.
2005	Is diagnosed with cancer. Subsequently spends a long time in hospital, undergoing operations, chemotherapy, and radiotherapy.
2008	Shoots *This Night* in Porto, Portugal.

More long stays in hospital.

Is awarded the Golden Lion of the Venice International Film Festival for his life's work. |
| 2009 | Directs operas and plays in Leipzig and Berlin.

More long stays in hospital.

Exhibitions: *Autrefois et Toujours: Photographic Works by Werner Schroeter, 1973–2009*, curated by Christian Holzfuss, Fine Arts Berlin; at the Galerie Jörg Heitsch, Munich, in January; and at the House on the Lützow-platz, Berlin, in December. |
| 2010 | On 19 February, receives the Teddy Award of the Berlin International Film Festival (the Berlinale) for his life's work.

On 24 March, an exhibition opens at the Gay Museum, Berlin, *Maria, Magdalena, and All the Others*, a tribute to Werner Schroeter for his sixty-fifth birthday, curated by Wolfgang Theis. Schroeter was able to see the exhibition in advance but was not well enough to attend the opening.

Dies on 12 April in a hospital in Kassel from the consequences of his cancer.

On 2 December, a comprehensive retrospective of his films opens at the Georges Pompidou Center, Paris. In parallel, the Goethe-Institut in Paris holds an exhibi- |

tion of works by Alberte Barsacq, who collaborated with Schroeter on set designs and costumes for over thirty years.

The Galerie Vu in Paris shows part of the exhibition *Autrefois et Toujours: Photographic Works by Werner Schroeter, 1973–2009*, curated by Christian Holzfuss, Fine Arts Berlin.

DISTINCTIONS AND FILM AWARDS (A SELECTION)

1969   Josef von Sternberg Prize at the Mannheim International Film Festival for *Eika Katappa*.

1978   Baden-Baden Television Prize for *The Kingdom of Naples / Neapolitan Siblings*.

Gran premio Taormina, Italy, for *The Kingdom of Naples / Neapolitan Siblings*.

Gran premio Festival delle nazioni, Italy, for *The Kingdom of Naples / Neapolitan Siblings*.

1979   German Film Prize in gold for *The Kingdom of Naples / Neapolitan Siblings*: best direction and best camerawork (by Thomas Mauch).

First Prize, Chicago International Film Festival for *The Kingdom of Naples / Neapolitan Siblings*.

Adolf Grimme Prize for *The Kingdom of Naples / Neapolitan Siblings*.

1980   Golden Bear of the Berlin International Film Festival (the Berlinale) for *Palermo or Wolfsburg*.

International Critics' Award, Venice, for *The Dress Rehearsal*.

1981   German Film Prize, best documentary, for *The Dress Rehearsal*.

1982	German Film Prize in gold for *Day of the Idiots*.
	Critics' Award, São Paulo, for *The Council of Love*.
1987	Adolf Grimme Prize for *In Search of the Sun*.
1989	Premio Bari, Bari International Film and Television Festival, for his life's work.
1991	German Film Prize in gold for *Malina*: best film, best director, best actress (Isabelle Huppert), best editing (Juliane Lorenz).
1996	Golden Leopard, Festival internazionale del film, Locarno, for his life's work.
	Film Prize of the Hof International Film Festival for his life's work.
	Prize of the German Film Critics for *Love's Debris*.
2000	ARTE documentary film prize, Documentary Film Festival, Duisburg, for *The Queen—Marianne Hoppe*.
2006	Premio a un Cineasta del nostro tempo, Festival internazionale del cinema e delle arti, Trieste, for his life's work.
2008	Golden Lion of the Venice International Film Festival (La biennale di Venezia) for his life's work.
	Tribute, Viennale (Vienna Film Festival), for his life's work.
	Best Friend Award, Estoril Film Festival, for his life's work.
2010	Teddy Award of the Berlin International Film Festival (the Berlinale) for his life's work.
	Friedrich Wilhelm Murnau Film Prize, Bielefeld, for his life's work, together with Elfi Mikesch.

ACKNOWLEDGMENTS

In line with the character of a memoir, this book is based first and foremost on Werner Schroeter's vivid recollections, his enjoyment in telling a story, and his interest in looking back at his life. But it is just as notable for the great confidence that he had in me. I must thank him, posthumously, for the candor with which he accepted my role as a listener, observer, researcher, and coauthor. The book began when a professional project evolved into a strong personal relationship. I would like to thank him for that too. From the first, and especially in the difficult phase after Werner Schroeter's death, my editor at Aufbau, Franziska Günther, brought great commitment to the project, and I thank her with all my heart for that.

Since Schroeter was not able to check the last of the work, having comments, documents, and materials from many of his colleagues was of inestimable value, and so was the help that I received from the institutions entrusted with his literary estate. I owe particular thanks to Monika Keppler, who actively supported the project and offered good advice. I owe her thanks not only for that and for drawing on her collection for the illustrations but especially for the comprehensive appendixes, documenting the scenographic, filmographic, and autobiographical facts concerning Werner Schroeter's life and work.

In addition, I would like to give special thanks to the following people and institutions: Digne Meller Marcovicz, for photographs from her huge archive, as well as her unerring judgment; Elfi Mikesch, for photos, advice, and wisdom; Frieder Schlaich and his colleagues at Filmgalerie 451, for information on the film *This Night*;

Gerrit Thies and Wolfgang Theis, for pictures and assistance when I was working in the archives of the German Kinemathek, Berlin; Stefan Drössler, of the Munich Museum of Film, for material on the early films; Peter Berling, Thomas Mauch, and Juliane Lorenz, for useful tips, memories, and filmed material; Christoph Holch and Anne Even, for information, material, and films relating to Werner Schroeter's work for television; Roswitha Hecke, Susa Katz, Ulrike Stiefelmayer, Monika Treut, Josef Schnelle, Wilhelm Roth, Wolfgang Storch, and the Arsenal Cinema, Berlin (Institute of Cinematic and Media Arts), for material and information; Katrin Seybold and Wolfram Schütte, for their evaluations; and Gina Berg, for her family memories. Not least, I would like to thank Ingrid Caven for the subtitle.

My thanks, too, to Christian Schiessler, for compiling the index of names, and to Matthias Braun, for his patience and sympathetic interest.

INDEX OF NAMES

Schlaich, Frieder, 214, 243

Schleef, Einar, 200

Schlingensief, Christoph, 223

Schlöndorff, Volker, 43, 123, 138

Schmid, Daniel, 5, 14, 39, 46, 49–55, 82, 97, 100–101, 105, 124, 126–27, 129, 148, 152

Schmidt, Trudeliese, 127, 189, 193

Schmidt-Reitwein, Jörg, 154–55

Schmitt, Christian, 88

Schneider, Maria, 126–28

Schneider, Romy, 115, 145–46

Schönberg, Arnold, 175, 197, 212

Schroeder, Barbet, 54

Schroeter, Werner: and alcohol, 165–66; aggression, dislike of, 241–42; El Angel, nickname of, 90, 94; *Anglia* (film), 46, 50; *Argila* (film), 20, 31, 34–37, 64, 67; as associative thinker, 242; awards of, 29–30, 42–43, 226; background of, 6–12; *The Bomber Pilot* (film), 23, 45, 48–50, 52, 55, 58, 73; bourgeois life, rejection of, 243; bullying of, 19; Callas, effect on, 13–14, 30–31, 52, 60; Callas, as spiritual mother, 5, 14; as charming, 225, 244; as Christian, 219, 226; cities, love of, 15; on collective art, 111; and comedy, 48–49; creativity, and longing for life, 97; *Day of the Idiots* (film), 113, 146, 150–52, 167, 171, 176, 180, 188; death, concern with, 239–40; death of, 227; *The Death of Maria Malibran* (film), 20, 44–45, 50, 52, 63–66, 71–72, 74, 79–80, 82–83, 101–2, 104, 148, 176, 212; depression of, 16; *Deux* (Two) (film), 11, 20, 95, 203–8, 214; on directing, 110–11; divorce of, 76; *The Dress Rehearsal* (film), 140–41; and drugs, 105; early films of, 30; early sexual experiences, 17; education of, 10–11, 13–17, 22; *Eika Katappa* (film), 14–15, 24–25, 29–30, 33, 37–44, 46–47, 52,

67, 113, 120, 188; fatalism of, 225–26; financial difficulties of, 104–5, 114, 123, 201, 225, 242; *Flocons d'or* (film), 44, 54, 78, 101–6, 108, 117, 144, 146, 176; Foucault, meeting with, 80–83; as generous, 241; God, belief in, 169; grief, attitude toward, 6; homosexuality of, 82; illnesses of, 19, 27–28, 32–33, 67, 212–14, 222–26, 244; as individualist, 240; influences of, 19–21, 30, 37–38; *In Search of the Sun* (film), 140, 176; *The Kingdom of Naples* (film), 14, 40, 44, 46, 48–49, 59, 103, 108, 117–26, 129; *Der lachende Stern* (The laughing star) (film), 59, 159, 160–61, 176–77; *Das Liebeskonzil* (The Council of Love) (film), 153–55; *Love's Debris* (film), 64–65, 140, 187–90, 193, 200, 204, 210, 227; *Malina* (film), 46, 59, 176–81, 191, 196, 200, 202–3, 215; Manson Family, encounters with, 99–100; marriage of, 73, 76; melodrama, as form of opera, 131; Mexico, attitude toward, 88–89, 92; *Monsieur Verdoux* (film), 195; Montezuma, Magdalena, relationship with, 22–26; mother of, 5–6; mother's death, grief over, 107; music, importance of to, 217–18; myth of Narcissus, fascination with, 204; Naples, love of, 14–15; *Nicaragua* (film), 46–47; *Palermo oder Wolfsburg* (film), 21, 46, 59, 71, 120, 126, 129–35, 138–39, 146; psychology, as against, 83; punk style, cultivating of, 45; *The Queen* (film), 140, 195, 222; as reader, 19–20; relationships of, 28–29; *The Rose King* (film), 24, 26–27, 74, 95, 161–65, 171, 174, 176–77, 179, 191, 203, 214; *The Sailors of This World* (film), 84, 126–27, 144–45; Schmid, friendship with, 50–55; self-expression, as inner necessity, 110; as self taught, 41; sense